Praise for
The Complex PTSD Treatment Manual

> "Arielle Schwartz has written THE guidebook for clinicians seeking to understand complex PTSD and how to treat it! On every page, she interweaves up-to-date theoretical ideas with practical clinical wisdom. Every word of this book can easily be implemented by therapists regardless of their training or approach."
>
> **— Janina Fisher, PhD,**
> Author of *Transforming the Living Legacy of Trauma*

"Dr. Schwartz's book is likely to be a big help to clients and also to therapists who treat individuals with severely traumatic life histories. It is very readable and accessible. Reading it gives a feeling of being in a conversation with Dr. Schwartz. The chapters give many examples of how cognitive behavioral therapy, somatic experiencing, and EMDR can be successfully integrated in therapy preparation, diagnostic assessment, and treatment planning. It also includes many transcripts of therapy sessions, which illustrate with clarity how particular interventions can be effectively used. This book is a significant contribution to our developing knowledge of the best ways to treat complex PTSD and dissociative conditions."

—Jim Knipe, PhD
Author of *EMDR Toolbox: Theory and Treatment of Complex PTSD and Dissociation*

"Dr. Schwartz guides us into a field of healing practices and possibilities founded in a resilient-informed approach. She offers portals into the untold and hidden stories of pain that live in the nervous system and the biology of people affected by chronic traumatization. She reminds us of the power and strength that lay at the core of human existence and put us in touch with our inner capacities. *The Complex PTSD Treatment Manual* is a rich, comprehensive, well-integrated, and immensely useful masterpiece that will support child and adult therapists working with C-PTSD in bringing healing to generations!"

—Ana M. Gomez, MC, LPC
Author of *EMDR Therapy and Adjunct Approaches with Children*

"Arielle Schwartz does it again, delivering clinicians a practical volume full of useful skills with her uncanny ability to translate complex neurological concepts into relatable language. I am especially impressed with the sensitivity and humanity that she employs in addressing parts work and dissociation. This is a marvelous foundational volume on complex trauma that I will be very happy to recommend to my students."

—Dr. Jamie Marich
The Institute for Creative Mindfulness
Author of *EMDR Made Simple, Trauma Made Simple*

"Dr. Arielle Schwartz has done it again. A thorough explanation of the reasons complex trauma exists, how it expresses itself in behaviors, and what treatment entails. An important foundation for therapists treating complex trauma. Knowing these foundational insights will make treatment easier and more effective."

—Annie Brook, PhD
Founder of The Brook Institute, Author of *Birth's Hidden Legacy*

"Arielle Schwartz has crafted an up-to-date synthesis of many of the best practices of the evolving science of resolving complex PTSD. This highly practical treatment manual is an essential guide for beginner therapists and a useful summary for seasoned clinicians. Bravo!"

—Will Van Derveer, MD
Cofounder of the Integrative Psychiatry Institute

"*The Complex PTSD Treatment Manual* is a must-have for any mental health professional who treats complex trauma. In this manual, Dr. Arielle Schwartz seamlessly integrates components of several evidence-based therapeutic modalities for the treatment of complex trauma and provides clinicians with concrete tools and techniques that help clients improve emotion regulation and attunement, process traumatic events, and ultimately regain their lives and sense of connection. Dr. Schwartz's compassionate, scientific, and client-centered approach to C-PTSD makes her a rare and valued voice in the field of trauma psychology!"

—Jennifer Sweeton, PsyD
Author of *The Train Your Brain Card Deck* and *Trauma Treatment Toolbox*

"*The Complex PTSD Treatment Manual* is an essential masterpiece for any clinician working in the fields of trauma, complex PTSD, and mind-body medicine. Integrative health providers will love it. Woven into the academic rigor of this masterpiece are practical healing practices and embodied exercises for the lucky reader. It is the perfect balance between a personal transformation roadmap and a scholarly treasure. Dr. Schwartz takes us on a highly attuned and compassionate journey through multiple trauma-healing modalities and presents them in a user-friendly, practical way. The psychological needs arising at this post-pandemic juncture are different than they've ever been, and this will surely be your indispensable reference book for years to come. This book is a must-have!"

—Dr. Ilene Naomi Rusk, Integrative Trauma Therapist and Clinical Neuropsychologist
Director at The Healthy Brain Program, Brain & Behavior Clinic

The
COMPLEX
PTSD

Treatment Manual

. . . .

An Integrative, Mind-Body
Approach to Trauma Recovery

Arielle Schwartz, PhD

Copyright © 2021 Arielle Schwartz

Published by
PESI Publishing
PESI, Inc.
3839 White Ave
Eau Claire, WI 54703

Cover: Amy Rubenzer
Editing: Jenessa Jackson
Layout: Amy Rubenzer & Bookmasters

ISBN: 9781683733799
All rights reserved.
Printed in the United States of America

For the purpose of protecting clients' privacy and confidentiality, all identifying details have been removed from the clinical vignettes shared within this book.

PESI Publishing
pesipublishing.com

About the Author

Arielle Schwartz, PhD, is a licensed clinical psychologist, Certified Complex Trauma Professional (CCTP-II), and EMDR consultant with a private practice in Boulder, Colorado. She is the co-author of *EMDR Therapy and Somatic Psychology: Interventions to Enhance Embodiment in Trauma Treatment* and the author of *The Post-Traumatic Growth Guidebook* and *The Complex PTSD Workbook: A Mind-Body Approach to Regaining Emotional Control and Becoming Whole.*

Dedication

. . . .

In dedication to the brave souls who have suffered from the
unbearable burdens of trauma. In gratitude to the therapists
who compassionately offer heartfelt care in a hurting world.
May this book illuminate a path of courageous transformation
that allows us all to move from pain into possibility.

Table of Contents

Acknowledgments

All books come about as a team effort. I am so grateful for the support I have received from my beloved family. Thank you to my husband, Bruce Feistner, for your trust in my vision and for giving me ample time to carry it forward into the world. Thank you to my children, Eliana and Ian, for all of the ways that you inspire me with your joy and laughter. You fill my world with light. Thank you to Carolyn Schwartz and Victor Goldman for believing in me and for tirelessly standing by my side. You have taught me what is possible when we are fully loved and accepted for who we are.

A book can be thought of as a legacy, a meaningful contribution to the world that lives on after us. Within these pages, I give you the best synthesis of my current knowledge and experiences as a psychologist and trauma treatment specialist. The inspiration for this writing has come as a result of many years of personal growth and study. I gratefully honor the wise teachers, authors, and healers whose work has influenced the theories and practices that have shaped this book. Most directly, I am appreciative of Betty Cannon, whose existential and relational tutelage has shaped my personal and professional world more than any other. Thank you to my colleague and friend, Barb Maiberger, for the spark in your eyes when you recognized that I had more books in me. Through our many years of teaching together, we were able to develop an integrative curriculum that brings the wisdom of parts work therapy into somatically informed EMDR therapy. I am grateful to Jim Knipe for providing my EMDR therapy consultation and for imparting to me your wisdom gained from many years of providing support for individuals with C-PTSD.

My somatic psychology roots were nourished by Christine Caldwell and Susan Aposhyan. Not only were you my first teachers of body centered psychotherapy at Naropa University, but you also nurtured my role as a teacher in this field. Less directly, this book rests upon the foundation of influential leaders in the field. Namely, Daniel Siegel, Pat Ogden, Kekuni Minton, Janina Fisher, Bonnie Badenoch, Kathy Steele, Bessel van der Kolk, Stephen Porges, Allan Schore, Deb Dana, Babette Rothschild, Francine Shapiro, Robin Shapiro, Richard Schwartz, Jon Kabat-Zinn, Eugene Gendlin, Viktor Frankl, and Rollo May. Your books and teachings are legacies that have shaped me in countless ways.

I am deeply grateful for my team at PESI Publishing. It has been an honor to work with you: Karsyn Morse, Jenessa Jackson, and Kate Sample. Like trusted midwives, you have helped me to birth this book into reality. I have felt completely supported along the way.

I am deeply grateful to my clients. Thank you for trusting me with your hearts. You are wonderful teachers who have helped me grow as a person. Finally, I am grateful to the many therapists who have allowed me to be their mentor and teacher. Your commitment to serving your clients and desire to cultivate excellence in trauma treatment inspires me daily and is the reason for this book.

Introduction

Many mental health practitioners are trained in the treatment of single traumatic events and the diagnosis of post-traumatic stress disorder (PTSD). However, more often, our clients come to therapy with an extensive history of trauma that begins in childhood and continues into adulthood with layers of personal, relational, societal, or cultural losses. This is complex PTSD (C-PTSD), a diagnostic term that accounts for the consequences of repeated or chronic traumatization. In some cases, this form of trauma begins in early childhood when individuals experience repeated abuse or profound neglect, though C-PTSD also arises as a result of ongoing social stress, such as racialized trauma, living in poverty, or growing up in a war-torn country.

Individuals with C-PTSD often feel overwhelmed by their pain and have organized their sense of self around survival. Their wounds might sound like:

- "I was physically abused as a kid. Now I have chronic health problems and pain. Sometimes I hope I'll die in my sleep."
- "It was never safe in my home. I watched my father hurt my mother again and again. My first memory was when he tried to choke her. I was only three. It was my job to take care of her."
- "I have grown up with a persistent feeling of fear and anger. As a Black American, I can't just drive my car or walk into a store without feeling on guard. I have to be vigilant about my surroundings. I have never known what it feels like to be 'safe.'"
- "My parents were survivors of the Holocaust. I can still remember the emptiness and fear in their eyes. They lost everything. Now I feel lost. Sometimes I just disappear."
- "I was raised in a cult where I was sexually abused. I survived by pretending that I was part of their world. Now I don't know what is true, whom to trust, or who I am."
- "My childhood was 'fine,' but no one really took the time to understand me. Now I feel so utterly alone in the world."
- "I grew up afraid for my life. Now I have lost my country. I am a refugee. I can never go home again. Each day I worry about the family that I have left behind."

It is common for individuals with complex trauma to have been in therapy for many years. They may feel cautious about therapy because of historical experiences where they have been misunderstood, misdiagnosed, or blamed for their symptoms. They may come to therapy reluctantly, with well-constructed defenses and somatic tension that serve as armor to protect them from underlying terror, helplessness, and shame. Some tread water in a sea of chronic overwhelm. They may struggle to sleep at night due to their heightened sensitivity to perceived threats and reliance on primitive survival instincts to defend themselves. Others have had to disconnect from their body and emotions altogether. For most, these protective behaviors have been necessary for their survival, and they will not surrender these sources of protection easily.

Clients who have survived persistent and chronic traumatization are savvy, and they will sense if we lack authenticity or genuineness in our approach to therapy. It is our job to earn their trust, which is a task that can be challenging, especially if they have experienced betrayal in previous relationships. However, if we do our jobs well, we might be given a sacred task: to bear witness to their suffering and attend compassionately to their wounds.

This book invites you to see these individuals for the incredible strength they carry within them. They are not "broken"; they are hurt and in need of empathy and compassion. Empathy reflects your ability to understand their perspective and stand in their shoes. Compassion involves your desire to be of service in relieving their suffering. The approach to treatment offered in this book will guide you to become this trustworthy companion so you can help guide a healing journey for another human soul. Therapy is always a combination of head and heart, of science and art. My hope is that this manual helps you to find the intersection of intuition and evidence-based treatment that allows you to openheartedly engage in this richly transformational interpersonal process. Not only will this approach help your clients, but it invites you to be willing to grow and change as well. In truth, many of us have become therapists because of our own wounds. We have had to walk our own healing journey because of the events we have faced in childhood or at other points in our lives. If left unaddressed, our own trauma can interfere with our work with clients. However, once addressed, these life experiences can provide a foundation for the compassionate presence that we offer to our clients.

The integrative, mind-body strategies presented here will allow you to effectively work with clients who have experienced multiple traumatic events and prolonged trauma exposure. These strategies are grounded within an approach to trauma treatment that is both strength-based and resilience-informed. A strength-based approach emphasizes our inherent capacity to heal from trauma when we have sufficient access to resources and support. A resilience-informed approach to care maintains that every human being has an intrinsic drive toward wholeness once those resources and supports are in place. Within these pages, you will learn essential healing practices drawn from relational therapy, mindful body awareness, parts work therapy, cognitive behavioral therapy (CBT), eye movement desensitization and reprocessing (EMDR), somatic psychology, and complementary and alternative medicine (CAM). **While this book provides guidance on the integration of these modalities into trauma treatment, it is recommended that you seek further training, consultation, or supervision on any modality that is outside of your area of competence as a clinician.**

Chapter 1 begins by distinguishing a diagnosis of C-PTSD from traditional PTSD and other diagnoses, such as mood, anxiety, personality, or dissociative disorders. It also explores the etiology of C-PTSD with attention to socio-developmental and cultural contexts. For example, I examine the significance of clients' early childhood history while also attending to the impact of chronic social disconnections that arise as a result of discrimination related to race, ethnicity, sex, gender, religion, age, or able-bodiedness. This chapter also emphasizes how to explore diagnosis and assess symptoms, as well as how to build a foundation of safety.

Chapter 2 elucidates the theoretical foundations of this integrative, mind-body approach, which is based on common factors research (Wampold, 2015), phased-based treatment recommendations for C-PTSD (Courtois & Ford, 2009; Herman, 1997; Schwartz, 2016), and the neurophysiology of trauma recovery (van der Kolk, 2014). I explore why the traditional approach to PTSD treatment—which involves directly targeting traumatic memories—can backfire with clients who have C-PTSD and discuss treatment modifications.

Chapter 3 describes the impact of chronic traumatic stress on the nervous system through the lens of polyvagal theory (Porges, 2011). Since C-PTSD is associated with dysregulation of the autonomic nervous system (ANS), the healing practices in this section focus on identifying symptoms of hyper- or hypo-arousal and strengthening clients' "social engagement system," which can enhance their sense of safety and connection.

Chapter 4 focuses on the role of the therapeutic relationship within the treatment of complex trauma. The greatest predictor of meaningful change in clients with C-PTSD is the quality of the therapeutic alliance (Pearlman & Courtois, 2005). Furthermore, mutual or co-regulation is a precursor for the development of self-regulation (Schore, 2019). This means that experiences of being understood and unconditionally accepted by another enhance our capacity to hold ourselves in a loving and compassionate manner. As therapists, we must attend to our own relational and attachment wounds, which, if left unaddressed, can interfere with our work with clients. The practices in this chapter focus on co-regulation and helping you, as the therapist, explore therapeutic relational dynamics that evoke discomfort, anxiety, or insecurity.

Chapter 5 emphasizes an embodied approach to mindfulness by focusing on the development of a felt sense that can keep both the therapist and client grounded in the present moment. As in the previous chapter, the practices here are not just a set of interventions for clients; they are also intended for us as therapists to practice our own mindful embodiment. Mindful embodiment helps create congruence between our words and body language, which enhances trustworthiness with our clients. From this foundation, we can guide clients to develop greater embodied self-awareness, which can help them build tolerance for distressing emotions and accompanying somatic sensations.

Chapter 6 provides an application of parts work therapy to C-PTSD with particular attention to dissociative symptoms. This chapter guides you through an integrative model of parts work that involves introducing clients to parts work, helping them identify and deepen their awareness of parts, anchoring the adult self, differentiating from a part, developing allies for a part, and repairing a missing experience. The practices offered in this chapter aim to help clients cultivate compassion so they can turn toward their painful past with greater care.

Chapter 7 focuses on the body in trauma treatment through the lens of somatic psychology. For many individuals with C-PTSD, building body awareness can initially be uncomfortable because many have difficulty staying present with their sensations, either because they feel flooded and overwhelmed, or numb and disconnected. In alignment with a phase-based approach to care, somatic psychology offers resources that can increase our clients' felt sense of safety. Once these resources are in place, awareness of somatic tension can guide clients to access the healing power of movement, which can help them resolve traumatic wounds from the past and empower them in the present.

Chapter 8 focuses on memory reprocessing through the lens of cognitive behavioral and EMDR therapies. This process involves purposefully reflecting on a traumatic memory within a trustworthy and safe environment. In doing so, we give clients an opportunity to confront the past while simultaneously integrating new, positive information that reduces the feeling of threat associated with traumatic memories. As applied to clients with C-PTSD and dissociative symptoms, this model involves building positive resources, reflecting on traumatic events using cognitive reappraisal, and safely reprocessing traumatic memories using dual-awareness strategies.

Chapter 9 focuses on the use of CAM to support trauma recovery, including bodywork, nutrition therapy, acupuncture, and yoga. This chapter explores the benefits of helping clients develop integrative healthcare teams to respond to the impact of trauma on both mental and physical health. The healing practices in this chapter will help you and your client identify healthcare goals and work through barriers that might inhibit them from exercising, eating healthily, or engaging in relaxation techniques on a regular basis. Moreover, you will learn a series of yoga-based interventions that you can easily integrate into psychotherapy.

Finally, **chapter 10** focuses on the third phase of trauma recovery: helping clients work through lingering feelings of anger, resentment, and sadness so they can cultivate a feeling of hope for the future. This concluding chapter explores topics of meaning, resilience, and post-traumatic growth.

Now that you know what to expect in this book, I invite you to pause and reflect upon your own work with your clients. It is a courageous choice to work with individuals who have suffered from trauma. To work in this realm asks that you bear witness to human suffering, a process that often involves confronting your own fears or unhealed wounds. While working with traumatized individuals is not easy, it is important to learn how to enter this difficult terrain without feeling vicariously traumatized. It is possible for you and your clients to come away from therapy feeling stronger and more resilient.

However, I imagine that you, like all therapists, have moments when you feel stuck with at least one particular client. There have likely been times when you feel that nothing you did made a difference. While frustrating, these experiences are common when working with individuals who have suffered from repeated traumatic events and extensive interpersonal wounds or betrayals. At these times, it is important to have supportive resources who can help you reflect upon these challenges. You can probably recall times when you reviewed a difficult case with a supervisor and discovered new perspectives and ways to help clients move through an impasse. While this book cannot replace supervision, I hope that you will allow the guidance in these pages to serve as a form of mentorship as you accompany your clients into the painful territory of their traumatic past.

> Throughout this book, you will find healing practices, reflection exercises, and clinical resources that you are welcome to reproduce. They are also available for download at www.pesi.com/cptsd.

1

Understanding Trauma and Complex PTSD

···

At some point in our lives, we all experience hardship and adversity. Facing traumatic events seems to be an integral part of the human experience. In fact, approximately 90 percent of us will face at least one traumatic event in our lifetime, with many of us being exposed to multiple traumatic events (Kilpatrick et al., 2013). Of course, not everyone who has experienced trauma will develop PTSD. Many individuals are remarkably resilient in the face of adversity. However, the capacity to bounce back from difficult events requires that we have sufficient support in the form of a loving family or caring community member who is invested in our well-being (Matheson, 2016). For example, children are more resilient to the chronic stress of poverty when they have at least one nurturing and protective adult in their lives (Haggerty et al., 1996). Being able to talk to someone helps us to process our thoughts and feelings about the traumatic experience and also helps to know that we are important.

In contrast, when individuals do not have someone who provides this compassionate understanding for their inner world, they are significantly more likely to develop PTSD. For example, children who grow up with a disengaged and emotionally unavailable primary caregiver will fail to get their needs met with regard to acceptance, love, and understanding. Furthermore, children who experience ongoing abuse from which there is no escape will experience extended periods of time in a state of fear or helplessness. These early childhood experiences can lead to learned helplessness and a loss of self-efficacy that follows individuals into adulthood, causing them to carry the learned experience and accompanying belief that their actions do not make a difference in the outcome of their lives.

In addition to these childhood origins of C-PTSD, some individuals experienced chronic, repeated traumas later in life, such as domestic violence, prolonged captivity, systemic racism, or refugee trauma. For example, consider a woman who experiences constant manipulation and verbal abuse from her husband. She fears leaving him because she would not be able to financially support herself or protect her children, so she copes with the threat of him day after day and globalizes her fear and mistrust of her husband to all men. Or consider an Arab American man who was targeted for years after the 9/11 attacks and has felt fear much of his life because of the color of his skin. He doesn't know whom to trust and does not feel like he belongs in this country despite the fact that he was born in the United States and calls this place his home. Again, the risk factors for C-PTSD significantly increase when there is no way to escape trauma and when individuals lack external support systems.

In this chapter, I will explore the symptoms of acute traumatic stress, single-incident PTSD, and C-PTSD. I will also focus on the diagnostic distinction between C-PTSD and other disorders, with consideration that these and other diagnoses can sometimes be comorbid. I will also explore how to develop a case conceptualization that considers social and cultural factors. Because establishing a sense of safety is paramount for trauma work, this chapter also provides two healing practices, which are intended to create an atmosphere of relational safety and teach your client the concept of the window of tolerance. These practices will allow your clients to better partner with you in their healthcare. Finally, therapists who specialize in the treatment of complex trauma recognize the impact that this work can have on their own mental, emotional, and physical health. Therefore, this chapter also offers an opportunity for personal reflection, which focuses on helping you find the resources to stay present with your clients as they experience helplessness, despair, uncertainty, disappointment, and loss.

Acute Stress Reaction

An *acute stress reaction* refers to the psychological and physiological responses that arise after exposure to a traumatic event. During and after traumatic events, most individuals will experience feelings of confusion, sadness, fear, anxiety, panic, irritability, agitation, anger, and despair. Additionally, it is common to experience physical symptoms, including rapid heart rate, sweating, shakiness, nausea, or dizziness. These reactions typically last for approximately two to four weeks. While these symptoms are unsettling, we as therapists are likely to exacerbate the problem if we join with our clients' fears about their emotions or sensations. Therefore, it is important to reassure our clients that these symptoms are normal and to be expected. The latest edition of the International Classification of Diseases (ICD-11; World Health Organization, 2018) has not only renamed acute stress disorder to "acute stress reaction" but also has moved its description out of the mental disorder section and into the "factors influencing health" section. The intention is to depathologize the experience of emotional distress after exposure to any highly stressful or traumatic event.

Post-Traumatic Stress Disorder

Although acute reactions to stress are normal, sometimes the physiological and psychological effects of trauma can develop into symptoms that remain for an extended period of time. Typically, this happens if the event threatens an individual's sense of survival and overwhelms their coping capacities. When this occurs, the traumatic experience can result in the development of PTSD.

The symptoms of PTSD fall into three categories: reexperiencing, avoidance, and persistent perceptions of current threat. Reexperiencing symptoms, also referred to as invasive or intrusive symptoms, interfere with our clients' ability to feel safe and relaxed. **Traumatic events are not simply remembered, they are relived as if they are still occurring.** Sometimes these symptoms arise as vivid images, nightmares, or flashbacks that are accompanied by strong emotions and disturbing sensations. Other times, reexperiencing symptoms are due to early childhood preverbal events for which there are no clear images or memories. As a result, clients might report feeling flooded by emotions and sensations with no known cause, or they may have somatic symptoms, such as chronic pain and illness symptoms, that flare up during times of stress.

Avoidance symptoms are behaviors that individuals adopt to prevent or push away reminders of the trauma. For example, they may avoid external situations, such as places, activities, or people, that are associated with the traumatic event. They may also push away internal reminders of the trauma, including related thoughts, memories, emotions, or sensations. They may deny that certain disturbing events ever occurred, repress their feelings, or minimize their pain. In some cases, clients may engage in substance use, emotional eating, or over-exercising to push away their pain. In addition, relatively common and socially accepted behaviors, such as chronic busyness, overworking, extended screen time, or sleeping extensively, can also function as avoidance behaviors.

The third category of symptoms, persistent perceptions of current threat, refers to having **an enhanced startle effect or hypervigilance, in which individuals feel as though they must remain on guard or are highly sensitized to their environment.** They may be highly sensitive to people's body language, facial expressions, and tone of voice. In addition, they might have very precisely controlled behaviors to manage their experience, such as always sitting close to the door in your office or frequently checking the clock.

There is also a dissociative subtype of PTSD. In contrast to the traditional PTSD diagnosis, which emphasizes hyper-arousal symptoms, the dissociative subtype is distinguished by symptoms of hypo-arousal, dissociation, emotional numbness, depersonalization, and derealization. In this case, clients might report times when they feel disconnected from their body, like their body doesn't feel real, or that the world around them feels surreal. They might report feeling as though they are living in a daze or a fog that is not medication induced.

In contrast to individuals who are hypervigilant, clients with dissociative symptoms are prone to under-responding or to feeling immobilized in risky situations. As a result, they do not take actions to protect themselves, which can lead to re-traumatization. For example, a client might not be aware of the fear-based sensory experiences associated with a dangerous dating partner, which can increase their vulnerability to sexual assault or cause them to remain in an abusive relationship for an extended period of time. Moreover, clients with dissociative symptoms often have greater difficulty remembering details about historical traumatic events. In some cases, clients can develop complex internal systems with parts that carry memories and emotions related to the traumatic event and parts that are invested in disconnecting from the pain.

In general, PTSD tends to be underdiagnosed (da Silva et al., 2018). Approximately 8 to 10 percent of those who seek mental health services receive a diagnosis of PTSD, although it has been suggested that an additional 15 percent would likely screen positive for the disorder (Lewis et al., 2018). In fact, research has found a large proportion of undetected PTSD among clients seeking care for other (non-PTSD) primary diagnoses, with clinicians failing to document the client's trauma history in their clinical records (Zammit et al., 2018). Moreover, a significant percentage of clients have "subthreshold" PTSD, in which they meet only partial diagnostic criteria. Nonetheless, these individuals report impaired social or occupational functioning as a result of their trauma and would benefit from treatment for their symptoms (Franklin et al., 2018). Not surprisingly, PTSD rates are higher among Latinos, African Americans, and American Indians given the extensive history of racism and discrimination in the U.S. and around the world (APA, 2013).

C-PTSD

In contrast to single-incident PTSD, C-PTSD occurs as a result of repeated or chronic exposure to extremely threatening events from which escape is impossible. C-PTSD is associated with a longer duration and greater intensity of traumatic stress. Situations that might elicit complex traumatization include torture, prolonged domestic violence, prolonged captivity, chronic discrimination, genocide, and the unrelenting distress of being a refugee separated from one's family and country. In addition, C-PTSD can arise as a result of developmental trauma, which includes childhood sexual abuse, physical abuse, neglect, exposure to domestic violence, having a parent with untreated mental illness, and having a parent who abuses alcohol or other substances.

Furthermore, children with learning disabilities seem to be at greater risk for abuse, which can increase their likelihood of developing C-PTSD. For example, one study revealed a strong correlation between dyslexia and physical abuse, with 35 percent of individuals reporting abuse before age 18 (Fuller-Thompson & Hooper, 2014). There is speculation that this correlation is bidirectional in that parents who feel triggered by their child's cognitive differences or impulsivity become abusive, and as a result of this chronic stress at home, children are at greater risk for continued learning problems. Here, we can imagine a vicious cycle in which parents and children react to each other in an exacerbated dynamic of mutual dysregulation.

The timing of developmental trauma appears to make a difference as well. Children go through critical growth periods in which they are more susceptible to the impact of trauma. One of these periods occurs during the first three years of life when infants and toddlers are in the attachment phase of development. When an infant's world is frightening, unpredictable, threatening, or neglectful, they cannot form a secure attachment with their primary caregiver. This rocky foundation can hinder their capacity to cultivate a sense of self or develop meaningful, healthy relationships in adulthood. In addition, adolescents are also highly vulnerable to relational trauma due to the unpredictable physiological changes that accompany this developmental period and the psychological tasks of identity formation.

The intensity and impact of traumatic events is worse when there is a secondary layer of betrayal (Courtois & Ford, 2009). Betrayal trauma occurs when victims are blamed for the event, when others develop an alliance with the abuser, or when others fail to protect them. For example, betrayal trauma can occur in the case of childhood sexual abuse when a parent tells their child that the abuse was their fault because they were "too pretty" or "seductive." This betrayal worsens if the other parent allies with the abuser, believing them instead of protecting the child. Betrayal trauma can also arise in the context of racial or cultural trauma when an individual's country and government fail to provide a safe haven or protect them. Betrayal is associated with a greater propensity of dissociative symptoms.

In some cases, clients may experience ongoing stress in their current lives in addition to the historical traumatization they have experienced. For these clients, their current lives reflect the instability that they felt as a result of childhood trauma, and in turn, they often come into the office with repeated crises that are unfolding in the present day. For example, they might live with chronic uncertainty due to homelessness, financial stress, or domestic violence. Or those who are immigrants might face current threats of deportation. Or those with chronic pain and illness might feel worn down by their symptoms. Understanding these contextualizing factors is crucial so that we, as clinicians, do not assume that the client "should" be more resilient, as this can lead them to feel blamed for their symptoms.

Diagnostic Criteria for C-PTSD

The most recent edition of the ICD (World Health Organization, 2018) has added the diagnosis of C-PTSD into the category of disorders specifically associated with stress. The diagnostic criteria include the typical symptoms of PTSD (reexperiencing, avoidance, and persistent perceptions of current threat), as well as three additional categories of symptoms: difficulties with affect regulation, negative self-concept, and interpersonal disturbances (Böttche et al., 2018; McElroy et al., 2019). Let's take a closer look at this additional subset of symptoms:

- **Affect dysregulation:** Chronic traumatization often leads to profound dysregulation of the *autonomic nervous system* (ANS), which regulates bodily functions such as our heart rate, blood pressure, body temperature, and breathing without conscious awareness. The ANS either mobilizes energy through our *sympathetic nervous system* (SNS) or conserves energy through our *parasympathetic nervous system* (PNS). Complex trauma is associated with imbalances in both PNS and SNS states, resulting in associated patterns of dysregulated affect. Some individuals have predominant SNS activation, resulting in a state of hyper-arousal that manifests as heightened reactivity, anxiety, emotional outbursts, and rage. These clients are prone to acting out with reckless, impulsive, or excessive risk-taking or self-harm behaviors. They may also present with difficulty concentrating and attentional challenges. In contrast, other individuals present with greater PNS engagement, which promotes a state of hypo-arousal associated with helplessness, hopelessness, despair, and depression. These clients present as emotionally numb and suffer from a reduced ability to feel pleasure and positive emotions. Many individuals alternate between these hyper- and hypo-arousal states.

- **Negative self-concept:** Individuals with C-PTSD are prone to an impaired sense of self-worth and struggle to form a coherent sense of self. These symptoms are sometimes referred to as changes in a client's *systems of meaning*, which is defined as alterations in core beliefs about oneself, the world, and one's future. When individuals are not able to flee from an abusive situation or fight off an abuser, they tend to feel as though they have failed. This can lead to pervasive feelings of shame, guilt, self-blame, and despair accompanied by beliefs that they are at fault, helpless, damaged, diminished, or worthless. They may also have difficulty trusting other people, leading them to doubt that others are capable of being good, kind, or generous. Some individuals experience a profound existential loneliness or sense of despair about the state of the world. Collectively, these feelings can interfere with a sense of meaning, purpose, or hope for the future.

- **Interpersonal disturbances:** Having a history of complex trauma, especially that which is due to interpersonal trauma, can markedly impair an individual's ability to develop trusting relationships with others. Fears of betrayal, abuse, and abandonment can fuel patterns of avoidance in relationships or over-dependence on others. Such patterns can interfere with the ability to form and sustain healthy and reciprocal relationships.

Although these symptoms of C-PTSD reflect the impact of trauma on clients' mental and emotional well-being, we also have to consider the profound impact of trauma on physical health. As evidenced by the Adverse Childhood Experiences (ACE) study, individuals with childhood trauma are especially susceptible to a range of chronic pain and physical illnesses (Felitti et al., 1998). The ACE study, which was conducted by Kaiser Permanente and the Centers for Disease Control and Prevention, surveyed over 17,000 patients regarding their reports of adverse childhood events, such as experiencing abuse or neglect, witnessing domestic violence, or growing up in dysfunctional household characterized by divorce, mental illness, substance use, or parental imprisonment. They found that the number of ACEs was correlated with a variety of harmful mental and physical health outcomes later in life. In particular, having an ACE score of four or more significantly increased the risk of developing depression, substance use, suicidality, obesity, heart disease, cancer, lung disease, and liver disease.

Assessment of C-PTSD

C-PTSD has traditionally been difficult to diagnosis, partly because the diagnosis has only recently been recognized and differentiated from PTSD and borderline personality disorder (Cloitre et al., 2014). Accurate diagnosis can also be challenging because the symptoms of C-PTSD can be similar to other disorders, including major depressive disorder, bipolar disorder, generalized anxiety disorder, panic disorder, obsessive compulsive disorder, eating disorders, learning disabilities, attention-deficit/hyperactivity disorder, substance abuse disorders, dissociative disorders, conversion disorders, and psychotic disorders.

Therefore, when assessing for C-PTSD, we want to carefully take our time to develop an accurate understanding of our client's symptoms within the context of historical traumatic experiences and current stressors. Oftentimes, these clients have been misunderstood, misdiagnosed, or inappropriately medicated. These clients entrust us with their care, so from our very first meeting with them, we must begin to gather information about their lives and their histories in a sensitive, yet thorough, manner. In addition to assessing for the six categories of C-PTSD symptoms, we must also attend to dissociative symptoms (e.g., depersonalization and derealization) to determine whether there may be a comorbid dissociative disorder. Furthermore, when clients have chronic difficulties with emotion dysregulation—especially when accompanied by fears of abandonment, interpersonal difficulties, a poor sense of self-worth, suicidal ideation, and impulsivity—we might also consider the presence of a comorbid personality disorder.

It is also essential that we consider social, developmental, and cultural factors when reflecting on a client's trauma history. For example, it is important to know if the client grew up in poverty, without sufficient medical care, or without access to healthy nutrition. We want to understand whether our clients were the target of racial oppression, discrimination, harassment, or threats. If you work with refugees, it is imperative that you recognize the ways in which these individuals have been betrayed by other humans. These individuals may have faced profound helplessness and powerlessness that led to a depletion of mental and emotional resources. For these clients, it can feel nearly impossible to retain a sense of being human or to trust that their actions will make a difference in the outcome their life (Ehlers, Maercker, & Boos, 2000). These types of experiences can drastically impact a person's ability to trust other people or the world at large (Matheson, 2016).

Including the client's social, developmental, and cultural contexts in the case conceptualization helps us avoid inadvertently blaming the client for their symptoms. **We must acknowledge how**

a client's self-protective, defensive reactions may continue to be necessary for their health and well-being. If we set a treatment goal to help a client restore a sense of safety or trust when systemic problems have not been addressed, we might be doing harm. For example, consider a woman who is struggling with anxiety and poor sleep but who still works in a setting where her boss has been harassing her for over a year. She cannot afford to leave her job because she is a single mother. Within this context, her fear and distrust are understandable given these ongoing challenges that are outside of her control. If we treat her fear-based symptoms without considering the contextual features at play, she will inevitably feel misunderstood. Thus, we must always consider situational factors when working with any client who is currently being mistreated or discriminated against, especially when the underlying bias (such as racism, classism, or religious bias) has not been addressed within the external community or societal context.

Finally, given the importance of maintaining a strengths-based and resilience-informed treatment approach, it is also crucial to conduct a thorough assessment of protective factors. Many individuals with C-PTSD have not only suffered from neglect, abuse, or ongoing threat but have also lacked protective factors that can mitigate the impact of these events. As previously mentioned, one of the most significant protective factors in childhood trauma is the presence of a supportive individual or community who understood, nurtured, and protected the child. Additional protective factors include participation in activities outside of the home and the development of positive peer relationships. Clients can also accumulate protective factors in adulthood through experiences that provide them with a sense of empowerment and success, as well as through the formation of caring relationships. Such positive moments help individuals cultivate "earned secure attachment," which refers to the learned security individuals can develop in adulthood despite insufficient nurturance from caregivers in childhood.

We gather information about our clients' history in order to form a case conceptualization, which is a narrative that provides an understanding of their predominant symptoms and their existing strengths within the context of their social and cultural history. However, a clinical interview needs to be offered at a pace that does not overwhelm the client, as rushing the process might impair their willingness to continue with therapy. Often, when working with clients who have C-PTSD, we must patiently and compassionately wait for them to feel safe enough to share their pain. While some clients are able to share a cohesive narrative that describes their past, this is less often the case with C-PTSD. More commonly, we have to listen for clues about their past as described in fragmented memories or stories of triggering events, or by paying attention to their distressing symptoms. Furthermore, clients may not be able to talk about their distress as a "symptom" because these feelings and behaviors are so thoroughly integrated into their identity. They might say, "This is simply who I am."

It can also be challenging to conduct a thorough clinical interview if the client has dissociative symptoms. Dissociation is both a built-in physiological survival mechanism and a psychological defense structure. It helps the individual disconnect from threatening experiences by creating a division between the part of the self that is trying to live a "normal" life and the part of the self that is holding onto trauma-related memories, emotions, and sensations. Dissociation can lead a client to disconnect from their distress, be highly intellectualized, or uphold idealized descriptions of abusers. Therefore, when we are exploring our client's history, some clients may have a tendency to underreport symptoms, or they may be too triggered by questions that they are unable to participate in a clinical interview.

For example, a client may hold a fantasized or idealized version of a family of origin to avoid confronting the reality of childhood abuse or neglect. In other cases, you might learn that the client feels as though the world is unreal, feels disconnected from their body, or has periods of "lost time." In some cases, it can be difficult to assess whether dissociative symptoms are present because clients do not want to come across as "crazy." This need to appear "normal" can override a willingness to talk about their distress. However, we may begin to notice that they have difficulty recalling recent events. We might notice subtle changes in their body language, such as a collapsed posture or faint tone of voice, that suggest they are no longer fully grounded and present. Or they might report feeling tired, foggy, dizzy, numb, lightheaded, or nauseous but not realize these are symptoms of dissociation.

Importantly, dissociation can occur in both hyper- and hypo-aroused states. Here are some examples of dissociation across the arousal continuum:

- **Running:** "The last thing I recall is the therapist asking me about my childhood. I was in the parking lot before I realized it. I don't remember leaving her office."
- **Raging:** "I lost control! I was told that I was choking him but have no memory of it. They showed me the video, and I couldn't believe that was me."
- **Foggy and dizzy:** "The room starts to spin, and I feel foggy and nauseous, but I don't know what triggered it."
- **Sleeping:** "Any time I have a conflict with a friend, I fall asleep afterward. Often, I stay there in my chair for hours. I become nothingness. I go blank."
- **Fainting:** "It starts with a queasy feeling in my stomach. I guess I finally faint, and I'm a mess when I come to. It's so embarrassing."

In some cases, it can take several months of treatment before you are able to form a thorough case conceptualization and related diagnoses, especially when dissociative symptoms are paramount. When the diagnosis is not clear, you can still utilize the treatment approaches discussed in this book to help deepen your understanding of your client's history, stabilize their current distress, and treat trauma-related symptoms.

The following section offers a series of questions that you can use to better understand a client's trauma history, symptoms, resources, and strengths. In some cases, it might be appropriate to explore these lists with your clients during a clinical interview. **However, there is little clinical value in focusing on lists of questions with clients when this interferes with the therapeutic relationship.** In most situations, I suggest that you use these questions to facilitate conversations with clients in a well-paced manner that helps you to learn about their lives. The primary goal is to develop a trauma-informed and strength-based case conceptualization that considers a client's developmental, social, and cultural life experiences.

The first set of questions allows you to assess your client's ACE score so you can better understand the client in the context of developmental trauma. The second set of questions goes beyond the client's ACE score by including a wider range of developmental, social, and cultural traumatic events that would be considered adverse life events. The third set of questions provides a comprehensive list of disturbances related to the six categories of C-PTSD symptoms, with an additional section devoted to dissociative symptoms. The fourth set invites you to focus on resilience as an integral part of treatment by examining the client's protective factors, strengths, and resources. Finally, the fifth set asks you to engage in self-reflection by examining how your own history impacts your ability to engage in trauma work with clients.

Adverse Childhood Experiences

The following list explores possible ACEs that may have occurred prior to the client's 18th birthday. These questions are based upon the 10 categories of trauma identified in the ACE study (Felitti et al., 1998), which provide insight into the association between developmental trauma and mental and physical health problems in adulthood.

Before your 18th birthday:

- Did a parent or other adult in the household swear at you, insult you, put you down, humiliate you, or act in a way that made you afraid that you might be physically hurt?

- Did a parent or other adult in the household push, grab, slap, throw something at, or hit you so hard that you were injured?

- Did an adult or person at least five years older than you ever touch or fondle you, make you touch their body in a sexual way, or sexually abuse you in any other way?

- Did you feel that no one in your family loved you or thought you were important or special? Did you feel that your family didn't feel close to or support each other?

- Did you feel that you didn't have enough to eat, had to wear dirty clothes, and had no one to protect you? Were your parents too drunk or high to take care of you or take you to the doctor if you needed it?

- Were your parents ever separated or divorced?

- Was your mother or stepmother pushed, grabbed, slapped, or had something thrown at her? Was she ever hit with something hard or threatened with a gun or knife?

- Did you live with anyone who was a problem drinker or alcoholic, or who used street drugs?

- Was a household member depressed or mentally ill, or did a household member ever attempt suicide?

- Did a household member ever go to prison?

Add up each question to which the client answered "yes" to find out their ACE Score: _____

Adverse Life Events

This list of adverse life events explores additional traumatic events beyond the ten ACE categories. These events may have occurred to the client in childhood or across the lifespan. You can explore these items with your client during a clinical interview, or if directly asking these questions would be too overwhelming for your client, you can use this checklist as you get to know your client across multiple sessions.

- Were you told that you were the result of an unwanted pregnancy?
- Were you separated from your mother for an extended period of time after birth?
- Were there any medical complications during or after your birth?
- Were your medical needs neglected in childhood?
- Did your mother experience postpartum depression?
- Did either of your parents have PTSD?
- Did either parent have strong narcissistic or borderline personality characteristics?
- Did you have family members who did not respect your boundaries?
- Did you experience a lack of emotional safety in your family?
- Was there competition with your siblings for limited parental attention?
- Were you chronically rejected, misunderstood, discounted, or shamed?
- Did you fear death or serious injury at any point in your life?
- Were you held in captivity with the inability to escape at any point in your life?
- Did you experience any unwanted or forced sexual encounter at any time in your life?
- Did you witness a serious injury or death of another person?
- Were you in or exposed to combat during military service?
- Were you the victim of a serious crime or robbery?
- Have you felt repeatedly discriminated against, harassed, or bullied?
- Have you been homeless at any point in your life?
- Are you a refugee, or have you been displaced from your country?
- Have you feared being deported or questioned your safety in your country?

C-PTSD Symptoms

This comprehensive checklist explores disturbances related to the six categories of C-PTSD symptoms, with an additional section devoted to dissociative symptoms. As with the previous checklist, you can explore these items with your client directly during a clinical interview, or you can use this checklist as you get to know your client across multiple sessions.

Reexperiencing Symptoms

- Do you experience flashbacks, such as vivid images, overwhelming emotions, or disturbing sensations?

- Do you have nightmares or wake up in a fright?

- Do you think about traumatic events at inconvenient times?

- Do you sometimes feel like you are reliving traumatic events or as if they are still occurring?

- Do you sometimes feel triggered in a way that leaves you feeling overwhelmed, shaky, and anxious (or shutdown, helpless, and collapsed)?

Avoidance Symptoms

- Do you stay away from people or places that remind you of traumatic events?

- Do you tend to withdraw or isolate yourself?

- Do you rely upon alcohol, substances, or food to avoid feeling your pain?

- Do you sometimes spend hours watching T.V. or playing video games?

- Do you find it difficult to admit to yourself that you were abused or neglected?

- Do you spend so much time caring for others that you ignore yourself?

- Do you tend to be a perfectionist or be highly critical of yourself and others?

- Do you focus so much on your work so you don't have to feel or think about the past?

Persistent Perceptions of Current Threat

- Do you feel hyperaware or on guard?

- Do you startle easily?

- Do you find yourself constantly checking your environment for signs of threats?

- Do you always need to have an escape plan?

- Do you tend to expect the worst to happen?

- Are you highly sensitive to subtle changes in other people's body language and facial expressions?

Affect Dysregulation

- Do you tend to cry uncontrollably, even after minor, everyday challenges?

- Does it take you a long time to feel better after stressful events?

- Do you frequently feel angry or irritable?

- Do you have a hard time controlling your anger?

- Do you tend to feel anxious or panicky?

- Do you often feel hopeless and depressed?

- Are there times when you feel like you would be better off dead or when you think about suicide?

- Do you sometimes feel the urge to harm yourself?

- Do you tend to spend time with people or in places that are dangerous?

- Do you tend to feel numb and cut off from your emotions?

- Do you feel incapable of feeling joy or pleasure?

Negative Self-Concept

- Do you feel like you have little control over your life no matter what you do?

- Do you often feel ineffective or powerless?

- Do you feel like a failure?

- Do you believe that you are damaged?

- Do you have little hope for your future?

- Do you often feel ashamed, guilty, or unworthy?

- Do you feel as though there is something wrong with you?

- Do you have a hard time finding a sense of purpose or meaning to your life?

Interpersonal Disturbances

- Do you feel disconnected from other people?

- Do you tend to avoid spending time with other people?

- Do you have a hard time trusting other people or knowing whom to trust?

- Do you have a difficult time doing things on your own or feel that you rely too heavily on other people?

- Do you often feel terrified of being left or abandoned by others?

- Do you find it difficult to hear other people's viewpoints or perspectives?

- Do you tend to avoid conflict?

Dissociative Symptoms

- Do you sometimes find yourself staring into space or realize that you have been daydreaming for long periods of time?

- Is it difficult for you to pay attention, or do you get distracted easily?

- Do you find yourself suddenly getting tired, feeling far away, or as if you're looking at the world through a fog?

- Are there times when people, objects, or the world feels unreal?

- Do you sometimes feel disconnected from your body or emotionally numb?

- Do you feel like you are different people in different situations?

- Do you sometimes feel, act, or talk like a younger person?

- Do you have difficulty remembering broad periods of your life?

- Do you ever arrive at places and don't know how you got there, or find things that you have bought but don't remember buying them?

Protective Factors, Strengths, and Resources

This list focuses on strengths and protective factors that may have mitigated the impact of complex trauma. It can be beneficial to assess the client's positive life experiences, as you can draw on these as a resource during treatment when the client feels overwhelmed or dysregulated.

- Do you recall times when you felt loved, nurtured, and protected by your mother, father, or other primary caregiver as a child?

- Do you recall having a trustworthy relative, caregiver, neighbor, coach, or teacher who cared about your well-being when you were growing up?

- Is there someone trustworthy in your life right now with whom you can talk?

- Do you believe that life is what you make of it?

- Do you consider yourself a go-getter?

- Have you experienced times when you felt successful or empowered?

- Are there activities you enjoy?

- Do you make time to focus on your health by attending to your nutrition or exercising?

- Do you make time for rest and relaxation, such as focusing on your sleep or getting a massage?

- Do you make time for social connections with family, friends, or at community events?

- Do you make time for religious or spiritual practices, such as praying, meditating, or spending time in nature?

- Do you have a sense of hope and optimism about the future?

- Do you have goals for your future, and do you take steps toward achieving your goals?

Therapist Self-Awareness Practice

Given the high prevalence of trauma exposure, many of us who work as healers have also had to work through challenging or traumatic life experiences of our own. As therapists, we must remain committed to our healing journey so we can stay present to the suffering of our clients. It is so very important to take care of yourself while caring for others.

Take some time to reflect on your own history. This process may illuminate a need for your own personal therapy, which is a process that can enhance your well-being and become a foundation of compassion for the difficulties your clients face.

- Review the list of ACEs and adverse life events. What is your own ACE score? What additional challenges have you faced in your life?

- Take a look at the list of PTSD and C-PTSD symptoms. Make note of the distress that you have experienced historically. Do you continue to struggle with some of these symptoms today?

- Is it difficult to feel compassion for your own symptoms or struggles?

- What has helped you navigate the challenges of your life? Have you been in therapy? If so, what were the therapeutic moments that helped you better understand yourself and allowed you to grow?

- Review the list of protective factors, strengths, and resources. What resilience factors did you have as a child? What supportive resources do you have in your life now? What are the self-care practices that help you during difficult moments?

Establishing Safety by Inviting Spacious, Relational Awareness

Although conducting a comprehensive assessment is important to develop an understanding of the client's historical circumstances, it is not always the place to start. In particular, **before you can focus on gathering information about the past, you must build a foundation of safety.** You can achieve this by orienting clients to the here and now, inviting them to pay attention to cues of safety, and reminding them that there is plenty of time for your work together. Taking the time to provide this spacious, mindful, and relational approach can provide an immediate corrective experience for clients who come in feeling anxious, rushed, or pressured. Let's take a closer look at my experience working with Susan:

When Susan first came into therapy, she appeared restless as she shifted uncomfortably on the couch. She spoke quickly, jumping from one subject to another. In quick succession, she spoke about her recent breakup with her boyfriend and how he had reminded her of her mother who had been abusive to her as a child. I learned that she hadn't been sleeping and had been having panic attacks. I could see that she was feeling overwhelmed.

In response, I immediately began to focus on finding my own center by deepening my breath and bringing attention to my own body sensations. This focus on regulating my own body and mind helped me connect to a calm and grounded place within myself. I then asked Susan if it was okay if I invited her to take a brief pause from speaking. She agreed, and I suggested that it was most important to me that she feel safe in the room with me. I then added that we had plenty of time to get to know each other. I continued to take several deep breaths and noticed that she began to slow down her breathing as well. I offered a reflection that I noticed that she had taken a deeper breath during the pause.

Acknowledging this subtle, yet significant, shift, I invited her to take a look around the room and to notice how she felt sitting in the room with me. She looked at the plant sitting near the window and said, "It has been a long time since I have slowed down." She returned her eyes to meet mine. I offered a kind smile in return and shared that I looked forward to getting to know her. This moment of connection spontaneously brought my hand to my heart, a reflection that I felt touched by our exchange.

As therapists, it is our job to pace therapy in such a way that we can stay present and grounded. Our own breath and mindful body awareness then serves as the foundation for our work with others. Once we have established this sense of relational safety, we can begin to gather information about a client's history. In my work with Susan, I eventually learned that in addition to the emotional abuse she experienced from her mother, she had a father who was often drunk. In her words, "When he was sober, he was loving. But when he was drinking, he would be angry and threatening." She had frequent nightmares as a little girl but had no one to turn to when she felt afraid. Now we were able to compassionately attend to her feelings of fear, hurt, anger, and sadness with a here-and-now emphasis on relational safety. The spontaneous lifting of my hand to my heart offered a nonverbal gesture that communicated to her that I felt moved by our connection. This moment of relational connection stood in contrast to the emotional abuse and neglect she experienced in her childhood. Slowing down and focusing on the here and now offered a reparative experience of being nonjudgmentally heard, seen, and understood.

Like Susan, our clients sometimes come into session wanting to share stories about their traumatic past. They might begin to feel a sense of urgency, or you might notice that they speak quickly in order to get the story out. As a result, our clients are more likely to feel overwhelmed or re-traumatized. We, as therapists, are also more likely to feel overwhelmed in this exchange. Using the next healing practice, we can encourage clients to slow down and focus on the present moment with simple statements that help them orient their attention to a more spacious, relational awareness. This allows therapy to focus on creating safety and a sense of connection right from the beginning.

Invite Spacious, Relational Awareness

Notice how you feel as you read the following statements, and explore offering these in session with clients. As with all of the healing practices in this book, you might only explore one of these statements at a time. I suggest timing and adapting the practice so that it is relevant to your client's experience. See if you can notice how the use of these statements enriches the quality of presence, deepens a feeling of connection, or encourages a sense of spaciousness within your sessions.

- It is important that you feel safe with me as you share your story. Is it okay with you if I periodically invite you to take a brief pause from the story you are sharing with me? This way, I can help you pace yourself and reduce the likelihood that you will leave here feeling overwhelmed.

- I would like to remind you that there is plenty of time and space for you. There is no need to rush.

- Can you take a moment to sense your body while you share your story? What sensations are you aware of?

- Can you take a moment to sense your emotions while you share your story? What are you feeling right now?

- What you are saying is important, and I want to be sure that I can stay present with you and all that you are sharing with me. What I am noticing right now is… [*a reflection of the expression that you notice on the client's face, an emotion or sensation that you are aware of in yourself, and so forth*].

- Notice how it feels to have me right here with you as you are sharing your story.

Window of Tolerance

Many clients with C-PTSD have spent extended periods of time in both hyper-aroused and hypo-aroused states. Therefore, treatment involves helping clients recognize when they are in their *window of tolerance*, a phrase that trauma expert Dr. Daniel Siegel uses to describe an optimal zone of nervous system arousal where clients can respond effectively to their emotions (Siegel, 1999). **We can tell that a client is in their window when they are aware of their body and breath, feel calm, are able to think clearly, and are able to express a range of emotions without getting "stuck" in their feelings.** When a client is above their window of tolerance, they may be prone to overwhelming feelings of anxiety, panic, hypervigilance, restlessness, irritability, aggression, or rage, and they may cry uncontrollably. In contrast, when a client is below their window of tolerance, they might feel tired, lethargic, emotionally dull, helpless, shutdown, numb, disconnected, or depressed.

Individuals who have suffered from chronic, repeated traumatization often sustain prolonged periods of SNS or PNS activation, or they alternate between these two states with little to no capacity to self-regulate into an experience of feeling calm and safe. Many individuals thus rely heavily upon coping skills that over-contain their distress. For example, they may focus excessively on their work and become a workaholic. Others manage their distress through over- or under-eating, smoking, drug or alcohol use, or dissociation. This process can create a "faux" window of tolerance in which individuals temporarily and superficially override their distress in a way that mimics safety; however, they quickly return to their dysregulated state (Kain & Terrell, 2018).

Because many individuals with C-PTSD have no internal experience of safety, creating a false sense of safety has been necessary for their survival. These pseudo-safety behaviors have allowed them to function despite being in chronic distress. For these individuals, the experience of true safety and connection can feel threatening because it requires allowing themselves to be vulnerable with another person, which often elicits memories of rejection or abuse. The work of Dr. Gabor Maté offers a compassionate approach to understanding these coping behaviors and asks that we recognize them as a survival strategy to help manage the pain of trauma (Maté, 2010).

This next healing practice focuses on building an understanding of the window of tolerance, which can help you and your clients compassionately communicate about different nervous system states that may arise during trauma work. Over time, you will work together to discover states of calm and connectedness by tapping into the social engagement system (chapter 3), engaging in co-regulation (chapter 4), and practicing mindful body awareness (chapter 5). In addition, in chapters 6, 7, and 8, you will help clients increase their distress tolerance by widening the window of tolerance at a pace they can tolerate.

Know Your Window of Tolerance

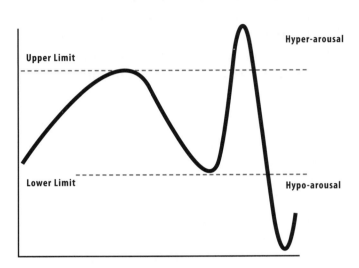

Window of Tolerance

- Your window of tolerance represents your ability to respond effectively to stress. You can think of this as your optimal zone of nervous system arousal. When you are inside your window of tolerance, you are more likely to feel connected to yourself, calm, and safe. However, there are times when you might be outside your window of tolerance, either above or below it.

- When you are above your window, you feel hyper-aroused. During these times, you might feel:

    o Anxious, frantic, or panicky

    o Restless, jumpy, or fidgety

    o Shaky or trembly

    o Tingly or breathless

    o Irritable

    o Angry or rageful

    o Out of control or overwhelmed

- When you are below your window, you feel hypo-aroused. During these times, you might feel:

    o Tired or lethargic

    o Emotionally dull

    o Helpless or powerless

    o Heavy or depressed

    o Floaty, dizzy, or nauseous

    o Shutdown, disconnected, or numb

- You might notice that you have a tendency toward one side of this nervous system imbalance, or you might alternate between both hyper- and hypo-arousal.

- It is common to engage in learned coping strategies to help you manage your distress. You might:

    o Work excessively hard or stay busy

    o Need to feel in control or be perfect

    o Abuse food by over- or under-eating

    o Use substances, such as cigarettes, alcohol, or drugs

    o Engage in reckless sexual activity

- These behaviors allowed you to survive the pain. They reflect your attempt to do the best you could to navigate an unspeakable situation. However, our work together will help you learn to relate to yourself and work through the trauma of your past so you no longer need to rely on these behaviors. You can discover a new sense of connection and safety.

2

Theoretical Foundations of an Integrative Approach to Trauma Treatment

It takes tremendous courage to confront traumatic memories and emotions. Successful treatment requires a compassionate therapeutic relationship *and* effective, research-based interventions. Therefore, this chapter examines the theoretical foundations of the integrative, mind-body approach presented in this book, which is grounded within common factors research, phased-based treatment recommendations for C-PTSD, and the neurophysiology of trauma recovery.

Common Factors in Trauma Recovery

Any integrative approach to therapy brings together two or more therapeutic modalities within a cohesive, conceptual framework (Zarbo et al., 2016). Integrative models of treatment often rely on *common factors*, or core ingredients, that underlie the efficacy of psychotherapy at large (Wampold, 2010; Wampold & Imel, 2015). These common factors are: the therapeutic alliance, therapist empathy, therapist congruence and genuineness, collaboration between the therapist and client, the establishment of agreed-upon treatment goals, cultural adaptation of interventions to meet the needs of the specific client, and client engagement in treatment (Wampold, 2015). Of note, an integrative approach is not the same as an eclectic approach. Eclecticism pulls in a vast array of techniques that can feel disjointed and confusing to the client. In contrast, an integrative approach has a cohesive feeling because of its emphasis on common factors. As therapists, we can further facilitate the cohesive quality of this integrated approach by ensuring that a common treatment goal underlies the various treatment approaches.

There are several unifying goals of the integrative model presented in this book, all of which are critical to the treatment of C-PTSD. The primary focus of treatment is to retain clients in therapy long enough for the therapist and client to find a way to work together with a shared understanding of the client's goals (Corrigan & Hull, 2015). Once we have a relationship with the client, we ask the client if they would like to work on the following treatment goals as related to the symptoms of complex trauma: (1) facilitating greater affect regulation and emotional balance; (2) reducing avoidance symptoms, including dissociation; (3) reducing the frequency and intensity of reexperiencing and heightened arousal symptoms; (4) facilitating improvements in self-concept and sense of self; and (5) enhancing success with interpersonal relationships.

Ultimately, the goal of this integrated model is to help our clients feel more resilient. *Resilience* is defined as having an increased capacity to handle stress and bounce back after difficult or traumatic life experiences (Schwartz, 2020). Resilience helps us recognize that we will all face difficulties at some point in our lives, but we can also learn the skills and tools that help us connect to our inner strength and sense of empowerment. We also must recognize that resilience is best attained and developed within supportive and unconditionally accepting relationships. Healing from C-PTSD involves helping clients become aware of their past and how it affects them in the present. We help them recognize how the past has shaped their thoughts and behaviors. In addition, we help them orient to the fact that these historical traumatic events are over by focusing on cues of safety in the here and now. When clients have a greater capacity to be mindfully attune to the present moment, it gives them a greater sense of choice about their thoughts and behaviors.

Some clients have been in therapy for many years with an accumulation of unsuccessful outcomes. They may come to therapy with a high degree of distrust and cynicism. Others face ongoing stressors, such as racial inequity, discrimination, homelessness, poverty, addiction, health challenges, or relationship losses. A compassionate approach to care asks us to nonjudgmentally accept each client within the context of their unique social and cultural challenges. An integrative approach to treatment allows us to adapt the focus of our work to meet the needs of each specific client by recognizing that there is no single therapeutic method that is appropriate or effective for all clients. Some clients will respond better to a cognitive approach, whereas others will appreciate emotion-focused or somatically oriented interventions. Most importantly, even when clients are facing current stressors, the interventions presented in this book will empower them as they navigate the obstacles in their lives by helping them to restore trust in the goodness of human connection and to build confidence in their own capacity to handle adversity.

Phase-Based Treatment

Rather than focusing directly on traumatic memories, therapy for C-PTSD relies upon a relationally focused, tri-phasic approach to care (Herman, 1997). Phase one focuses on establishing stability and safety; phase two focuses on helping clients process traumatic material in a well-paced, regulated manner; and phase three involves integrating new experiences into identity and relationships. In many cases, phase one is the longest and most important phase in the treatment of C-PTSD.

Phase one of complex trauma treatment emphasizes the paramount importance of the therapeutic relationship, mindful body awareness, and parts work therapy. The relational focus builds therapeutic rapport and trust through a client-centered and collaborative approach to treatment. Without a collaborative approach, the therapeutic relationship risks recapitulating power dynamics of dominance and control, which can mirror damaging elements of relationships from the client's past. A collaborative approach views the client as a partner with an active role in their treatment. This encourages clients to develop a sense of control and self-efficacy as they take ownership of their therapeutic experience.

A collaborative approach to care stands in contrast to a traditional biomedical model in which the client is seen as a passive recipient of treatment, the client's belief systems are viewed as irrelevant, and healthcare professionals are seen as the determiners of treatment (Gatchel, 2004). Individuals with C-PTSD may not have a framework for trust because they have been repeatedly betrayed by relationships in the past. It is our job to move at a pace that creates safety. Relational moments of compassion can eventually build a foundation for the client to develop a revised, healthy sense of self within the interpersonal world.

Phase one also focuses on helping clients develop coping strategies and positive resources to enhance stabilization through a readily accessible feeling of safety in body and mind. In part, this is facilitated through mindfulness-based interventions (offered in chapter 5) that invite clients to increase awareness of their mental, emotional, and somatic experiences with an emphasis on staying grounded in the present moment. Mindfulness has been increasingly viewed as a valuable asset to successful therapy outcomes (Germer & Neff, 2019; Kabat-Zinn, 1990) because it helps clients build tolerance for distressing emotions and sensations, and also increases their capacity for self-compassion and acceptance.

Clients with C-PTSD may block self-compassion or resist positive emotions. For example, they may have an unrelenting inner critic or deep-seated feelings of unworthiness that lead them to dismiss and push away the nourishment of positive emotions. Therefore, phase one of treatment also involves developing a deeper understanding of the client's inner world through parts work therapy (Schwartz, 1997; van der Hart, Nijenhuis, & Steele, 2006). Parts work helps clients deepen their understanding of internalized messages from their family of origin and address dissociative symptoms. When children have grown up with an abusive parent and there is no way to escape, it is common to develop a dissociative split between the part of the self that upholds the attachment to the caregiver and the part that holds the reality of the abuse (Fisher, 2017). These dissociative symptoms often persist into adulthood as a means for clients to avoid acknowledging the abuse. Integrating parts work therapy into the first phase of treatment for C-PTSD becomes an essential tool to help clients differentiate from parts of themselves that are self-critical or self-harming so they can sustain positive affect and eventually work through the painful memories of historical traumatic events.

Phase two of trauma treatment typically involves the direct targeting of traumatic memories through exposure and desensitization techniques. However, this approach to treatment can be re-traumatizing and injurious to clients with C-PTSD, and some clients may not be able to tolerate it (Cloitre et al., 2012; Szczygiel, 2018; van Vliet et al., 2018). Therefore, it is wise to proceed with caution into this phase of treatment with respect to clients' access to resources and readiness for trauma reprocessing. If we open up clients' access to these distressing memories, emotions, or sensations too quickly, we risk triggering dissociative symptoms or leaving them feeling overwhelmed. Instead, it is important to build up their capacity to tolerate both positive and negative affect and sensations prior to working through traumatic events. With some clients, this can take quite a bit of time and, in some cases, too much emphasis on safety can delay treatment (de Jongh et al., 2016). Importantly, we can counterbalance the targeting of traumatic memories by simultaneously helping them build positive resources and emotion regulation skills (Karatzias et al., 2018). In addition, we can empower clients through a collaborative and open conversation regarding the timing and appropriateness of memory-focused interventions so they feel like they have choice about when to reprocess traumatic material.

In addition, phase two of trauma treatment also involves a balance of top-down and bottom-up processing (Ogden & Minton, 2014). Top-down processing engages the upper brain centers, such as the prefrontal cortex, through psychoeducation and cognitive interventions to regulate emotional distress. Top-down strategies include talking about traumatic events, identifying negative thought patterns or thinking errors, and cultivating resources, such as positive beliefs or imagery. In contrast, bottom-up processing engages the lower brain centers, such as the limbic system and brainstem, by bringing attention to sensations and emotions to access the way trauma is held in the body. Bottom-up strategies include focusing on emotions and sensations while processing traumatic events, engaging in mindful breathing, and inviting movement to facilitate somatic release. In the treatment of complex trauma, we can draw on both top-down and bottom-up strategies to adjust the pacing of therapy. For example, clients who are prone to flooding might benefit from top-down interventions to help them connect to a sense of safety in the moment, whereas clients who have a difficult time connecting to their bodies might benefit from a bottom-up approach focused more on sensing their body and emotions.

As you proceed through the book, you will learn how to implement well-paced therapeutic interventions to help clients work through traumatic memories without becoming overwhelmed or shutting down in the process. The interventions in this second phase are primarily drawn from somatic, cognitive behavioral, and EMDR therapies, as these help clients to work through disturbing images, emotions, and sensations. Importantly, when a client has experienced neglect and a lack of attachment during infancy or early childhood, there may not be specific traumatic memories to desensitize. Instead, you can address the impact of these deficient early experiences by building a caring therapeutic relationship and by helping the client cultivate other nurturing resources for the part of the self that experienced abandonment or neglect.

Phase three aims to help clients sustain a positive sense of self, strengthen their resilience, and sustain a feeling of hope for the future. Here, we remember that even positive change can be challenging to accommodate. Sometimes we must help clients work through barriers to integrate a new or emerging sense of self into the world. This can be especially important for clients whose physical health is compromised as a result of unresolved C-PTSD. Research shows that unresolved trauma—including childhood attachment wounds, poor sleep, lack of exercise, social isolation, and poor nutrition—can exacerbate chronic pain and illness conditions (Grant, 2016). In addition, clients with long-term trauma often have lives that reflect their debilitating symptoms. They might identify as the "sick one," and they might have family members or friends who reinforce their diminished sense of self. In some cases, we must help clients let go of the deeply engrained beliefs and behaviors that reinforce these symptoms. This process may cause clients to go through an extended period of grief as they attempt to develop a new sense of self. They may report that life feels meaningless and carry immense despair, or they may have a crisis of faith in other people and the world. A strength-based approach helps clients to cultivate the resilience needed to enact these difficult, yet positive, changes and even allow them to grow in response to complex traumatization (Schwartz, 2020).

In phase three, we also assist clients in creating sustainable lifestyle changes that reinforce this new sense of self (Schwartz & Maiberger, 2018). For example, we can assist clients in developing integrative, trauma-informed healthcare teams that might include an exercise coach, yoga teacher, sleep expert, or nutrition therapist. Additionally, we can attend to our clients' strengths, spiritual lives, meaning making, personal values, and sense of purpose. Our aim is to help clients strengthen their capacity for positive emotions, sense of self-efficacy, feelings of empowerment, and capacity for reciprocally nourishing interpersonal relationships. Ultimately, we help clients make meaningful connections out of the complexity of diverse life experiences (Siegel, 2010).

The Neurophysiology of Trauma Recovery

Neuropsychotherapy is a term that refers to the process of applying neuroscientific research within psychotherapy. It used to be thought that the brain only exhibited neuroplasticity, or the capacity to change, during early childhood. However, we now recognize that brain development continues throughout our lifespan (Amen, 2015; Doidge, 2007). Our brains are malleable and have the capacity to develop new neural connections even as we age. That means that the effects of childhood trauma, which are known to adversely impact the developing brain, are not immutable. With therapy, the brain can rewire itself and heal from the emotional injuries of the past (Rousseau et al., 2019).

All of our life experiences form neural networks in the brain. A *neural network* is a group of interconnected neurons in the brain that fire together and that form the basis of all of our memories. For example, if you are learning a new piece of music on the piano, you are forming a neural network that includes the muscle memory of your hands, the sound of the music, and the feeling that you have in your body as you play the keys. Each time you practice the written music, you reinforce this neural network, and over time, it becomes easier to play. Eventually, you no longer need to look at the musical notes on the page; you can play by memory.

Ideally, all your memories are integrated into an overall sense of who you are as a person. However, a trauma-related memory is considered an impaired neural network because it is disconnected or isolated from neural networks associated with positive and nourishing memories (Bergmann, 2012). It forms an encapsulated self-state that does not integrate into your overall identity. These impaired neural networks form the basis of many disturbing symptoms related to trauma, such as intrusive thoughts, disturbing somatic sensations, flashbacks, and other reexperiencing symptoms. For example, when a trauma-related neural network is activated, a client may feel like they are reliving the traumatic event, causing them to experience distressing imagery, disturbing sensations, and a feeling of terror. Moreover, it is often very difficult for them to reclaim a sense of safety.

In this triggered state, clients are more likely to have difficulty shifting their thinking toward positive resources that counter the fear-based state (Shapiro, 2018). They have a harder time accessing their resources of feeling cared for by a loved one or feeling grounded in the present moment. When this occurs, the impaired neural network is reinforced. In time, it can become increasingly difficult for clients to experience themselves as cognitively constructive and emotionally adaptive.

At any given moment, we can either strengthen existing neural connections or develop new ones. To facilitate neuroplastic change in the case of complex trauma, we must help clients build new neural connections throughout the brain. Therapy accomplishes this goal by helping clients talk about traumatic memories while also encouraging them to focus on present resources of safety in which they feel socially connected to the therapist and grounded in the present moment. This helps create a bridge between the distressing self-state of the traumatic memory and the resourced and empowered self-state of the here and now. Importantly, when we invite clients to talk about traumatic memories, we want to be mindful that they are doing so in a purposeful, reflective manner so cognitive reappraisal can occur (Ford, 2018). *Cognitive reappraisal* is defined as the process of reinterpreting the meaning of events in order to reduce their disturbing emotional impact (Cutuli, 2014).

Our memories are influenced by our current social environments and are subject to change in response to suggestive cues and questions (Siegel, 2001). Traumatic memories are particularly malleable. Therefore, we must refrain from being overly interpretive about a client's symptoms, especially when they are experiencing somatic sensations with no known cause. For example, a client might wonder if they were sexually abused because they had an upsetting dream or felt an uncomfortable sensation in their body. In some cases, they might view therapy as a process to uncover repressed memories. Since we want to avoid the construction of false memories, it is important for both clients and therapists to resist the urge to "tell a story" about these symptoms. Instead, when working with clients who have somatic sensations without explicit memories, we ask them to describe their present-moment experiences while suspending our own or their urge to apply a narrative. We can reassure them (and ourselves) that we can still work with and respect the somatic discomfort even if we don't know the exact cause.

We can apply our understanding of neuroplasticity into trauma treatment by inviting clients to explore difficult memories from the past while simultaneously focusing on new positive resources that are available in the present moment. For example, we can encourage clients to sense the safety of the present moment, to feel the warmth of our relational exchange, or to remember times when they felt loved or understood by another. When we invite them to recall a distressing memory from the past, they pull forward the old neural circuit *and* also have an opportunity to construct a new neural circuit that integrates these positive resources. This process can also facilitate a new sense of meaning about historically painful life events.

Our brains have a built-in negativity bias, which leads us to pay more attention to cues of threat than to cues of safety (Vaish, Grossmann, & Woodward, 2008). If clients are currently living in an unsafe environment or relationship, we want to pay attention to their feelings of fear and prioritize their physical and emotional safety. However, when this negativity bias is a remnant of historical trauma, it can lead to a *false positive* in which the client perceives a situation or person as threatening when they are actually safe. In this case, you invite a client to focus their attention on positive resources to reduce the negativity bias. Through this process, you are asking them to engage in *attentional control* (Bardeen & Orcutt, 2011). Even if a client is experiencing ongoing stress related to homelessness or poverty, you can invite them to notice how the safe environment of the therapy office provides a brief respite and a necessary contrast to the threats the client is experiencing in their external environment.

Although focusing on resources can provide a temporary reduction of distress, this typically does not resolve the underlying cause of the client's dysregulation. As a result, symptoms may re-emerge during times of stress. We ultimately find a sustainable resolution of C-PTSD symptoms when we help clients work through the distressing thoughts, emotions, and sensations associated with traumatic memories. Instead of overriding their somatic distress, you eventually invite clients to turn toward their discomfort in a slow, modulated manner by focusing on small, manageable amounts of discomfort and returning their attention to a resource as needed. This alternation of attention allows clients to develop *dual awareness* in which they learn to attend to the distress of traumatic memories while also staying connected to a sense of safety in the here and now (Rothschild, 2010; Shapiro, 2018). Dual awareness is a key element of trauma treatment modalities discussed within chapters 7 and 8 of this book.

Bringing Attentional Control, Choice, and Containment into Therapy

C-PTSD is associated with the sense that one has lost authority over the process of remembering. For example, clients may even become triggered by traumatic memories when parenting their children. In this case, we want to help clients reclaim a sense of choice about when and where they think about traumatic events. To do so, we can teach clients the skill of *containment*, which is defined as temporarily putting thoughts about trauma aside and reorienting attention toward resources (Shapiro, 2018). For example, clients might imagine putting their disturbing memories in a container and storing them there for the time being, or they can write down disturbing thoughts in a journal and then close it. When clients exhibit symptoms such as intrusive memories, flashbacks, or nightmares, these serve as signals to focus upon the skill of containment.

Successful containment requires that clients have a predictable time set aside during which they can begin to work through their disturbing emotions, thoughts, and sensations. Often, that time occurs in therapy. Clients sometimes come into the office feeling panicky, anxious, overwhelmed, or shutdown. When this occurs, we can help them practice containment by orienting their attention to cues in the current environment that help them recognize that they are safe in the here and now. In addition, you can use the therapeutic relationship to strengthen clients' sense of safety by inviting them to listen to sound of your voice while offering a calm reminder that you are there for support. Once a client has successfully shifted their focus to a positive resource, you can then invite them to notice the reduction in defensive activation throughout their body.

The following two healing practices invite the client to practice attentional control and containment. Importantly, it is wise to ask the client's permission to redirect their attention away from their distress, or they otherwise might be afraid that we will not adequately attend to their pain. **Giving them a sense of choice helps to honor their process.** We can reassure them that there is plenty of time to work with their distress by returning to the statements offered in the healing practice from chapter 1 on inviting spacious, relational awareness. As with all of the healing practices in this book, you might only explore one of these statements at a time. I suggest timing and adapting the practice so it is relevant to your client's experience. For the first practice, I suggest keeping several sensory items in your office, such as a basket of differently textured items (e.g., rocks, seashells, pinecones) and several essential oils from which to choose.

Develop Attentional Control

- I notice that you are feeling… [*e.g., anxious, unsettled, overwhelmed, disconnected, restless, irritable*]. I would like to offer a few suggestions to help you feel safe right now. Is that okay with you?

- Would you be willing to let me know if you start to feel overwhelmed or overly distressed during our time together? I'd love to help you feel like therapy is a safe place.

- Would you be willing to look around the room? Take your time. Notice any details that help you recognize that you are safe. Perhaps you find a piece of artwork or a plant that helps you feel more relaxed and at ease. Notice how you are able to move your head and eyes to look around the space. Notice where your eyes would like to rest.

- Can you take a moment to notice the contact between your body and the chair or couch? Can you notice the points of contact between your back and legs? See if bringing your attention to these sensations helps you feel more present and connected to yourself.

- Explore how it feels to take several deep breaths while focusing on the rise and fall of your belly. Or perhaps just notice the air moving across the tip of your nose or in and out of your mouth.

- Perhaps you would like to take a sip of water or warm tea. Notice how it feels to move your tongue around the inside of your mouth. Notice the taste or temperature. You might choose to sense the back of your teeth or the roof of your mouth with your tongue.

- What sounds are you aware of in this room? How does it feel to listen to the sound of my voice or to notice the… [*e.g., hum of the air conditioner, sound of traffic, quietness of the room*]?

- If you would like, choose an item to hold in your hands, such as a rock, pinecone, soft pillow, or stuffed animal. Notice the texture, temperature, and weight of this object as you hold it in your hands. What do you notice as you shift your attention to this object?

- If you would like, choose an essential oil and place a few drops on a piece of cotton. What do you notice as you shift your attention to this scent?

- Notice how you feel as I say to you the words "you are safe now." How does your mind respond? What emotions do you feel?

- Let me know when you feel connected to yourself and safe. As we refocus our attention on the difficult experience that you were speaking about, let me know if you begin to feel anxious or shutdown again. We can revisit these strategies as needed.

31

Cultivate Choice and Containment

The following strategies encourage you to mindfully choose when to think about the traumatic events from your past:

- Make an agreement with yourself that you will only focus on traumatic memories when you have support and resources. Keep in mind that you might only feel safe while in therapy. Or you might choose periods of time to journal and reflect.

- Take several deep breaths and remind yourself that you have a choice about whether this is a good time to think about any distressing memories from your past.

- If you choose to journal about traumatic events on your own, it may be instrumental to set a timer for 10–15 minutes. When the timer goes off, check in with yourself to ensure that you feel safe with your process. Remember, you can close your journal and know that any upsetting material will be held safely inside until you feel ready to return to the process. You may not want to address these events until you *return to therapy*.

- If at any point you feel triggered or overwhelmed, give yourself permission to distance yourself from any disturbing thoughts, emotions, or images. You can be creative in this process. For example, you can imagine a box, file, or room that is big enough to hold your distress. Then imagine placing any images or thoughts into the container until you return to therapy. Or you can imagine the traumatic event getting farther and farther away so it becomes smaller and smaller in your mind. Remember that you can open your container or bring these images or thoughts into your mind when you are in therapy.

3

The Neurophysiology
of Complex Trauma

....

As human beings, our bodies are physiologically equipped with built-in protective mechanisms that help us survive threatening situations by mobilizing our defenses or disconnecting us from our pain. When we experience a threat, our SNS helps us move into self-protection through the release of adrenaline, cortisol, and norepinephrine throughout the bloodstream. Just as animals seek to flee or fight predators, we too rely upon these defense mechanisms to survive. However, fight and flight are not sustainable over the long term, and when there is no way to escape an event that threatens our lives, we shift into an immobilization response in which we feel frozen, shutdown, or collapsed. We can see this "feigned death" in animals who stop moving or literally faint as a last-ditch attempt at survival. Individuals who have a history of chronic, repeated traumatic stress can feel trapped by this immobilization response, leading them to feel disoriented, disconnected, and disembodied.

We now understand that the body "bears the burden" and "keeps the score" of traumatic events (Scaer, 2014; van der Kolk, 2014). Psychotherapists who emphasize talk therapy may predominantly focus on the role of the mind as influencing physical well-being; however, a mind-body approach to trauma recovery is now recognized as essential to successful treatment. We simply cannot think our way out of our innate, physiological stress and trauma responses. Therefore, the integrative mind-body model of care presented in this book emphasizes a bidirectional relationship between the mind and body. This approach balances the traditional top-down approach of talk therapy with bottom-up interventions that focus on sensations and emotions in order to access the way that trauma is held in the body.

In this chapter, I examine the neurophysiological impact of complex trauma on the nervous system through the lens of polyvagal theory (Porges, 2011). Given the role of ANS dysregulation in C-PTSD, healing practices in this chapter focus on identifying symptoms of hyper- or hypo-arousal and strengthening clients' social engagement system to enhance their present-moment experience of safety and connection. Through small experiments, we invite clients to explore how subtle changes in posture, breath, movement, and somatic awareness can help them develop a felt sense of trust, connection, safety, and stabilization.

The Polyvagal Theory in Trauma Treatment

Initial conceptualizations of the ANS posited that it had two branches: the SNS and PNS. These two branches were thought to function in a reciprocal manner, meaning that when one was active, the other was disengaged. Within that model, the SNS was described as our "stress response" system, whereas the PNS was associated with our ability to recover from stress through a "relaxation response" that allowed the body to rest and digest. More recently, however, the work of Dr. Stephen Porges (2011) has advanced our understanding of the ANS as it relates to trauma and PTSD. His work suggests that the ANS actually has three branches and that these branches are not simply reciprocal; rather, they work in a hierarchical fashion. In particular, he identified that the PNS has two presentations: In times of safety, the PNS facilitates the classically understood relaxation and regenerative responses, but in times of threat, the PNS has a defensive mode in which we collapse, feel helpless, or immobilize into a feigned death or "faint" response.

We can better understand these two expressions of the PNS through Porges's polyvagal theory, which provides a deepened understanding of the vagus nerve. The vagus nerve is primarily associated with cranial nerve X, though it also has shared neurology with cranial nerves V, VII, IX, and XI. The term *vagus* is Latin for "wandering," an appropriate descriptor for this nerve, which runs down from the brain and connects to the muscles around our eyes, mouth, and inner ear. The vagus nerve then moves downward to innervate the larynx and pharynx in the throat, as well as the heart and lungs. It then descends through the diaphragm into our digestive organs, including the stomach, spleen, liver, kidneys, and small and large intestines. The vagus nerve can be thought of as a bidirectional information highway that communicates between the mind and body.

The vagus nerve governs the nervous system's parasympathetic response, and it comprises two vagal circuits. The first vagal circuit, which is the most recently evolved part of our vagus nerve, is called the *ventral vagal complex*. Porges also calls the ventral vagus the *social engagement system* because it connects to the muscles and organs above the diaphragm that are primarily involved in helping us feel socially connected and safe in the world. The social engagement system gets its name because it is responsible for facial expressivity, which helps us understand or communicate emotions. In addition, the social engagement system is responsible for both the expressive and receptive domains of verbal communication. This guides the rhythm, tone, and inflection of our speech, which helps provide meaning to our communications. Furthermore, the social engagement system enhances our ability to listen to others and allows us to pick up on emotional nuances within communications. We communicate a sense of care and kindness to others when we offer a soft smile that extends from our face and eyes, or through a resonant tone in our voice that is then received by the ears of the listener. Given the connections between the vagus nerve and the heart and muscles of our face, we are also more likely to engage in empathic responses.

The second vagal circuit is an evolutionarily older part of the PNS called the *dorsal vagal complex*. Here, the vagus nerve extends below the diaphragm into the digestive organs. When we feel safe, the ventral vagal and dorsal vagal circuits coordinate a nourishing PNS response that has an inhibitory effect upon the SNS. Indeed, this allows us to soften into a state of nourishing relaxation. However, an evolutionarily older expression of the dorsal vagal complex can become dominant in situations of ongoing threat from which there is no escape. This is an immobilization state of collapse associated with low muscle tone, slowed heart rate, nausea, dizziness, and numbness.

From an evolutionary perspective, this "feigned death" response is instinctual in animals who faint so predators will lose interest in them—because, unlike scavengers, predators will typically not eat animals who are already dead. This immobilization response is accompanied by the release of endogenous (i.e., naturally produced) endorphins that have a numbing effect on pain. In small amounts, these endorphins can provide temporary relief. When complex trauma survivors remain stuck in this immobilization response, it can lead to dissociation, depression, and chronic physical health problems.

When we feel threatened, we typically move through a hierarchical sequence of three ANS pathways, each aimed for survival. When possible, we first try to activate our social engagement system to reestablish a sense of connection and safety. For example, a young boy who is facing separation from his mother might initially try to smile or reach out for his mother's hand for reassurance or to prevent her departure. If the boy is unable to secure a safe, relational bond, he will begin to cry or cling. This might evolve into feelings of fear or anger, which may manifest in terms of the boy running away or beginning to hit his mother. These behaviors indicate that the child has mobilized into fight and flight through SNS activation, which represents the second step in the hierarchy. Again, the purpose of these defense behaviors is to reestablish safety. However, this is often not possible in situations of ongoing threat, such as when a child is being abused or when a person is held in captivity. For example, if we imagine that this boy has been repeatedly abandoned and neglected, then he might progress to the third step in the hierarchy, in which he experiences feelings of defeat and helplessness that are driven by the evolutionarily older expression of the PNS.

According to Porges's model, both branches of the PNS serve as a metaphorical "vagal brake" for the SNS, though they implement this brake in unique ways (Porges, 2011). It is akin to the process of putting on the brakes when driving a car: We can either slow down by pressing on the brakes smoothly, or we can slam on the brakes and come to a hard, fast stop. The dorsal vagal complex functions like an abrupt brake by sending the body into a state of collapse and immobilization. In contrast, the social engagement system functions as a refined brake that facilitates increases in physical health and emotional well-being. Although the vagal brake functions to dial down activation of the SNS, trauma activation sometimes presents as rapid alternation between or simultaneous activation of both hyper-arousal and hypo-arousal (Kain & Terrell, 2018). In this case, we can imagine the individual driving with one foot on the gas and one foot on the brakes. **When the nervous system is imbalanced, it is often difficult to find nourishing relaxation or restful sleep, yet equally challenging to feel emotions of joy, pleasure, and excitement.** Here, we see a classic combination of being both wired and tired as clients describe oscillating between feelings of panic and exhaustion.

Not only are there two branches of the vagus nerve, but we can also blend the social engagement system with both the SNS and dorsal vagal complex to create "hybrid" nervous system states. The social engagement system on its own is associated with feeling calm, connected, curious, clearheaded, competent, and capable in choosing how to respond to a range of feelings and experiences. When we feel safe, we can blend our social engagement system with the SNS, which supports play, laughter, and sexual intimacy. As you can see, this blend allows us to evolve the crude functions of the SNS into a broader range that supports our adaptive and creative capacities. When we feel safe, we can also blend our social engagement system with the dorsal vagal complex so we can connect to the restorative side of the PNS, which allows us to choose to immobilize into an experience of relaxation, intimacy, and spiritual states often found in meditation.

The F's of Trauma Reactions

Drs. Maggie Schauer and Thomas Elbert, developers of narrative exposure therapy for the treatment of PTSD, describe six stages of trauma reactions: *freeze, flight, fight, fright, flag,* and *faint* (Schauer & Elbert, 2010). The initial stage in their model is a freeze response, which is a high arousal immobilization response managed by the SNS. This stage is like the proverbial "deer in headlights" and involves the orienting response of the lower brain regions. The second and third stages involve flight and fight, respectively, which are also maintained by the SNS. These two stages facilitate mobilization by increasing blood flow to the heart and muscles of the arms and lungs. The fourth stage is a fright response, which they describe as dual autonomic activation that involves abrupt alternations between SNS and dorsal vagal states. In this stage, an individual begins to feel symptoms of panic, dizziness, nausea, lightheadedness, tingling, and numbness.

The fifth stage in their model is the flag response, which is dominated by the dorsal vagal complex and leads to feelings of helplessness, fogginess, disorientation, fatigue, numbness, and physical immobilization. Within this stage, speech can become more difficult, sounds feel distant, and vision can be blurry. Physiologically, heart rate and blood pressure can rapidly drop, which can lead individuals into the sixth stage: a faint response. While the faint response is often used figuratively to represent a collapsed physiological state, in this model, fainting is referred to as a literal, vaso-vagal syncope. The faint response typically occurs when individuals are confronted with a life-threatening experience from which there is no escape. The faint response also serves the survival purpose of placing the body into a horizontal position to increase blood supply to the brain. Fainting is connected to the emotion of disgust, which leads the body to reject toxic material; however, this disgust response can also arise when an individual has a witnessed a violent or horrific event that is perceived as toxic to the psyche.

Psychotherapist and C-PTSD specialist Pete Walker adds another "F" to our complex trauma terminology (Walker, 2013). In particular, he proposes a "fawn" response that occurs when an individual engages in appeasing or pleasing behaviors for survival. For example, a child might try to forestall or dissuade an abuser or attacker by caring for the assailant's emotional or physical needs. The child bypasses their own needs—and in some cases, sense of identity—for the sake of attending to the needs of others. This caretaking system has elements of social engagement because this submissive response is driven by a need for attachment. Children who experience abuse are faced with a biologically driven conflict between their need to flee the dangerous environment and their need to attach to caregivers (Fisher, 2017). This can lead to a dissociative split between the part of the self that upholds the attachment to the caregiver and the part of the self that holds the reality of the terror. (We will discuss dissociation in greater depth in chapter 6.)

The Neurobiology of Chronic Traumatization

When children are exposed to repeated or chronic trauma, their developing nervous system and physiology are shaped within the context of this dangerous environment. In some cases, ongoing developmental trauma primes the nervous system to progress more quickly into immobilization because infants and young children do not have the option to flee or fight an abusive situation;

activation of the SNS is fruitless (Ogden & Minton, 2014). When this occurs repeatedly, this can lead to a conditioned immobilization response (van der Kolk, 2006), which can also be thought of as *learned helplessness,* a quality identified by Martin Seligman (1975/1992) to describe the powerlessness and hopelessness that is commonly experienced in situations of abuse.

Martin Teicher, a biopsychiatrist at Harvard, has researched the impact of childhood trauma on the developing brain of young infants and children (Teicher & Samson, 2016). His findings suggest a loss of gray matter in the prefrontal cortex and more specifically the orbitofrontal cortex. The orbitofrontal cortex is the part of our frontal lobes that helps regulate activity in the lower brain centers. It also has many extensions into the sensorimotor cortices of the brain, which help us consciously reflect on our sensations as related to our memories of the past. According to neuroscientist Antonio Damasio, somatic awareness is required to help us learn from our past so we can successfully plan for the future (Damasio, 1999). Our sensations help remind us of the negative consequences of historical behaviors, meaning that the body can be thought of as our conscience. However, individuals whose prefrontal cortex is compromised due to trauma may tend toward impulsivity and immediate gratification of needs without thinking about the long-term consequences of their behaviors.

Brain scans also reveal decreased hippocampal volume in individuals who have experienced childhood trauma (Teicher & Samson, 2016). The hippocampus is the part of the limbic system that is involved in the storage and retrieval of long-term, explicit memories. Explicit memories help us recall the factual details about events, such as the time, place, and order of events. They provide the basis for a verbal narrative that helps us develop a coherent sense of self across time. Therefore, individuals with reduced hippocampal functioning may have a harder time paying attention, focusing, and recalling factual information.

Also within the limbic system we find the amygdala, a small, almond-shaped structure involved in the development of implicit memories. In contrast to the verbal narrative associated with explicit memories, implicit memories maintain the emotional and sensory components of our experiences. When a traumatic event occurs, the amygdala stores this experience in the form of fear-based sensory fragments of memories. It is for this reason that specific sensory details surrounding traumatic events, such as the associated smells, sounds, and felt experiences, are often so strongly imprinted and vividly recalled. Given that the amygdala is fully formed by the third trimester of pregnancy, our implicit memory system is also involved in the formation of preverbal memories during infancy and in utero exposure to stress.

The implicit memory system can also carry the impact of trauma across multiple generations, with research finding that the descendants of ancestral trauma are more vulnerable to the development of PSTD after trauma exposure. In particular, research in the field of epigenetics has found evidence of DNA methylation changes among offspring of trauma survivors, including women who were pregnant during the 9/11 attacks and children whose parents were survivors of the Holocaust (Yehuda et al., 2005, 2009, 2006). These methylation changes are associated with alterations in a child's capacity to handle stress and may result in greater sensitivity to sounds and fear of unfamiliar people (Matthews & McGowan, 2019; Wolynn, 2016). While the sensations and emotions that arise with implicit memories are often strong, we must also remember that they are not always accurate. In many cases, they only represent fragments of sensations; they do not necessarily represent an exact replay of the original set of events.

The amygdala receives input from the basal ganglia, a set of brainstem structures that activate our most primitive defense reactions. For example, when we sense danger, the brainstem initiates an orienting response that brings our attention to the source of the threat through an instinctual turning of our head and gaze. This reflexive action is often accompanied by marked anger and fear. In response to real or perceived threats, the limbic and brainstem structures work together as the hypothalamus signals the pituitary gland to initiate the release of both catecholamines (epinephrine and norepinephrine) and cortisol from the adrenal glands via the hypothalamic-pituitary-adrenal (HPA) axis. This process initiates several physiological reactions, including increased heart rate, quickened breath, increased muscle tension, dry mouth, disrupted digestion, and the release of glucose to prepare the body to fight or flee (Ford, Grasso, Elhai, & Courtois, 2015).

Once the immediate threat is over, cortisol communicates back to the HPA axis via a negative feedback loop that stops the release of our stress hormones. However, chronic stress and ongoing trauma exposure recalibrate our stress response system and lead to modifications in the functioning of the HPA axis. In particular, individuals with chronic PTSD tend to have lower levels of cortisol, which reduces sensitivity in the negative feedback loop and interferes with the body's ability to achieve homeostasis. As a result, individuals who have been exposed to ongoing trauma exhibit an overall ability to recover from stress, interferences in their circadian rhythm, and digestive disturbances.

Overall, the brainstem and limbic centers become highly sensitized as a result of chronic and repeated traumatic events. This can contribute to a hyperawareness of facial expressions or body language, which is a process that can occur with or without conscious awareness. For example, compared to individuals without a trauma history, those with PTSD are more likely to perceive neutral faces as aggressive and fearful faces as angry (Bardeen & Orcutt, 2011). In addition, they are more likely to experience feelings of shame or terror in response to images of smiling faces (Steuwe et al., 2014). As a result, individuals with a trauma history can falsely perceive current situations as threatening even when there is no danger. It can be difficult for them to differentiate between experiences that occurred in the past and what is happening in the present moment. Moreover, once they perceive that a threat exists, they are more likely to perseverate on that threat, making it increasingly difficult for them to feel safe. This process can lead to a vicious cycle of anxiety.

Neuroscientist and author Dr. Joseph LeDoux describes two circuits in the brain associated with our fear response (LeDoux, 1996): a post-cognitive circuit and a pre-cognitive circuit. The post-cognitive circuit allows incoming sensory information to be routed to the prefrontal cortex, which allows us to assess and reflect on our interactions with other people and our environment. However, when we sense a dangerous situation, a pre-cognitive circuit sends sensory information directly to the amygdala, which can initiate a defensive response without engaging the prefrontal cortex. From an evolutionary perspective, this secondary circuit allows us to mobilize self-protection resources without conscious thought. For example, it would be life-saving to instinctively climb a tree to escape a lion rather than to have waited too long while we thought about our options. As we can see, the nervous system can initiate a full-body defensive reaction before we even fully assess what is happening. Psychologist and author Dr. Dan Goleman calls this process *emotional hijacking* to account for the ways in which limbic activation suppresses the regulating functions of the prefrontal cortex (Goleman, 1995/2006).

Trauma is also associated with impairments in communication between upper and lower brain centers. Although PTSD is typically associated with increased limbic arousal, decreased frontal lobe activity, increased SNS arousal, and elevated levels of cortisol in the bloodstream, individuals with the dissociative subtype exhibit paradoxical increases in frontal lobe activity and decreases in limbic activity. They also tend to have decreased activity in the somatosensory cortices, resulting in impaired bodily awareness (Felmingham et al., 2008; Lanius et al., 2012; Nicholson et al., 2017). In other words, they tend to feel detached and disconnected from their emotions. Moreover, individuals with the dissociative subtype tend to have lower cortisol levels and parasympathetic dominance (Yehuda, 2009; Zaba et al., 2015). Given that cortisol is directly related to our circadian rhythm, this can cause sleep disturbances among those with dissociative PTSD. Our body's typical circadian rhythm tends to peak in the morning, dip after lunch, lift in the late afternoon, and dip again in the evening for healthy sleep. However, individuals with the dissociative subtype tend to have a flattened circadian rhythm, which is associated with reduced alertness in the morning and reduced capacity for restful sleep.

Another interconnected set of brain regions that has been linked to trauma symptoms is the default mode network. This interactive network of neural structures is associated with brain activity that occurs when we are not focused on a specific task, such as when we are daydreaming, reminiscing about the past, and fantasizing about the future. These freely associated thought processes help us find creative solutions to navigate through challenging situations. However, alterations in the default mode network have been discovered in individuals with anxiety, depression, PTSD, and chronic pain (Daniels et al., 2011). As a result, when these individuals experience or perceive cues of danger and threat, they switch into survival mode with symptoms of rumination, hypervigilance, and dissociation.

In addition to impaired communications between the upper and lower brain centers, Teicher and colleagues have found associations between childhood trauma and impaired connections across the corpus callosum (Teicher & Samson, 2016). Neural connections within the corpus callosal region allow the right and left hemispheres of the brain to communicate with each other, which helps us to feel our emotions, put our experiences into words, and counterbalance negative feelings with positive resources. However, individuals with C-PTSD exhibit reductions in the area and integrity of the corpus callosum, resulting in poor communication between the left and right hemispheres of the brain.

The right side of the brain is primarily associated with our ability to express and recognize emotions. Because the right brain is dominant during the first three years of life, it tends to hold our earliest attachment memories and patterns of affect regulation. When right-brain activity is dominant, we tend to feel more emotionally connected to ourselves and others. However, traumatic memories, especially those related to childhood relational injuries, are also held within the right brain (Schore, 2010). Therefore, individuals who hold traumatic memories are more likely to harbor negative emotions and perceptions in the right brain.

In contrast, when left-brain activity is dominant, we tend to feel more analytical and logical. The rational capacities of the left brain can help us to work through difficulties in a sequential manner. As related to trauma recovery, the left frontal lobes help us to detach from our distress, which can allow us to more easily reflect upon on the positive events of our lives (Silberman & Weingartner, 1986). While the left brain can help us to create distance from our emotional distress, too much left-brain activity can leave us feeling disconnected. The left side of the brain also houses Broca's area, which supports our language capacities. Given that traumatic stress compromises Broca's area, this can make it more difficult for individuals to talk about traumatic experiences (van der Kolk, 2014).

Individuals with C-PTSD also tend to be hypersensitive to sound, light, and touch. Again, we can see a brain-based explanation for these symptoms. All of our memories go through a process of consolidation, which allows the sensory components of our experiences to be held throughout the association cortex. This is the part of the brain that unites each of our sensory experiences to produce a unified perceptual experience of the world. Each sensory system has its own area within the association cortex that is connected to the lobes of the brain. For example, the parietal lobes house the somatosensory cortices that are responsible for our sense of touch. The temporal lobes contain the auditory cortices that help us process sounds and comprehend language, and they also house the olfactory cortices that are responsible for our sense of smell. Deep within the fold between the parietal and temporal lobes we find the insula, which houses our sense of taste and our interoceptive awareness of internal body states, such as hunger, fullness, thirst, and changes in heart rate. Finally, the occipital lobes are involved with processing visual information.

Teicher has identified specific areas within the association cortex that are overdeveloped in children as a function of the type of trauma they have experienced (Teicher & Samson, 2016). In particular, his findings indicate that witnessing trauma (such as domestic violence) is associated with overdevelopment within the visual cortex, exposure to verbal abuse is linked to hypersensitivity in the auditory cortex, and sexual abuse is associated with hypersensitivity in the somatosensory cortices. Importantly, these neuroplastic cortical changes function to protect the child from the sensory processing of specific abusive experiences and form a neurobiological basis for dissociative symptoms (Heim at al., 2013).

Returning our attention to the vagus nerve can provide insight into *hyperacusis*, or hypersensitivity to high and low frequency sounds, that individuals with C-PTSD often exhibit. The ventral vagus nerve extends into the inner ear and, in times of safety, functions to tone the stapedius muscle— which, in turn, engages the tensor tympani to regulate the middle ear bones. This process helps reduce sensitivity to high- and low-vibration sounds, which allows our ears to be sensitive to the range of the human voice. However, when we feel unsafe, the stapedius muscle loosens to increase our sensitivity to high- and low-frequency sounds. In the natural world, animals communicate danger by using high-pitched screeching sounds, as we often hear with birds or monkeys, and by attuning to lowpitched growls from predators. Unfortunately, chronic and repeated trauma can leave an individual hypersensitive to these high- and low-frequency sounds.

Ultimately, having an understanding of the impact of chronic traumatization on the brain and body provides insight into the different ways that clients with C-PTSD might present in therapy. Imbalances in the vagus nerve and the subsequent physiology of the ANS can lead them to present as overwhelmed, anxious, panicky, distracted, unfocused, or hypomanic. At other times, they might present as shutdown, fatigued, lethargic, or depressed. They can also present as disorientated, may have difficulty speaking coherently, or may even come across as paranoid and delusional. Without an understanding of each individual's trauma history, it is easy to misunderstand and misdiagnosis these symptoms. However, once we grasp the profound impact of complex trauma, we can better understand the variable nature of clients' symptoms. Such understanding allows us to approach treatment with greater wisdom and compassion.

Neuroception and the Social Engagement System

Underlying polyvagal theory is the concept of *neuroception*, which is a term that Dr. Porges coined to reflect the process by which the ANS constantly scans for and responds to internal and external cues of safety or danger in our environment. This process is one that happens largely out of conscious awareness. For example, I once worked with a woman who had been violently attacked many years prior and who started having flashbacks and acute anxiety symptoms again after starting a new job. She was frustrated because she had previously worked through this traumatic event in therapy and thought she was "over it." At first, she didn't realize why her symptoms had re-emerged. However, in therapy she reflected on her new work environment and realized that one of her coworkers had similar physical features to the man who attacked her years ago. Although she consciously recognized that her coworker was not her attacker, her body unconsciously responded to these similarities and made her feel triggered without realizing why. Even as she spoke about this in session, her heart began to beat rapidly and her breathing changed. We were able to recognize that this experience was giving her access to an incomplete part of the trauma that she still held in her body. She was able to work through these feelings safely, and her symptoms remitted.

We can build a more conscious relationship with the process of neuroception by increasing our awareness of changes in our nervous system, such as increases in heart rate, changes in our breath, patterns of tensions in our chest, or subtle changes in our gaze and posture. Doing so in the context of the therapy session can help clients notice more easily when they are feeling keyed-up or shutdown. They then have a choice to become curious about these reactions and why they might be occurring. In addition, in the safety of the therapeutic environment, they can release unnecessary physiological and emotional activation.

Empathic Attunement and the Vagus Nerve

The vagus nerve develops between the first and second year of life, concurrent with the development of the attachment relationship. Therefore, the quality of the mother-infant relationship has a strong initial influence over the tone and functioning of the vagus nerve (Insel, 2000). A sensitive caregiver attunes to the infant's nonverbal cues—paying attention to the child's facial expressions, vocalizations, gestures, and body movements—and this attunement guides the caregiver's use of touch, eye contact, and tone of voice, as well as the timing of interactions. Through this attuned relationship, primary caregivers help regulate the immature physiology of the infant and young child. In particular, the mother's ANS regulates the infant's physiologic state via a right-hemisphere-to-right-hemisphere limbic system influence (Bornstein & Suess, 2000; Schore, 2001), which has a long-lasting impact on the nervous system.

Over time, the accumulation of empathic attunement helps reinforce children's internal sense of self, which includes ownership of their body and emotions. This process strengthens their capacity for neuroception. As individuals develop into adulthood, they carry with them this capacity to sense their own somatic and emotional changes, and they internalize the capacity to be responsive to their own changing needs, which reflects their ability to engage in self-regulation. Importantly, the ability to self-regulate is an acquired process that develops in the context of a secure relationship wherein individuals learn to regulate themselves through mutual regulation or *co-regulation*. Co-regulation is an interactive process in which individuals reciprocally regulate each other's nervous system by tapping into their social engagement system to promote feelings of safety and connectedness.

Oftentimes, individuals with C-PTSD have a compromised capacity for self-regulation because they did not receive sufficient co-regulation in childhood. They did not grow up in a caring environment characterized by attunement, connection, and safety. However, these individuals can learn how to self-regulate in the safety of the therapy office by co-regulating with their therapist when working through distressing emotions or somatic experiences. In this respect, therapy provides another opportunity for clients with C-PTSD to experience relational attunement, co-regulation, and the development of neuroception. It also provides them an opportunity to strengthen vagal tone, which is associated with a greater ability to tolerate or recover from stress (see chapter 9). Through this process and through repeated practice clients can create new patterns of ANS regulation.

This next series of clinical interview questions can be used to help your client better understand the common symptoms of nervous system dysregulation that individuals with C-PTSD experience. If appropriate, you can explore this list of questions with clients during a clinical interview. However, if doing so would interfere with the therapeutic relationship, you can use these questions in the context of more informal conversations intended to get to know the client better.

The list of clinical interview questions is followed by three healing practices. The first practice guides clients in building neuroception and increasing awareness of their nervous system state, which can help them recognize when they are unnecessarily engaging in a defensive state. The second practice enhances the social engagement system by inviting clients to engage in small experiments in which they explore how subtle changes in somatic awareness can help them develop a felt sense of trust, connection, safety, and stabilization. The third practice focuses on widening the client's window of tolerance by increasing their capacity to tolerate emotional or somatic distress. It is important to let clients know that it is their choice to participate in any of these practices and that there is no "right" or "wrong" answer. You might only explore a single practice or even just one part of a practice in a session, and I suggest only integrating a practice as it feels relevant to the moment. For example, a client might share that they have tension in their eyes and jaw, which could prompt you to engage in a somatic exploration of these areas.

Clinical Interview Questions

Know Your Nervous System

This list of clinical interview questions explores some of the common symptoms of nervous system dysregulation that individuals with C-PTSD experience. To help identify imbalances within the ANS, the list is broken down into hyper-arousal (or sympathetically dominant) symptoms and hypo-arousal (or parasympathetically dominant) symptoms. You might explore these items with your client directly during a clinical interview, or if doing so would be too overwhelming, you can use this checklist as you get to know your client across multiple sessions.

Hyper-Arousal Symptoms

- ☐ Do you have difficulty relaxing or sleeping?
- ☐ Do you experience shortness of breath or feel like you can't take a deep breath?
- ☐ Do you sometimes have a rapid heartbeat or feel pains in your chest?
- ☐ Have you been diagnosed with hypertension?
- ☐ Do you tend to sweat profusely?
- ☐ Do you get frequent colds?
- ☐ Do you have frequent food cravings for sweet or salty foods?
- ☐ Do you have a difficult time regulating your blood sugar?
- ☐ Do you grind your teeth or clench your jaw?
- ☐ Do you have muscle tension in your shoulders, arms, back, or legs?

Hypo-Arousal Symptoms

- ☐ Do you frequently feel lethargic or tired?
- ☐ Do you find yourself intolerant of exercise?
- ☐ Are you lightheaded or dizzy?
- ☐ Is your vision blurry or dimmed?
- ☐ Do you urinate frequently?
- ☐ Are you nauseous frequently?
- ☐ Do you get migraines?
- ☐ Do you faint easily or frequently?
- ☐ Do you have non-epileptic or psychogenic seizures?

Build Neuroception and Discern Awareness

- Would you be willing to explore a brief experiment aimed at increasing your awareness of your nervous system? I invite you to allow yourself to be curious about your experience and, as much as possible, to become aware of your experience without judgment.

- There are three levels of nervous system arousal, which include feeling: (1) safe and connected, (2) mobilized for fight or flight, and (3) immobilized and collapsed. There is nothing inherently wrong with any of these nervous system states. You might notice different emotions or memories connected to each. However, it can be valuable to notice changes that occur during our sessions.

- You can build self-awareness of cues that give you feedback about the state of your nervous system. Take a few moments to observe your body movements, posture, breath, heart rate, or level of energy that give you feedback about these three states.

- Does your breath feel short or quickened? Can you sense your heartbeat in your chest? Are you aware of tension in your belly, chest, or throat? Do you notice if you are holding yourself upright in a rigid manner, or does your posture feel collapsed? Do you feel calm, energetic, restless, or fatigued? What do these cues from your body tell you about your nervous system state?

- Our minds are constantly scanning for cues of threats. These cues might come from our external environment, our body, or our relationships. We engage our defenses when we perceive that we are not safe. If you notice that you are moving into a fight-or-flight response or are feeling immobilized and collapsed, see if you can notice what is leading you to feel unsafe.

- I invite you to share with me when you notice changes during sessions, as this will allow us to work together as a team to create a safe environment for trauma recovery.

- You can also enhance your awareness of your nervous system states between sessions. This will help give you feedback about how you are responding to your environment. It may also be helpful to ask yourself if you are responding accurately to a threat that is happening right now. Or perhaps you are reacting unnecessarily to a feeling that is connected to a memory from your past. Can you sense if your defensive response is necessary for the present circumstances?

Healing Practice

Awaken Your Social Engagement System

- Would you be willing to explore a brief experiment aimed at helping you connect to your social engagement system? Your social engagement system represents one branch of your vagus nerve, which passes through your face, throat, lungs, heart, and belly. Gentle movements and breaths through these areas of your body can help you feel safe and connected to yourself and others. I invite you to allow yourself to be curious about your experience and, as much as possible, to become aware of your experience without judgment.

- Let's begin by noticing your eyes. See if you can sense any tension or fatigue in this area of your face. Explore some movements in your eyes by widening them or squeezing them shut. Then begin to explore how it feels to soften your eyes into a gentle expression of warmth. If you'd like, think of someone you care about, and imagine sharing with them a loving smile from your eyes. Notice how the changes in how you express yourself through your eyes resonates in other areas of your body.

- Bring your attention to your mouth. Once again, see if you notice any tension in your jaw, lips, or cheeks. If you would like, find some movements to explore any sensations here by opening your mouth and closing it tightly. You might even fake a yawn until you induce a real yawn, as this can release tension in the jaw and soft palate in the back of your mouth. Then soften your jaw and allow your teeth to gently separate from one another. As with the eyes, you might imagine a loved one and engage a soft smile. As you release tension around your mouth, notice if you experience any corresponding release of tension in other areas of your face or body.

- Bring your attention to your throat. Notice if you are aware of any sensations or tension in this area of your body. Sense your breath as it moves through the back of your throat and encourages a deepening of your awareness into this area of your body. Perhaps explore any sighs or sounds that resonate with the sensations in your throat. If you would like, explore slowly dipping your head forward and lifting your head up. Notice the feeling of contraction in your throat and subsequent opening. Pause in stillness and notice any related sensations in other areas of your body.

- Bring your attention to your chest. If you notice any tension around your chest or shoulders, explore rolling your shoulders forward and back. Continue moving until you feel more connected to this area of your body. Now imagine your heart nestled into your lungs and how they are deeply interconnected. Your breath is a wonderful way to connect to your heart. Perhaps you would like to bring your hands over your heart and begin to sense the subtle movements of your breath in the lifting and lowering of your chest. With this quality of interconnection in mind, explore how it feels to reflect on a friend or a pet that enhances your sense of connection, gratitude, and love. As you breathe into this loving feeling, notice any related sensations in your body.

- Now bring awareness to your belly, and begin to notice any sensations, tension, or discomfort here. If you would like, bring your hands over your belly and begin to focus on breathing through your diaphragm, allowing your belly to rise with each inhale. See if you can release tension by softening your belly with each exhale. You might choose to close your eyes and settle into your chair. Notice how you feel as you let yourself be heavy or relax into support. See if you notice any subtle shifts in your digestion, such as a soft gurgling in your stomach or intestines, as a result of the deepening of your breath. Can you sense any other signs that your body is relaxing in response to your belly breathing?

Widen Your Window of Tolerance

- Would you be willing to explore a brief experiment aimed at helping you stay present with distressing sensations and emotions? This practice can help you widen your window of tolerance and ultimately prepare you for trauma reprocessing.

- Take a few breaths, and begin to notice if there is any distressing emotion or body sensation that is present for you in this moment. Rather than trying to make this distressing feeling go away, this practice invites you to notice what happens when you allow yourself to focus your awareness on this emotion or sensation. You have a choice during this process, and you can take your attention away from the distressing feeling at any point.

- You might notice an urge to judge your experience as bad or scary. Instead, see if you can describe the sensations or emotions you are having. As you bring your awareness to the distressing emotion or body sensation, see if you can notice whether it has a temperature. Is it hot or cold? Does it have a texture? Is it dull or sharp, dense or dispersed, radiating or prickly? Is there a weight to the sensation, such as feeling floaty or heavy? Is there a color or shape to it?

- You might notice that you have an urge to tell a story about this emotion or sensation. For now, see if you can return to your intention to stay with the feeling, and observe any subtle changes as you bring your awareness to your experience.

- Perhaps you notice a negative thought or belief that interferes with your ability to stay present with this emotion or body sensation. For example, you might believe you are weak if you feel sad, or you might fear something bad will happen as a result of the sensation in your body. See if you can return to an intention to observe your experience.

- Now that you have brought your attention to your distressing emotion or body sensation, take some time to notice if the feeling has changed in anyway. Were you able to stay with your experience just a little bit longer? Has the sensation lessened in intensity, or has it perhaps increased? Either way, I invite you to take a moment to appreciate yourself for bringing your awareness to your distress. In time, this practice builds your capacity to heal from trauma.

4

The Therapeutic Relationship in Complex Trauma Treatment

C-PTSD tends to interfere with our ability to feel safe, calm, and connected to others. Interpersonal trauma often betrays our trust in other people and impairs our ability to form secure, nourishing relationships. However, **the greatest predictor of meaningful change in clients with C-PTSD is the quality of the therapeutic alliance.** When we develop rapport with our clients, it increases the likelihood that they will remain in therapy long enough to benefit from additional trauma-focused interventions (Pearlman & Courtois, 2005). Therefore, our journey through this integrative, mind-body approach begins with relational therapy, which invites us to focus on building trustworthy relationships while understanding that our clients' symptoms are best understood within socio-developmental and cultural contexts.

As human beings, we are shaped by the significant relationships in our lives. Relational therapy focuses on our clients' relational experiences as they exist both inside and outside of therapy. Relational therapy is rooted in a psychodynamic approach in which we aim to understand ourselves and our clients within the context of our earliest childhood relationships, seeing as these have a profound impact on our sense of self and our interpersonal dynamics with others. Furthermore, relational therapy as developed by psychiatrist Dr. Jean Baker Miller explores the impact of our clients' historical or current social disconnections that developed as a result of abuse, racism, sexism, class prejudice, and homophobia (Banks, 2006; Frey, 2013).

The goal of relational therapy is to provide a safe place for clients to attend to their relational wounds while also experiencing new, reparative relational experiences. This asks us to attend to the impact of power differentials and privilege dynamics within therapy and as they relate to our clients' lives outside of therapy. Since relationships are a two-way street, this chapter asks you to explore your own developmental and cultural history through self-awareness practices. This allows you to compassionately attend to possible clinical blind spots that can interfere with your work with clients.

This chapter also offers healing practices focused on co-regulation and relational repair. Ultimately, the relational learning that occurs in therapy through reparative moments of disconnection can strengthen our clients' ability to respond and handle the interpersonal challenges in their lives with greater care and sensitivity. This chapter concludes with an additional opportunity to reflect on your experience as a therapist with guidance for self-care around vicarious trauma and compassion fatigue.

Attachment and Identity

Connection is at the core of all human experience. We all share the need to be seen and understood. We long to belong and to experience ourselves within the context of loving, respectful *relationships*. We form our sense of self in the context of others. This process begins in our earliest attachment relationships and continues throughout the lifespan. During infancy, our nervous system is dependent upon others to help us feel safe, connected, and calm. Our sense of self develops through the ways in which we were touched, the quality of the eye contact we received, the facial expressions or body language we witnessed, and the tones of voices that we heard. Good-enough caregivers attune to an infant's needs and respond by providing basic needs for care, nourishment, excitement, and rest. This empathic attunement helps reinforce the child's internal sense of self, which includes ownership of their body and emotions.

When infants and their caregivers interact, there are natural cycles of engagement and disengagement that occur. During the engagement phase, the infant might make a sound, widen their eyes, and open their mouth. In response, the caregiver responds by mirroring sounds and facial expressions. This exchange builds into a playful burst of excitement that is often followed by a period of disengagement, which the infant initiates by turning their head to the side and looking away. This period of disengagement initiates a resting phase during which the attuned caregiver responds by averting their own gaze to honor this temporary quieting. The disengagement phase allows both the caregiver's and infant's nervous system to recalibrate until they are both ready for another round of playful interaction. Sometimes caregivers misread the infant's cues for disengagement, leading them to override the infant's need for rest. While this is a relatively common occurrence, when this pattern continues over time, an infant learns to override the natural rhythm of their nervous system for the sake of connection.

We continue to learn patterns of emotional expression throughout childhood and adolescence. For example, perhaps you can recall times when you felt afraid as a child. Maybe you have memories of how your mother or father responded. Were they comforting and caring? Or did they respond with their own fear or anger? Depending on the nature of these interactions, we may learn that it is acceptable to express our thoughts and feelings in relationships. Or we may learn to keep parts of ourselves hidden from others, which can lead us to sacrifice our authenticity in order to maintain a semblance of belonging.

In situations of abuse or neglect, children are profoundly misunderstood, dismissed, or harmed, which can lead them to experience intense emotional and physiological distress for extended periods of time. Abusive caregivers are emotionally dysregulated and not available to help their children feel calm and safe. As a result of these relational dynamics, children internalize the message that their distress is unacceptable and intolerable. They may begin to believe that they are unlovable or that they are "too much" for others to handle.

Attachment theory explains how these early developmental experiences provide the basis for our sense of self. **Our memories of these relational interactions are held deep within the implicit memory system.** Children who grow up with caregivers who are predictable, consistent, attuned, and trustworthy will develop a secure attachment style. They can reach for connection yet also differentiate themselves from their primary caregiver. They feel supported in having boundaries and, thus, are able to develop an embodied sense of self. As adults, these individuals are able to move with relative ease between their needs for closeness and their needs for separateness.

In contrast, children who grow up with distant or disengaged caregivers might adapt by avoiding closeness, disconnecting emotionally, or becoming overly self-reliant. As adults, they may develop an insecure-avoidant attachment style, leading them to dismiss their own and other people's emotions or needs. Other children may grow up with caregivers who are highly perceptive but can also be intrusive or invasive. This unpredictable parenting style can lead children to feel as though they cannot consistently depend upon their caregiver for connection. Consequently, they may develop an insecure-ambivalent attachment style that is characterized by uncertainty, anxiety, fears of abandonment, and a sense that relationships are unreliable.

In the most extreme situations of abuse, individuals may develop a disorganized attachment style. In these situations, children grow up with a parent whose behavior is a source of alarm or terror. Children are born with an innate, biological drive to attach with their primary caregiver and an equally strong drive to escape any source of threat. Since infants and young children are completely dependent upon their parents, those who grow up in an abusive environment must attach to the very person who is abusing them, and they must disconnect from the reality of the abuse in order to survive. This pattern often leads to dissociative symptoms in clients with C-PTSD.

Because we carry our relational experiences inside of us, these implicitly held memories can lead to relationship problems in adulthood that replay the painful dynamics of childhood. We engage in behaviors and interactional styles that are consistent with what we know and who we know ourselves to be. You can think of these early attachment relationships as teaching us a series of dance steps. We tend to look for others who dance in a similar manner, and if they don't, we hand them the instructions. For example, someone who was chronically rejected in childhood might continue to experience feelings of isolation or carry a belief that they are unlovable. They might feel overly dependent on others or unintentionally behave in a manner that leads someone to pull away from them. Conversely, they might carry a deep fear of intimacy that leads them to push others away when they get too close. Sometimes they might act aggressively or impulsively when intolerable emotions arise. As you can see, all of these relationship interactions can mimic abuse experienced during childhood. As a result, it is harder to navigate the typical challenges that arise when forming intimate relationships, parenting children, or developing meaningful friendships.

Authenticity and Embodied Culture in Relational Therapy

So often, therapists feel pressured to focus too heavily on diagnosis and protocol-based treatment interventions—a process that can sacrifice the genuineness that is necessary to build relational trustworthiness. The basis for trustworthiness in any relationship is authenticity and mutuality (Frey, 2013). Mutuality is the foundation of a sense of belonging and social connectedness, and it is defined as a bidirectional relational exchange in which both individuals are willing to be changed and impacted by the other. A commitment to authenticity requires that we, as therapists, work through our own developmental wounds so we can be available for the relational work with our clients. Often, we build these capacities within a supervisory relationship that allows us to discuss our clinical work and reflect on our reactions and emotions as they arise in the context of this work. As a result, we can wisely differentiate between authentic responses that are relevant to the client's growth and goals versus responses that are reactive or self-aggrandizing.

Supervision also gives us an opportunity to explore ruptures in the therapeutic relationship so we can nondefensively acknowledge when our behaviors have negatively impacted our clients. **Our willingness to be changed by our clients and our ability to admit when we have made mistakes reduces the power differential within the therapeutic relationship.** This process aligns with our intention to reduce the impact of oppression, discrimination, and marginalization in our clients' lives. Here, supervision can help us explore our own history as related to culture, ethnicity, race, sex, and gender and how our own embodied experiences of privilege and power might show up in therapy.

All of our culturally and socially informed experiences are held in our bodies (Bennett & Castiglioni, 2004; Kimmel, 2013; Nickerson, 2017). We adopt social and cultural rules because this provides us with a sense of belonging. Our posture, use of eye contact, use of gestures, and use of space are all reflections of these learned experiences. We develop our own cultural identity in this way. Inevitably, our interactions with others have embedded dynamics of power and privilege. This shows up in our willingness to initiate conversations, speak freely, or take up space. Conversely, historical experiences of feeling disempowered, disrespected, or violated might show up as withdrawal behaviors, defensiveness, reactivity, or fearful reactions to another person.

We all carry within us perceptions of ourselves and others based on our cultural heritage. These form the basis of stereotypes, prejudice, and discrimination based on attributes such as race, ethnicity, sex, gender, religion, age, or able-bodiedness. Often, these dynamics occur outside of conscious awareness, but we can learn to take responsibility for our unconscious culturally-based behaviors. Even if we grew up in a family that endorsed prejudice, we can reflect on our conditioning and develop new, respectful, and kind ways to relate to people who are different from ourselves. This process is a cornerstone of successful relational therapy in an increasingly multicultural world. This requires tolerating the discomfort that can accompany change and new learning.

Therapist Self-Awareness Practice

Take a moment to reflect on your role as a therapist. There are likely many times when you have felt secure in your work with others. Perhaps, like many of us, there are times when you have also felt anxious or insecure. The following descriptions invite you to notice any therapeutic relational dynamics that may or may not feel familiar to you. Explore how they relate to your own and your clients' relational, socio-developmental, and cultural histories.

- **Feeling defensive:** Bring to mind a time in therapy when you felt the urge to distance yourself from a client. Perhaps you began to focus on their thoughts instead of their feelings. Or maybe you felt detached and dismissive of their experience. You might have also begun to feel disconnected from your own body and emotions. Or you might have felt tired and distracted. Perhaps you began to inadvertently push your client away.

- Can you recall other times in your life when you have felt this way outside of therapy? Is there a resonance with this relational stance from your own childhood or attachment history? Were either of your parents distant or dismissive? In what ways might your history help you understand your own feelings about your client? Can you sense if this dynamic is connected to your or the client's cultural background? Do you notice any parallels between your feelings and your client's relational or attachment history? In what ways might this introspective process help you deepen a sense of compassion for yourself or empathy for your client?

- **Feeling protective:** Bring to mind a time in therapy when you felt so strongly connected to the experience of a client that you had a difficult time separating yourself from their experience. Perhaps you felt strong emotions and body sensations during the session. Maybe you continued to feel these emotions and sensations even after the session was over. Perhaps you felt responsible for the client's experience or an urge to rescue them.

- Ask yourself if this experience of merging with another person is familiar for you. Do you tend to carry the emotions of others? Can you recall other times in your life when you felt this way outside of therapy? Is there a resonance with this relational stance from your own childhood or attachment history? Did you feel responsible for a parent's emotions when you were a child? In what ways might your history help you understand your relationship style with your client? Can you sense if this dynamic is connected to your or the client's cultural background? Do you notice any parallels with your client's relational or attachment history? In addition, in what ways might you create a little more space to feel yourself as different from your client?

- **Feeling fearful:** Bring to mind a time in therapy when you felt anxious and unsettled before, during, or after a session with a client. Maybe you felt uncomfortable or restless. Perhaps you could feel your heart rate increase or noticed that your breath became shallow. You might have noticed feelings of aggression toward your client or that you were feeling victimized by them. Or you might have felt confused and as if you couldn't think clearly. All of these are signals that your mind and body were responding to a feeling of being threatened.

- Can you recall other times in your life when you felt this way outside of therapy? Is there a resonance with this relational experience from your own childhood or attachment history? In what ways might your history help you understand your own feelings about your client? Can you sense if this dynamic is connected to your or the client's cultural background? Do you notice any parallels with your client's relational or attachment history? In what ways might this introspective process help you deepen insight into the reenactment that is occurring in therapy?

- **Feeling secure:** Bring to mind a time in therapy when you felt centered and grounded. Perhaps you noticed that you felt more attuned to your client's needs and emotions. The session may have had a feeling of flow and ease, or you might have felt less aware of time. Maybe you even felt more connected to yourself, your body, or your breath. Can you recall other times in your life when you felt this way outside of therapy? Can you sense if this feeling is connected to your or the client's cultural background? Take a moment to recall these moments of feeling connected, calm, and secure both within and outside of therapy. Allow your own nervous system to be enriched by these memories. Can you imagine cultivating more of this feeling within your work with others?

Connection and Co-Regulation

Co-regulation, also called mutual regulation or social affect regulation, refers to the ways in which our connections with others help us learn to hold ourselves in a more loving manner. Co-regulation in psychotherapy provides opportunities for our clients and ourselves to have new, socially learned experiences of connection, attunement, acceptance, and compassion. **Simply put, we learn to compassionately respond to our own painful emotions when we have experiences of being unconditionally accepted by others.** In this way, we can think of co-regulation as a precursor to self-regulation.

Psychotherapy that focuses solely on skill building as a means of developing self-regulation is often limited because this "one-person" approach to therapy is not as transferable to the relational world we live in. As described by Dr. Allan Schore, we need to shift from a "one-person" approach into a "two-person" psychology (Schore, 2019). With an interpersonal focus, we can observe the complexity of two minds and two bodies in a moment-by-moment exchange. Here, we must go beyond the verbal narrative to attend to the nonverbal communications of both the therapist and client by paying attention to the ways that our body language, facial expressions, and tone of voice inform our relational experiences.

When we, as therapists, attune to our own body during session, we can sense subtle changes in our own somatic experience that might provide insight into the experience of the client. For example, you might notice a subtle tightening in your chest and, as a result, place your hand over your heart and take a deep breath. By developing this embodied awareness, you model your own self-regulation. This can then become a nonverbal invitation for the client to breathe more deeply, or you might use this information to encourage them to sense their body and breath. **Your capacity to regulate your own nervous system not only helps with the client's ability to regulate their body and mind, but it also provides a foundation for self-care.** For example, tracking your somatic experiences during session allows you to notice if you are leaning forward in a way that would eventually leave you feeling fatigued. Or perhaps you notice that you begin to breathe in a shallow manner as you attune to your client's anxiety. Such awareness allows you to make subtle changes to your posture or breathing, which therefore allows you to attend to your own needs throughout session.

The process of developing this somatic awareness in session allows therapists to apply polyvagal theory to therapy (Dana, 2018). Here, we facilitate co-regulation as an interactive process that activates the social engagement systems of both the therapist and client. Although it is common for clients with C-PTSD to alternate between hyper-aroused and hypo-aroused states, by engaging in co-regulation, we can help them feel safe and connected even in the midst of a wide range of difficult emotions and body sensations. Co-regulation requires our own comfort with a wide range of affective responses and states of arousal. **Clients with developmental trauma may have never had another person who was able to be with them in their distress without that person becoming anxious, shutting down, or leaving them in the midst of their pain.**

Tapping into the social engagement system is not the same as offering support. Many clients have had their basic needs met by caregivers who did not meet their needs for connection. Social engagement refers to having experiences of mutuality and reciprocity in which we are open to receiving clients as they are. When we, as therapists, offer our openness and receptivity to clients, they feel accepted and understood. By attuning to your own body, it is more likely that you will notice somatic experiences, such as body sensations and emotions, that parallel the experience of the client. Somatic psychologist Stanley Keleman calls this process *somatic resonance* (Keleman, 1987). Within somatic psychology, therapists are encouraged to pay attention to these sensations as opportunities for transformational moments in therapy. For example, you might share a momentary heaviness in your chest and accompanying sadness in response to a client's experience. This communicates that you have been moved or changed by your client. For the client who was rejected in childhood, this moment of being received can be profoundly reparative. You have let them know that they are important, that their presence is felt, and that they make a difference—all because they have had an impact on you.

The goal of regulating emotions is not to make feelings go away. **Rather, the aim is to help clients build their capacity to ride the waves of big emotions and sensations.** Initially, clients work through overwhelming emotions and somatic experiences with the knowledge that we are willing to join them in these difficult moments. In time, this process helps them learn that temporary experiences of contraction can resolve into a natural expansion of positive emotions, such as relief, gratitude, empowerment, and joy. Ultimately, this process helps clients trust their own capacity to handle their feelings.

We offer co-regulation through a steady, compassionate, and attuned relational presence. We are self-aware and offer our observations of the client's somatic cues. We help clients build their own capacity for self-observation by directing their attention to changes in their tone of voice, movement, posture, or use of eye contact. For example, we might gently point out their flattened facial expression, collapsed posture, or disengaged eye contact. In addition, we can help clients build conscious neuroception by inviting them to observe cues regarding their changing nervous system states. In this case, we might suggest that they notice whether their heartbeat has quickened, if they are holding their breath, or if they are feeling frozen and immobilized. Perceiving these somatic indicators of nervous system changes can allow them to better respond to their varying needs.

The next healing practice offers relational interventions to bring co-regulation into therapy. This practice begins by inviting you to focus on your own breath and body sensations to understand what you are bringing into the therapy room. This self-awareness then serves as the foundation for rest of the practice, which invites you to notice cues about your client's nervous system state, to share your observations with them, and to explore changes in eye contact or spatial positioning to facilitate greater regulation in relationship. I suggest integrating this practice when it feels relevant to the moment, with consideration that some clients might feel embarrassed or ashamed to have their somatic patterns seen or named.

Explore Co-Regulation

Explore the following relational interventions to bring co-regulation into therapy:

- **Notice your own body and sensations:** What do you notice in your body? Do you find it easy or difficult to connect to your emotions? Do you find that your mind is racing, or do you feel foggy-headed and tired? Do you feel relaxed or anxious? Are you having difficulty paying attention? How might your experiences be related to the client's nervous system state? What allows you to stay present and feel safe? Do you need to adapt your posture, move your body, or change how you are breathing so you feel connected to your social engagement system?

- **Observe the client's nervous system arousal:** Notice cues and signals regarding your client's state of ANS arousal. Are they restless, fidgety, or having difficulty sitting still? Or are they unusually still and lethargic? Is their posture rigidly upright or collapsed? How quickly or slowly are they speaking? What is the quality of their eye contact?

- **Offer your awareness:** Ask your client for permission to share an observation of changes in their affect, sensation, and alertness. Explore how the client's self-awareness and your observations are similar or different. Pay attention to when these changes happen as related to content that is being discussed at the time.

- **Reflect and accept:** Before offering any interventions aimed toward regulation, provide your understanding about the client's current experience within the context of their developmental, social, and cultural history. For example, if they are angry, firmly validate why this anger makes sense in the context of their experiences in the world. Compassionately reflect their emotions, allowing your tone of voice or body language to mirror the intensity of their experience. Even if you or the client are feeling stuck in the midst of difficult emotions, explore how it feels to nonjudgmentally accept them and yourself just as you are.

- **Explore regulation in relationship:** Regulation in relationship involves recognizing the client's cycle of engagement and disengagement by honoring their needs for space and connection. For example, you might change how close or far away you are sitting from each other. Or you might invite the client to stand up and explore how it feels to stand facing you, or if they prefer to stand side by side. Notice your client's use of eye contact.

There may be times when their eyes widen or look to you for a sense of reassurance and connection. Notice how you feel as you meet their gaze. In contrast, there might be times when your client looks down or away. In this case, ask if it is okay with them if you look away too, and invite them to let you know when they are ready to reengage with eye contact while verbally reassuring them that you are still there and that you care. Explore how you both feel as you respond to the cycles of engagement and disengagement. What do each of you need to stay connected to yourselves while being in relationship to each other?

Rupture and Repair

When we attune to nonverbal communications, we can sense our clients' subtle longings for connection or cues that we have been poorly attuned to their needs. For example, the client might lean forward toward us or avert their gaze. As therapists, we will sometimes misread some of our clients' cues, leading them to feel hurt or rejected, but these small ruptures in therapy can offer opportunities for repair. Acknowledging these vulnerable moments can offer a contrast to the experiences of childhood in which relational ruptures were never addressed.

At the same time, a buildup of poorly attuned moments in therapy can result in feelings of confusion, frustration, and disconnection. Both the therapist and client might play out injurious patterns from their pasts, which can impair the client's trust in the therapist. If we do not take the time to understand our own countertransference, we might engage in behaviors that inadvertently push clients away or make them feel rejected. For example, we might nonverbally communicate discomfort through our body language by unconsciously angling our torso away from a client or carrying tension in our tone of voice. Unfortunately, the accumulations of these misattuned interactions can lead clients to lose faith in therapy over time.

It is common for shame to arise when our longing for connection goes unmatched or is denied. Shame is an interpersonal emotion that shows up as embarrassment, humiliation, and shyness. In the body, shame causes us to blush, look away, hide our face, or collapse our posture. You can think of shame as a physical act of turning away from something that, in actuality, is deeply desired. When shame goes unacknowledged, it is common to feel angry and sad. Or when shame feels intolerable, it may be accompanied by behaviors that lead individuals to disconnect from their sensations and emotions because it is simply too painful to remain vulnerable. We may see this in clients who have a difficult time staying with their emotions or sensations.

In a healthy relationship, we recognize and receive these vulnerable emotions as part of a repair process. This becomes an opportunity to repair moments of disconnection and restore our client's trust in us. **Relational ruptures that are followed by repair help our clients recognize that interpersonal conflicts can be resolved.** They learn that they are capable of working through challenging experiences of disconnection, that they can handle the discomfort, and that they will come out stronger. They learn to share their fears and express vulnerable emotions with someone who will not reject them or take advantage of them. As therapists, we offer an intention to accept clients (and ourselves) as they (and we) are. This foundation of acceptance is the ground from which change and growth is possible. The result is an atmosphere of compassion that is mutually nourishing. Let's take a closer look through my process working with Jessica, a Caucasian woman in her fifties who grew up in a neglectful and emotionally abusive household:

Jessica had a tendency to hold herself to unrealistically high standards. At times, this manifested as unrelenting self-criticism and perfectionism. She struggled in her relationships and described feeling exasperated by others' inadequacies. Nonetheless, she had a tenacious capacity to keep an optimistic attitude. Often, Jessica would begin therapy appointments by telling me about her accomplishments or talking about positive moments from her week. Her upright posture and bright smile were uplifting and contagious. I often felt compelled to compliment her on her accomplishments.

However, toward the end of many of our sessions, her affect would abruptly change. She would suddenly announce that she was not getting her needs met in therapy. The warm smile on her face was replaced by an aggravated expression as she proceeded to tell me of all the ways that I had disappointed her. Initially, I didn't know what to make of this shift and struggled with repairing these experiences, which led to feelings of disconnection for both of us.

As we deepened our work together, I began to explore Jessica's childhood. I learned that she grew up in a neglectful and emotionally abusive household. Her mother was only 20 when Jessica was born and would often talk about how she hadn't wanted a pregnancy that early in her life. Her mother proudly told Jessica that she had taught herself to walk by 9 months, potty trained herself by age 1, and after that, she was "on her own." Those words "after that, she was on her own" captured the wound that Jessica carried with her into adulthood.

Jessica was taught not to have needs. Moreover, she learned there was no place for painful emotions of sadness, hurt, jealousy, or anger. Instead, Jessica became "mommy's little helper" and was rewarded for her competence, self-reliance, and ability to care for her two younger sisters. By the time she was 16, Jessica was relatively independent. She worked two jobs, continued to help around the house, and drove her siblings to school. While her self-reliance helped her to survive, it also covered up her underlying unmet needs for care, tenderness, affection, and understanding.

Despite this deepened understanding of Jessica's attachment history, I continued to feel my own anxiety build as I anticipated our painful moments of disconnection in sessions. In supervision, I explored my fear of her becoming angry with me. I identified how this feeling was reminiscent of wounds from my own childhood. I recalled memories of myself as a little girl who had to be good in order to avoid being the target of criticism from a parent. This realization also helped me understand how my fears had led me to avoid Jessica's feelings of anger, hurt, and disappointment. This process deepened my capacity for empathy.

In the next session, I shared with Jessica my sense that her history of having to be the "strong one" left little space for her feelings of hurt and anger. I also acknowledged that I had not sufficiently attended to her distress in our work together. Jessica sighed in relief, as she could feel that there was more room for her feelings. I let her know that it was okay for her to be angry with me. This statement offered an important repair, especially considering that she was never able to express her anger toward her mother. This session was a turning point in our work together. The dynamic did not continue to play out between the two of us, as we were able to create a safe place to attend to a wide range of her feelings. She shared how grateful she was to know that her painful experiences and her phenomenal strengths were all welcome in our relationship.

Within a relational approach to therapy, we recognize that we all make errors sometimes and that these moments are often a fundamental part of how change happens in therapy (Bromberg, 2011). We will sometimes misunderstand our clients, look at the clock at the wrong time, or say something inadvertently hurtful. We are all human, are we not? However, it is through a commitment to a process of repair that allows for new learning. This process requires that we take responsibility for our own part of the dynamic. Through personal introspection, supervision, or therapy, we can increase self-knowledge of our own attachment histories and relational learnings. Furthermore, supervision can help us handle the emotional intensity that can arise during difficult moments of disconnection or conflict in therapy without relying on defensiveness, withdrawal, or blame. In many cases, these moments can also become catalysts for our own growth. The next healing practice provides steps to repair disconnection and ruptures when they happen in therapy.

Initiate Relational Repair

- **Acknowledge the disconnection:** Begin the process of repair by letting the client know that you are aware of the disconnection. You might say, "I notice that you became quiet and looked away."

- **Offer your understanding and express your willingness to learn more:** Let the client know that you are invested in a process of repair. You can begin by stating your best guess of how the disconnection happened. You might say, "I think I missed something when…" Ask them if you have an accurate understanding about what happened. And let them know that you are interested in their perspective about what you got wrong.

- **Reflect their experience nondefensively:** Acknowledge their experience. You might start by saying, "You're right, I did…" and "I hear that you felt…" Take your time to articulate your deepened understanding of the cause of the disconnection. In some cases, it might be helpful to explain your reasoning for saying something or for behaving in a way that inadvertently hurt the client. However, be sure that you do not come across as though you are making an excuse or minimizing the client's experience. You might also offer an apology to the client. In doing so, invite the client to notice how it felt to receive an apology, as this may provide contrast to events in their past that were never acknowledged or repaired. Stay with this process until repair has happened.

- **Appreciate the resolution:** Acknowledge the courage that it takes to stay with discomfort so you can move from disconnection back into an experience of connection. You might ask, "How do you feel about this conversation?" You can also recognize their willingness to stay engaged with the process by saying, "Thank you for telling me how you felt. I feel closer to you now."

Therapist Self-Care

Therapists whose practices specialize in the treatment of clients with complex trauma recognize the impact that this work has on our own mental, emotional, and physical health. Through our work, we are in relationships with clients who have experienced intensely disturbing life events. Sometimes they share the content of those events, which can result in us vividly imagining their occurrence. Other times clients experience highly distressing physiological and emotional states in our presence. They might be overwhelmed by anxiety or dissociated and numb.

Working with traumatized clients can evoke feelings of helplessness, hopelessness, despair, isolation, loneliness, injustice, unfairness, suffering, and rage. A sensitive therapist might feel the residue of these relational interactions well after the session has ended. If left unaddressed, these experiences can increase a therapist's risk for vicarious trauma and compassion fatigue. Importantly, we can also reflect on the positive effects that arise as we witness the healing, recovery, and resilience of persons who have survived severe trauma in their lives, a process that has been termed *vicarious resilience* (Edelkott et al., 2016; Killian et al., 2017). We too have an opportunity to grow. We can be changed for the better through our work with our clients.

Therapist Self-Awareness Practice

Take a few moments to reflect or write your responses to the following questions, which are aimed at helping you identify resources that can support your work in the world:

- What helps you stay present with your clients as they experience helplessness, despair, uncertainty, disappointment, and loss?

- How do you take care of yourself when a client becomes emotionally overwhelmed, shuts down, or has dissociative symptoms during a session?

- What support systems do you have in place for times when you feel emotionally unsettled from your work? What helps you to feel regulated, grounded, or connected to your center?

- Do you have a supervisor who helps you when you experience challenging moments with clients? In what ways has your own therapy supported your role as a therapist? What additional supports might you need when you feel stuck in your work with clients?

- What meaning-making, spiritual, or self-care practices help you attend to the weight of trauma processing with clients?

- In what ways have you been changed for the better by your work? Can you recall moments when you learned more about yourself as a result of your clinical work? Are there any specific clinical moments that have inspired you or provided you with a sense of hope?

5

Cultivating Presence with Mindfulness-Based Therapies

Mindfulness-based therapies invite us to observe our mental, emotional, and somatic experiences with an emphasis on orienting to the present moment, staying curious and nonjudgmental, and cultivating self-compassion. Within the integrative mind-body approach to treating C-PTSD, mindfulness is applied to help clients build tolerance for distressing emotions and sensations. *Distress tolerance* involves learning to observe and stay present with difficult feelings while resisting urges to react or behave impulsively. Over time, this skill helps clients learn that painful experiences are not permanent; uncomfortable sensations and emotions eventually change.

Sustaining mindful body awareness can be especially important when working with clients with dissociative symptoms. However, clients might have a difficult time tolerating somatic awareness because our body sensations have a direct connection to trauma-related memories and emotions. Therefore, we build their capacity to stay present with sensations at a pace they can tolerate. When applied during phase one of trauma treatment, mindful body awareness can help clients access a felt sense of safety that can stabilize dysregulating symptoms. The ability to observe and tolerate body sensations also supports clients in successfully working through traumatic memories during phase two of trauma treatment.

There are many therapeutic approaches that integrate mindfulness into psychotherapy. These include mindfulness-based stress reduction (Kabat-Zinn, 1990), dialectical behavioral therapy (DBT; Linehan, 1993) acceptance and commitment therapy (ACT; Hayes, 2005), mindful self-compassion (Germer & Neff, 2019), and the Hakomi method of mindfulness-centered somatic psychotherapy (Kurtz, 1990). Rather than applying a single modality, this chapter explores the common factors inherent to mindfulness, which include developing a "witness" capable of nonjudgmentally observing our experiences, engaging in mindful body awareness, and strengthening self-compassion. Based on these shared principles, the healing practices in this chapter offer several different ways that you can guide clients to strengthen mindful body awareness, all of which can be adapted to meet the needs of each individual.

Mindfulness in Psychotherapy

The integration of mindfulness into psychotherapy begins with cultivating a witness within ourselves who invites us to become the observer of our thoughts and feelings. Becoming the witness is like sitting at the side of river, watching your thoughts and feelings float downstream. This invites healthy detachment in that we observe our thoughts and emotions rather than identify with them. We see these experiences as temporary rather than reflections of a static, unchanging reality. The witness also lets you see the "big picture" or a "bird's-eye view" of your inner landscape. Here, you might imagine thoughts and feelings as the clouds and weather patterns that pass through. Becoming a witness can be especially helpful when these weather patterns feel turbulent or overwhelming. Mindfulness also relies upon curiosity, which is akin to having a "beginner's mind." When we are curious, we are open to new learning, we are inquisitive about novel experiences, and we awaken our senses.

Mindfulness practices invite us to be nonjudgmental and to be kinder to ourselves and others. This compassion invites an awareness of our shared humanity, which can reduce our sense of isolation as we realize that our own suffering is interconnected to the suffering of others (Germer & Neff, 2019). Together, these practices invite self-acceptance, which helps us embrace ourselves just as we are. Rather than attempting to deny our suffering, to rid ourselves of pain, or to aggressively change ourselves, acceptance invites us to turn toward our discomfort. Having a history of C-PTSD can drastically reduce our client's capacity to stay present with emotions and sensations. The goal of building distress tolerance is to help our clients widen their window of tolerance in preparation for trauma reprocessing. Paradoxically, acceptance of our negative emotions also tends to naturally generate greater access to positive emotions, which gives clients greater access to the nourishment of positive states.

Healing Practice

The North Wind and the Sun

- Aesop's classic fable, *The North Wind and the Sun*, offers a powerful metaphor about the use of gentleness versus brute force to initiate change.

The North Wind and the Sun were arguing about which one was stronger. In the midst of their dispute, they looked down to see a traveler walking along a path. The man was wearing a cloak and scarf. The Wind boastfully said to the Sun, "I bet you that I can get the man to take off his jacket faster than you can!" Agreeing to the bet, the Sun sat back and watched as the Wind blew gusts that whisked the man's cloak around his body. However, as the Wind blew harder and harder, the man only wrapped his cloak closer to his body and tightened his scarf. All of the Wind's efforts were in vain. When it was the Sun's turn, the gentle beams of sunshine warmed the air. Within several minutes, the man began to loosen his scarf and unfasten his cloak. Soon he removed them both.

- This fable is a powerful metaphor for the ways in which the gentleness and warmth of self-acceptance can soften our defenses and open our hearts.

- In what ways do you approach creating change in your life as if you are the Wind?

- In what ways do you approach creating change in your life as if you are the Sun?

Various neuroimaging studies have found that mindfulness practitioners exhibit enhanced functioning in the prefrontal cortex and decreased activation in the amygdala, suggesting that these practices can increase our ability to reflect upon our emotional reactions and make decisions grounded in logic instead of resorting to our automatic survival reactions (Larrivee & Echarte, 2018; Raffone, Tagini, & Srinivasan, 2010). Mindful body awareness, in particular, seems to increase blood flow in the insula, a brain region associated with interoceptive awareness of sensations, as well as the sensorimotor cortices, which are associated with awareness of our external senses. Likewise, mindfulness has been associated with improvements in attentional control, emotion regulation, and PTSD symptoms (Hopwood & Schutte, 2017).

The term *mindfulness* is often confused with the practice of meditation, which can lead to some misconceptions about what the practice involves. For example, many individuals may inaccurately believe that it is necessary to learn specific meditation techniques in order to apply mindfulness into therapy. Others may associate mindfulness with a specific religion. In actuality, mindfulness simply encourages individuals to pay attention to present-moment experiences. As applied to trauma treatment, the goal of mindful body awareness is to draw attention to inner experiences by attuning to our emotions and sensations with an intention of nonjudgmental curiosity.

Somatic psychologist Dr. Christine Caldwell suggests that mindfulness is better described as the cultivation of "bodyfulness," since much of what we are building is our ability to stay present with somatic awareness (Caldwell, 2018). We develop an embodied sense of ourselves when we focus our attention to sensations, emotions, body shape, and movements (Fogel, 2009). As we cultivate our ability to stay present with our sensations, we also become adept at recognizing when we disconnect from the body. We must remember that many individuals with C-PTSD have dissociative symptoms. They might already feel as though they are "observing" their lives instead of "living fully" within themselves. A mindful body awareness approach offers an alternative to meditation practices that emphasize detachment, which might lead individuals with complex trauma to feel further disconnected or disembodied. In this way, we can still integrate mindfulness into psychotherapy in a manner that does not inadvertently reinforce a client's dissociative symptoms.

Mindfulness practices can help clients connect to their inner source of wisdom, allowing them to notice the effects of impulsive behaviors and develop greater coping strategies. Within DBT, Dr. Marsha Linehan refers to this process as developing *wise mind* (1993), which represents an optimal balance between our "reasonable mind" and our "emotional mind." Within ACT, Dr. Steven Hayes proposes that difficult emotions are normal responses to painful life events. Mindfulness can help clients to turn toward these feelings with acceptance, kindness, and self-compassion—which, in turn, helps reduce their reliance upon avoidance behaviors. Likewise, the practice of mindful self-compassion helps clients learn to love and accept themselves just as they are (Germer & Neff, 2019).

The goal of therapy is not to get rid of emotions but to reduce reliance upon reactive and impulsive behaviors, such as self-harm, substance use, or lashing out toward others. Through the use of mindfulness practices, we encourage our clients to reflect on their thoughts, emotions, and sensations prior to taking action. Encouraging a mindset of acceptance helps them to recognize that uncomfortable experiences do not require that they engage in escape or avoidance strategies. Instead, they can learn to stay present with difficult emotions and sensations, which increases their ability to tolerate distress. Here, we offer a new experience that helps them learn that difficult feelings are not destructive or the result of a bad attitude; these emotions, as painful as they might be, are simply meant to be felt. This capacity to tolerate distress has been found to promote treatment retention, reduce reliance on substances, enhance readiness for trauma processing, and help with relapse prevention after therapy ends (Boffa et al., 2018).

When incorporating mindfulness into therapy, we must remember that the practice is just as important for therapists as it is for clients. If we are uncomfortable with our clients' emotions, we might inadvertently shut down their process or give them the message that they are "too much." In contrast, we can use the co-regulation tools discussed in chapter 4 to provide compassion and acceptance for their pain. This can be especially important for clients who struggle with self-compassion. When a client is judging their feelings, then we can offer our compassion and nonjudgmental acceptance, which then provides a foundation for their own self-compassion. In time, clients can learn to internalize these experiences and cultivate an attitude of acceptance and compassion toward themselves. The interpersonal experience helps the client connect to their own core of wisdom.

Given the importance of mindful body awareness for therapists and clients alike, the healing practices in this chapter are not just a set of tools or interventions for clients. They are also tools that therapists should practice in order to cultivate their own mindful embodiment. **When we engage in our own embodied awareness, we nourish the therapeutic environment.** Building upon the relational approach discussed in chapter 4, we are more likely to sense our own somatic countertransference or resonance with our clients when we attend to our own body sensations. Mindful body awareness allows us to sense subtle shifts in ourselves that might provide insight into the inner world of the client. Such awareness can also amplify awareness of what we are bringing into sessions from our own personal experiences as related to current or historical events. Increasing self-awareness helps us close the gap between our verbal and nonverbal communications. Such congruence between words and body language enhances trustworthiness with our clients.

Therefore, I suggest that you explore the mindful body awareness practices provided in this chapter for yourself prior to introducing them to your clients. These practices offer a nourishing antidote to a world in which many of us are often rushed, distracted, and divided in our attention. Some practices may feel easier or more accessible to you than others. You may need to work through your own discomfort with certain somatic sensations or a tendency to disconnect from your body. If so, I invite you to be patient with yourself and to return to the practices on a regular basis. Perhaps you will also view this as an opportunity to enhance compassion for your clients if they find it difficult to connect to their sensations.

When introducing any mindfulness practice to clients, remember that it is never worth pushing an agenda that forsakes connection. You can gently encourage mindful awareness in psychotherapy by making statements such as "Take a moment to check in with your body" or "Notice the sensations and emotions that you are aware of right now." If the client is afraid or reticent to connect to their body, you can suggest that they proceed slowly by focusing on one area of the body at time and introduce more somatic awareness as the client is ready. It can be helpful to draw their attention to peripheral areas of the body that tend to be less triggering, such as the fingertips or toes. It can also be helpful to introduce the concept of *grounding,* which involves focusing on sensory awareness in the legs and feet.

In addition, clients can build their tolerance for somatic sensations by alternating between paying attention to body sensations and paying attention to external sensory stimuli. For example, a client who is afraid may describe feeling chilled, shaky, and tense around their core. In this case, you can encourage them to pay attention to what they can see, hear, smell, taste, or touch in their current environment. You can then gently encourage them to return their attention to their somatic experience for a few breaths at a time. With practice, this can help them to sustain awareness of sensation for longer periods of time.

Let's take a closer look at the integration of mindfulness in psychotherapy with two clients. The first is Zachary, a middle-aged Caucasian man who suffered from alexithymia and C-PTSD related to his experiences growing up as a single child with a mother who was clinically depressed:

> Zachary had a difficult time feeling his body and his emotions. I learned that his mother had been diagnosed with depression and that she was distant and dismissive of him in childhood. He was highly intellectual and could talk about his history with little emotional engagement. At times in therapy, I would find myself becoming emotionally detached and disconnected from my own body and sensations. My somatic resonance had led me to feel emotionally cut off.

> I recognized that my clinically detached stance was a reenactment of Zachary's history. Once aware of our pattern, I was able to structure our work in a new way that led to a more effective outcome. I asked his permission to begin each session with a short practice that invited him to bring his awareness to his body. I also focused my own awareness on my sensations. Initially, Zachary continued to report feeling numb and cut off. However, I was able to track subtle changes in my own body during sessions. I asked Zachary if I could share with him my experiences of these changes in sensations and emotion when they arose. Then I guided him to pay attention to his body while I reflected my observations about changes in his tone of voice or his engagement and disengagement with eye contact.

> In time, these moments of mindful, relational attunement helped him connect to his body sensations and increased his awareness of his emotions. He was eventually able to enhance his mindful body awareness outside of session and reported improvements in his relationships to others.

In contrast, Victoria, a Hispanic woman, was prone to emotional flooding and overwhelm related to her experiences growing up in a home with domestic violence. She would often describe times when she "couldn't stop crying" that would leave her feeling exhausted or depleted for days:

> Victoria came into session and began to describe a stressful argument she had with her wife the day before. While she and her wife had resolved their conflict, Victoria still felt angry, shaky, and agitated when she walked into my office. After several months of working together, I had already learned that Victoria felt afraid of connecting to her body. She spoke about how she would often feel "everything at once." She was fearful of getting flooded by her tears, as she would often get headaches after crying.

> I suggested that we explore a mindful body awareness practice with a focus on grounding. She agreed but identified that she felt tentative, as she was still fearful about focusing on her body and emotions. In order to create safety, I suggested that we begin by focusing her

attention to her feet. She immediately described feeling less threatened. After a few breaths experimenting with sensing and moving her feet, I suggested that she bring her attention to her legs by firmly pressing her feet into the floor so she could feel an engagement of the muscles in her legs. She took her time to orient to the sensations in her legs, and this time she reported that she felt more present. She looked at me and around the room and said she was surprised that she was feeling calmer.

At this point, I invited Victoria to tell me more about her argument with her wife. She spoke about how the fight had brought up a memory of her parents fighting when she was a young girl. She recalled feeling helpless and frightened as a young child. Momentarily, she looked as though she might cry, and then she froze with a look of fear on her face. Noting this abrupt shift, I gently guided her attention back to her feet and legs and invited her to take as much time as she needed until she felt grounded and safe. She said that she felt tightness in her chest. As she brought her awareness to her chest, she started to cry but then reiterated her fear of "feeling everything at once." I suggested that she could pace herself by bringing her awareness to her legs and feet anytime she felt overwhelmed by her feelings of fear and sadness.

Our session continued as she alternated between paying mindful attention to her sensations related to the past and refocusing her attention to her feet and the here and now. By the end of the session, she described feeling more connected to her body and emotions without being overwhelmed. She also described feeling more compassion for herself and more loving toward her wife.

When introducing any mindfulness practice, it can be helpful to engage in the process along with your client. For example, explore your own awareness of your breath and somatic sensations as you invite your client to do the same. Or, if a client brings their hands over their belly, you can place your hands over your own belly as well, mirroring their movement as a gesture of support. Notice what changes across sessions as you both include awareness of somatic experiences.

You can offer each of the following healing practices as an opportunity to participate in an experiment. Remind clients that they have a choice about whether or not they would like to engage in the practice. Should they choose to continue, let them know that there is no "right" or "wrong" response to the practice. Remind them that they can end the experiment at any point. As with all of the healing practices in this book, tailor these to meet the needs of the client. For example, you might only choose a small part of any practice as it is relevant to the client's experience in the moment. If you notice that a client has difficulty with cultivating a witness or sustaining self-compassion, it may be beneficial to move into parts work therapy as described in chapter 6 to explore parts that may be blocking or interfering with the practice.

Awaken the Witness

- Would you be willing to experiment with a short mindfulness practice focused on developing your ability to witness your thoughts and emotions? Take a moment to notice where your attention is flowing naturally. Are you more aware of your thoughts or your sensations? Are there any particular thoughts or emotions that you are aware of in this moment? Without judgment, gather a general sense about how you are feeling right now.

- By becoming a witness to your experience, you invite curiosity and an openness to new or previously unexplored experiences. As you explore this practice, simply notice your thoughts with a sense of wonder. Notice how your body speaks in a language of sensations, emotions, and images. Perhaps set an intention to explore something new about yourself.

- If you would like, begin to study your experience of the present moment as if you are looking at the world with beginner's mind, as if you are looking around at this room and experiencing yourself for the very first time.

- Becoming the witness allows you see the "big picture" or a "bird's-eye view" of your inner landscape. If you would like, imagine your thoughts and feelings as if they are clouds and weather patterns. You might notice that you feel calm and relaxed, like on a sunny day. Or you might feel as though you are inside a tornado. Or you might notice storm clouds building off in the distance. Can you make space for your experience without judging yourself?

- If you would like, begin to observe your breath. Notice the way your breath moves air across your nose or mouth. Notice whether your breath feels relaxed or forced. Notice the areas of your body that move in response to your breath, such as the rise and fall of your belly or chest. Now perhaps you can experiment with deepening your breath by softening your diaphragm and lower belly. See if you can allow your belly to expand with each inhale and relax a little more with each exhale.

- It can helpful to remember that all of your experiences are meant to come and go. Begin to observe the ebb and flow of your breath. As if watching water moving in a stream, notice your thoughts, and imagine releasing them downstream. Observe how your emotions and sensations rise up in your awareness and then let them go. If you find it difficult to let go of your thoughts, feelings, or sensations, then focus on your exhale. Explore a simple phrase with your breath. Inhale as you say to yourself "I am," and exhale as you say to yourself "letting go." Notice how you feel in your body now.

- There are times when you might notice resistance to painful feelings or sensations. Becoming the witness is about allowing your thoughts, emotions, and body sensations to be there without pushing them away or needing to change them. Notice how it feels to accept yourself just as you are. You might notice a sense of relief as you embrace your discomfort.

- Take your time with this practice, and let me know when you feel complete.

Explore Mindful Body Awareness

- Would you be willing to experiment with a short mindfulness practice focused on body awareness? I will guide you to focus your attention on your body, one area at a time.

- Take a moment to bring your awareness to your feet. Taking a deep breath, notice the sensations of your feet on the ground. Allow yourself to fully inhabit your feet as you notice your contact with the floor beneath you. You might wiggle your toes or press your feet more firmly into the ground. If you would like, press your feet downward to expand your awareness to include your legs.

- Begin to sense the muscles in the front and back of your thighs. You might even bring your hands to touch your upper or lower legs. Take several breaths as you focus your attention on your legs and feet. Notice how you feel as you allow yourself to live fully inside of your legs and feet.

- Take a moment to sense your hands. Now allow yourself to fully inhabit your hands as you wiggle your fingers, curl your hands into fists, or open your fingers wide. If you would like, expand your awareness to include your arms and shoulders. You might bring one hand across your body and gently massage the opposite arm, working from the shoulder down to the hand, and then repeat on the other side. Notice how you feel as you allow yourself to live fully inside of your hands and arms.

- Take a moment to bring your attention to the back of your body. Perhaps you notice your back pressing against your chair. Allow yourself to fully inhabit the back of your body as you sense the support of your chair. Notice how it feels to sense your lower back, and then bring your attention to your upper back and the area between your shoulder blades. Notice how you feel as you allow yourself to live fully inside of the back of your body.

- Take a moment to bring your attention to the front side of your torso. Perhaps place a hand over your belly and another over your heart. Notice the movements here that happen with your breath. Notice how you feel as you allow yourself to live fully inside of the front of your body.

- Take a moment to bring your attention to your neck and throat. You might lean your head forward and back or do some gentle circular movements to increase sensations here. Then bring your attention to your face and head. Notice your mouth and eyes. Perhaps you would like to place one hand on the back of your skull and another on your forehead to amplify your awareness of the sensations in your head. Continue to explore your sensations in your head and face for as long as you would like, and then notice how you feel as you allow yourself to live fully inside of your neck, throat, and head.

- I invite you to complete this mindful body awareness practice by taking several deep breaths—noticing your thoughts and emotions after increasing awareness of your sensations.

Offer Relational Compassion

- Take a few breaths to connect to your body and emotions. What are you bringing with you into the room today?

- I invite you to reflect on a difficulty that you are currently experiencing in your life. As you reflect on this experience, notice your thoughts, emotions, and body sensations.

- Now, as you take a deep breath, explore offering care and kindness toward yourself. Can you love yourself just as you are? Without judgment, notice if you are able to receive this care and compassion from yourself. Do you feel more relaxed and at ease? Or do you experience an increase in tension? There is no right or wrong answer.

- If you find it difficult to feel kindness toward yourself, see if you can become curious about your experience. Is there a belief or somatic experience that arises that blocks you from receiving this compassion? Do you find that you are judging yourself for your experience?

- How do you feel knowing that I am here, accepting you as you are? I am not judging you. Is it easy or difficult to receive this care from me? What do you notice in your body? What emotions are you noticing?

- Can you imagine another person who loves you and treats you with kindness? Notice how you feel as you imagine receiving care and kindness from this person. Again, what do you notice in your body? What emotions are you observing? Is it easy or difficult to imagine receiving this care?

- There is nothing that you need to do in order to deserve this kindness. This care is the birthright of all beings.

- If you would like, you might also imagine another person or a group of people who are experiencing a similar kind of pain or suffering. Explore how it feels to offer this same care and kindness to that person or those people. As you explore offering compassion to others, observe how you feel in your body. What emotions are you noticing?

- Return your awareness to yourself and your own need for love and care. Once again, take a deep breath as you explore how it feels to love and care for yourself.

- Without judging your experience as "good" or "bad," simply notice your emotions and sensations. Take your time here, and let me know when you feel complete.

6

Attending to Dissociative Symptoms with Parts Work Therapy

Parts work therapy recognizes that we all have different states of mind and emotion. Often, we will deem certain emotions, needs, or sensations as acceptable while pushing away and rejecting others. It might even feel as if some feelings are more "real" while others are fake or phony. In truth, all parts of our self are real, important, and necessary. However, it is common to experience conflicts between opposing emotions or needs. For example, there may be times when we both love and hate a parent. Or we might have a part that longs to be close to a loved one while another part feels fearful of intimacy. Sometimes these internal conflicts may be too disruptive for us to hold within our sense of self. In this case, competing needs can become polarized within us, leading to anxiety, indecision, procrastination, or self-sabotaging behaviors.

When an individual has a history of chronic, repeated trauma, there can be a greater divide between these different parts of the self and a greater likelihood of dissociative symptoms. In some cases, they might feel an unrelenting need to be perfect, be plagued by a harsh inner critic, or exhibit self-aggressive tendencies that lead them to feel at war with themselves. They might also feel as though they are cut off from their feelings or as if they are going through the motions of their lives without meaning or a sense of connection. Often, individuals with C-PTSD report alternating between feeling disconnected from their emotions and overidentifying with their pain.

There are several different approaches to parts work, including ego state therapy (Forgash & Copeley, 2008; Shapiro, 2016; Watkins & Watkins, 1997), Internal Family Systems therapy (IFS; Schwartz, 1997), structural integration theory (Fisher, 2017; van der Hart et al., 2006), and Gestalt therapy (Perls, 1992). Rather than applying a single model of parts work therapy, this chapter offers a common factors approach that focuses upon three key premises. The first premise is that the human mind is capable of conflicting thoughts, feelings, and needs. The second is that our parts are reflections of our family of origin. The third is that all parts are important. Based upon these common factors, this chapter guides you through a model of parts work that begins by helping clients understand the value of parts work. From here, we help them deepen awareness of their own parts. In some cases, this requires support to help them stay oriented in their adult self so they can differentiate from younger or self-sabotaging parts. Ultimately, this process helps clients repair missing experiences of nurturance or protection that they needed at earlier times in their lives.

Parts, Ego States, and Dissociative Symptoms

Different parts of the self can be considered different ego states (Forgash & Copeley, 2008; Shapiro, 2016; Watkins & Watkins, 1997). For example, there may be times when we feel younger than our current age, such as when we return to visit our childhood home. This "inner child" connects us to the emotions and sensations related to events or memories from childhood. Additionally, we tend to internalize our relational experiences with parents and primary caregivers. That's because when we attach to another person, they become a part of us. In Gestalt therapy, this process is called *introjection*, which is defined as adopting or incorporating the behaviors and attitudes of another person so strongly that they can no longer be separated from our own sense of self.

Introjection can be thought of as a loss of boundaries between the self and other, or a loss of the self. As a result, it may be difficult to differentiate between this sense of "other" and our own identity. For example, a critical parent might become the voice of our own self-critic, or a neglectful parent might lead us to dismiss our own or others' feelings and needs. Or a client who experienced abuse in childhood might introject the abuser. When individuals overidentify with abuse, this can manifest as self-loathing, negative self-talk, self-harm behaviors, and urges to act aggressively toward others.

You can think of introjection as the process that occurs when children form an attachment to a parent or caregiver even when that person is also the source of pain, fear, confusion, or rejection. In these situations, children might respond by taking care of the parent or by restricting any expressions of their anger or distress toward the parent in the hope that doing so will reduce the likelihood of more neglect or abuse. In many cases, children begin to turn these negative feelings toward themselves. In Gestalt, this process is referred to as *retroflection*. In adulthood, retroflection is often the root of depression, somatic symptoms, and self-harm.

Children will attach to a parent, even when that person is a source of danger or abuse, because they are completely dependent upon their parents for food, shelter, clothing, medical care, and a sense of belonging. Attachment is necessary for their survival. Because there is often no way to leave the abusive household, children must make the dangerous environment tolerable. In many cases, they must uphold an image of a "normal family" when going to school or church as part of an unspoken expectation of loyalty. In addition, children often receive praise and attention from the very adults who abuse them, which can lead to a profound sense of confusion. Similar dynamics can occur when the abuse is perpetrated by a teacher, coach, or religious leader. Feelings of powerlessness and shame tend to exacerbate a sense of isolation, leading children to refrain from sharing the "secret" of the abuse.

Psychologist and complex trauma specialist Dr. Janina Fisher describes this core conflict among young children who are being abused: They are caught between their biological drive to attach to the parent and their survival instinct to flee the dangerous environment (Fisher, 2017). In some cases, children begin to rely heavily on fantasy in order to survive. They might create an idealized mother or father in order to dissociate from reality. These fantasies often incorporate inaccurate beliefs about the self as being at fault or responsible for the abuse. Psychologist Dr. Jim Knipe (2015) suggests that it is utterly unfathomable for a child to contemplate that they are a "good kid" relying on "bad parents," so they form the narrative that they are a "bad child" relying upon "good parents." In turn, they conclude that something is wrong with them, that the abusive situation is entirely their fault, or that they do not deserve to exist. This process displaces the blame of the abuse or neglect onto the self. These thoughts may also arise because it gives the child a semblance of control in believing that they are the source of the problem.

Even well into adulthood, individuals with C-PTSD tend to uphold an allegiance to their abusers from childhood. This form of Stockholm syndrome can be seen in persistent idealization of family members or a need to maintain loving emotions toward abusers. Clients with a history of complex trauma might feel guilty if they speak poorly about their family, or they might feel as if the abuser still has control over their life. In some cases, clients might have difficulty acknowledging that the traumatic event happened, or they might minimize the significance of the event. For example, a client might talk about a "wonderful father" and then share incongruent memories about substance use or domestic violence. This lack of realization about the impact of traumatic events can feel disorienting to both the client and therapist. Sometimes this can lead the therapist to sense the unrealized feelings or sensations in themselves. For example, you might feel anger, sadness, or fear while the client reports feeling nothing at all.

From the framework of parts work, individuals avoid acknowledging or remembering the abuse by cutting off the parts of the self that hold trauma-related emotions and memories or sending them into "exile." They cannot integrate these feelings into an overall sense of self (Schwartz, 1997; van der Hart et al., 2006). It can feel threatening when these emotions of fear, dependency, rejection, or rage come to the surface. In these moments, they might try to manage their experience by pushing unwanted emotions away, working excessively, or becoming controlling with themselves and others. In addition, because reminders of the trauma exist within the body, individuals with C-PTSD often disconnect from their sensations. This can lead to derealization and depersonalization symptoms in which they feel as if the world around them isn't real, as if their body and actions are not part of them, or as if they are living in a fog.

Pushing away the emotions, sensations, and memories that are connected to traumatic events can leave individuals feeling disconnected or as if they are just going through the motions of their lives. Over time, they might feel like an imposter. The structural dissociation model calls this the "apparently normal part" of the personality (van der Hart et al., 2006). However, we must remember that this part helped the individual survive. This part helped a child growing up in an abusive situation to find a safe haven by continuing to go to school, attend church, or visit with friends. In these safe environments, children could act as if they were living a "normal" life even if they could not speak about the reality of their home environment.

In some cases, clients develop complex internal systems with several "exiled" parts that are stuck as if they are living in the time of the trauma. Some parts of the self might present in a state of hyper-arousal, as expressed by hypervigilance, restlessness, irritability, aggression, rage, anxiety, panic, or uncontrollable crying. Other parts might present in a hypo-aroused state, leading to them to feel lethargic, emotionally dull, helpless, tired, shutdown, numb, disconnected, or depressed. **In other words, dissociative symptoms can be thought of as dysregulated states of physiological arousal that are outside of the client's window of tolerance.** You might begin to sense that a client is experiencing dissociative symptoms even if they do not tell you directly. For example, you might notice that they do not recall a notable conversation you had with them or that they do not recall writing you an email that you received. Or you might notice changes in their tone of voice or posture that indicate that they have connected to feelings held by a young part of the self. Furthermore, you might notice changes in how you feel in the room with your client, such as suddenly feeling tired or having difficulty focusing.

Dissociation is also often experienced as disorientation in regard to the timing of traumatic events. The client might inaccurately believe that frightening events from the past are still happening or could easily happen again. For example, a woman had a historical experience of living in an unsafe home that had been repeatedly burglarized. As a result, she suffered from hypervigilance that prevented her from falling asleep at night, even though she was living in a safe home and community at this stage of her life. Another client would shift into a young part of himself that was connected to memories of physical abuse. In these moments, he would reexperience the emotions and sensations as if the abuse was currently happening. Clients might also describe feeling as though their body is foreign and not a part of them. For example, one man described his experience to me as though he were an astronaut floating through space.

Often, a caring, nonjudgmental conversation about dissociation—as well as its associated symptoms, such as addiction and self-harm—can help reduce the sense of stigma the clients carry, which increases the likelihood that they will speak openly about their symptoms (see the clinical interview questions from chapter 1). Take some time to explain to clients that developing an awareness of their dissociative symptoms can help them to take better care of themselves. It can also be helpful to let them know that recognizing the early signals of dissociation can allow them to respond before symptoms worsen. Throughout this process, you can help the client stay grounded by returning to the healing practices that focus on the window of tolerance (chapter 1), attentional control (chapter 2), the social engagement system (chapter 3), co-regulation (chapter 4), and mindful body awareness (chapter 5).

Parts Work Therapy

The goal of parts work therapy is to help clients realize and integrate the disowned emotions and traumatic memories held by exiled parts of the self. Initially, this often involves helping the client become aware that a part is present. A part might show up in emotional states, such as when a client feels overly dependent upon others, feels helpless, begins crying uncontrollably, or speaks like a young child. Other common signs of parts include self-criticism, perfectionism, self-aggressive tendencies, idealization of an abuser, a tendency to dismiss their own emotions or needs, procrastination, and indecision. You might also notice changes in posture, tone of voice, or use of eye contact, which suggest that the client is in another ego state. Or you might notice dissociative symptoms in which the client suddenly feels dizzy, foggy, tired, or numb. Physical symptoms of pain also suggest the presence of a part that has been somaticized. For example, you might notice that the client gets a headache, experiences a sudden pain in their body, or feels nauseous before, during, or after sessions.

We can also help clients identify parts of the self by inviting them to bring into session a photograph of themselves as a child. What do they notice as they look at the photograph? What emotions do they observe in their face or body language? What emotions are they aware of now? How do they feel toward this part of themselves? Alternatively, you can invite the client to draw a picture or create a collage that represents a part of themselves. Upon completion of this creative process, have them explore the colors or images they chose to represent the part and how they feel as they look at the drawing.

Another way to help clients identify parts is to invite them to create a meeting place for all of their parts, either in their mind or on a piece of paper. This might involve imagining a conference table, campfire, or other gathering place. Invite the client to bring in parts of all different ages, such as a baby, inner child, teenager, or adult part. Or they might have parts that represent different emotions, such as a shameful, fearful, angry, joyful, courageous, or loving part. In addition, you can suggest that they include parts that represent strengths or challenging aspects of their personality, such as a creative, hard-working, critical, perfectionistic, or neglectful part. Once the client places each part in the meeting place, you can ask them to describe the relationship between different parts of themselves. If they have created a drawing, you and the client can explore the placement of each part. For example, you might notice that some parts are located close to one another while others are placed far away. Or you might discover that there are parts who reject or feel threatened by other parts of the self.

Once you are aware that a part is present, you can help the client deepen their awareness of that part. One way to help clients differentiate from this part is to use the empty chair technique from Gestalt therapy. This process involves inviting the client to imagine a part of the self in an empty chair and facilitating a dialogue. You can place any kind of part in the chair, whether that be a part that represents the client's inner child, self-critic, parent, or abuser. Since all parts are important, it is important to give each part a chance to have a voice. If a client is struggling with self-criticism, you can invite them to put the inner critic in a chair and invite a dialogue between the part of the self who is critical and the part who is feeling criticized. Or, if the client is having difficulty making a decision, you can have two chairs, each representing the two possible sides of the decision. For example, a client who has an ambivalent relationship with a historically abusive mother might say, "Part of me wants to talk to my mom, and part of me is scared to call her." In this case, each chair represents the two sides of the decision. In most cases, you can invite the client to move in and out of each chair while encouraging a dialogue that allows them to hear the voice and needs of both parts of the self. In each seat, they have an opportunity to mindfully increase awareness of their emotions or sensations.

As we progress into parts work, you might notice that the client is strongly identified or "blended" with a part (Schwartz, 1997). They might be overidentified with a young part of the self or with a critical part. Blending is the result of a behavior that once allowed the individual to "fit in" with others and, in some cases, to survive an abusive environment. Children typically adopt the attitudes, beliefs, body language, and tone of voice of their caregivers—and in an abusive environment, this means the child might internalize the harmful messages, behaviors, and body language of an abuser as a part of the self. This process helps children predict future abusive behaviors by allowing them to recognize the facial expression or tone of voice associated with episodes of abuse. As adults, not only might these clients remain blended with their abuser, but they also might identify with the adaptive strategies they relied upon as a child to survive the abuse, such as remaining docile or subservient to avoid upsetting the abuser.

When clients are blended with a young part of the self, they will be more likely to rely upon these same behaviors in their adult relationships. In psychotherapy, we aim to help clients differentiate or unblend from these parts. Paradoxically, we often need to help clients hear the voice and understand the needs of each part before they will differentiate from that part. However, in many cases, the client is so blended with a part that we must help them anchor their awareness in the "adult" self that is oriented to the here and now. Within IFS, this process involves connecting to the "Self," which is described as the core of the individual that has qualities of compassion, confidence, creativity, courage, clarity, calmness, connectedness, and curiosity (Anderson et al., 2017; Schwartz, 1997).

When we invite our clients to connect to their adult, present-centered self, we help them access the internal resources that can help them respond more effectively to distressing emotions. With their awareness anchored in the adult self, it is easier for them to recognize choices that may not have been available to them when they were a child. In the past, they might not have been able to set boundaries, leave an abusive situation, or speak up for themselves. Orienting to the present moment helps clients realize that these events are over and in the past so they can now protect or nurture themselves in a new, healthy manner. **As clients strengthen their relationship to their own adult self, they can become a source of consistency, reliability, and love for themselves.**

When using parts work in the treatment of C-PTSD, it is important to help clients unblend from any parts that are overidentified with their abuser prior to working directly with the parts that hold their vulnerable emotions and memories. The goal of this process is to help clients redirect their feelings of anger, repulsion, hatred, and disgust to their rightful source. Most often, we must honor the client's pace in letting go of an overidentification with a young part of the self or with an abuser. In some cases, this process can feel threatening to the individual's conscious sense of self-identity. Clients may fear that they will lose a part of themselves or that they will no longer be able to protect themselves. This process can feel like a tremendous loss of identity, which can involve grieving the remnants of hope that their abuser would finally meet their needs for attachment, love, and acceptance. **We can remind clients that we are not getting rid of any part of them. Rather, we are giving them access to more of themselves.** We can also help them recognize that their needs for protection and nurturance can and will be met through other, healthy relationships, including the therapeutic relationship.

Once a client is no longer identified with the abuser, parts work can turn toward the vulnerable emotions and unmet needs of young or exiled parts. Often, this involves facilitating repair scenarios using imaginal techniques. In particular, clients can engage in visualization practices that focus on resolving the wounds they experienced when they were young. We can remind clients that all children deserve to be nurtured, protected, unconditionally accepted, and have their boundaries respected by caring, safe, and wise adults. We can facilitate repair by inviting the client to imagine the needs of a young part of the self. Once clients have identified a need, we can invite them to imagine attending to this young part by providing care, protecting it, or rescuing it from an unsafe environment. This process might also involve retrieving a part of the self that is stuck in the past and bringing it into the present. If it is difficult for a client to hold compassion for a young part, you can have them imagine another adult who can serve as an ally for the young part. Let's take a closer look at parts work through the experience of working with Mateo, a young man in his early twenties who was diagnosed with C-PTSD and struggled with dissociation and self-harming behaviors:

Mateo described feeling like he was in a daze, but at times, his pain would penetrate the numbness. That is when he would cut himself. In the months that I had worked with Mateo, I learned that he grew up in a house with a physically abusive and alcoholic father. Not only was he abused, but he also witnessed his father attack his mother. In one of his most disturbing memories, Mateo described seeing his father threaten his mother while holding a gun in his hand. The worst part of the experience was feeling frozen and helpless.

I asked Mateo to imagine his young self in that scene, and his face contorted into a look of disgust. Talking about himself in the third person, he stated, "That boy could never stand up to his father. That boy is repulsive!" Mateo had internalized the anger he felt toward his father and was directing this feeling toward himself. I suggested that Mateo imagine his father sitting in an empty chair across from where he was sitting. Then I asked Mateo what he would like to say to his father, perhaps something that he could not have said to his father when he a child.

At first, Mateo became very quiet. He lowered his gaze and seemed to touch into the helplessness and shame that he felt as a young child. He looked frozen. After several minutes, he shook his head as if to say, "I can't speak." I offered that he could take a moment to look around the room and sense that he was here, now. I reminded him that he was 23 years old and that his father could not hurt him now. I knew that he had been practicing tae kwon do for several years and suggested that he imagine connecting to his center. In response, Mateo took several deep breaths and nodded.

Once he was feeling grounded and resourced, I asked him to once again imagine what he wished he could have said to his father. This time, Mateo lifted his gaze toward the empty chair and he said, "I hate you! You were the one who was repulsive, not me." His face was red and his eyes widened. Then he began to cry as he continued to speak. "It wasn't my fault! It never was. I didn't do anything wrong!" After several minutes, he quieted. When I asked what he was noticing, he said, "I can see more clearly, like a fog has lifted."

Next, I asked Mateo what he imagined he needed most when he was a young boy. He shrugged his shoulders. After a period of silence, I asked him if there was anyone from his life now who he wishes could have supported him when he was a young boy. He shared that his martial arts teacher was the first person to whom he ever spoke about his childhood. It was this teacher who suggested that he come to therapy. I suggested that he imagine his teacher going back in time and talking with him as a young boy. I asked, "What would it have been like to have your teacher with you?" He recognized that his teacher would have seen how afraid he was and how helpless he felt. His teacher would have helped to protect him and would have stopped his father from hurting his mother. Once again, Mateo began to cry as he imagined this scene.

As the session came to a close, we acknowledged that we couldn't change the past, but we could help him stop blaming himself for these events from his childhood. A therapy progressed, he had several more "conversations" with his father. During one of the empty chair dialogues, Mateo was sitting in his father's seat and shared a new awareness. He said, "My father was abused as a child too. He didn't know how to be a dad." This realization evoked a spontaneous feeling of compassion for his father and for himself.

Importantly, we must remember that, as therapists, we have parts too. At times, our clients' parts can trigger parts in us. When this occurs, we might approach therapy from a part of our self, rather than from our adult self. For example, if we have parts that are phobic of the emotions that a client's parts carry, we might collude with the client's defenses in an attempt to keep these emotions at bay. Therapy might begin to feel stagnant, and we may feel stuck with a client. In this case, we can utilize supervision or consultation to explore any countertransference dynamics the client is evoking within us and identify whether we are blending with a part of our self.

The rest of this chapter offers healing practices that introduce clients to parts work and that help them identify and deepen awareness of parts, anchor the adult self, differentiate from a part, find resources for a part, and repair a missing experience.

The Beach Ball Metaphor

Through the use of a beach ball metaphor, this practice emphasizes the importance of pacing in therapy and the value of attending to the emotions connected to traumatic memories.

- Imagine a beach ball that is being held under water. This beach ball represents unwanted emotions, sensations, images, and thoughts related to your traumatic past. Initially, you might desire to push the ball under the water. In the short term, this might not feel difficult and can even feel good.

- However, over time, you might begin to grow tired. It takes a lot of energy to hold all of this underwater. It wants to come to the surface. It is increasingly effortful to push it all down.

- Inevitably, you get distracted. Maybe you lose focus because of a fight with a family member, a bad dream, or an incident where you drank too much. The next thing you know, the beach ball slips through your hands and bursts out of the water, creating a big splash. All of your feelings and memories come to the surface. This can feel like a crisis, and you are left cleaning up the mess. This can lead to a vicious cycle as you quickly push the ball back under the water.

- In order to heal the trauma from the past, it is important to allow the beach ball to come to the surface slowly. To do so, you must attend to the pain in small bits. Each time you bring your awareness to your memories, sensations, and emotions, you reduce the pressure, and the ball comes a little closer to the surface but at a pace that you can tolerate.

- Once you have worked through enough memories connected to your traumatic past, you no longer feel threatened by these feelings or images. Now the beach ball rests on the surface of your awareness. You no longer need to push any part of yourself away. You have freed up all of the energy that was bound inside of your effort to push it all down. This energy is now available for your life.

Introduce Clients to Parts Work

We bring parts work into therapy by helping clients recognize that we all have different states of mind, emotion, and physiological arousal. This healing practice provides psychoeducation to help clients understand parts work and invites them to be curious about their own parts.

- All of us have parts of ourselves. For example, you might recall times when you have felt young, small, or helpless. Other times, you might have felt self-critical or controlling of others. Or there may be times when you feel disconnected from yourself.

- Some parts may be easier for you to like or may feel more familiar. You may have other parts that you would rather push away. For example, some people feel capable or confident when they go to work but lonely or sad when they come home at the end of the day. It is common to experience conflicts between parts. Additionally, there may be a part of you that wants to heal and part that is afraid of feeling your emotions.

- Even if you do want to make room for your emotions, you may feel blocked by a part who criticizes, rejects, or blames the part of you who is vulnerable. Or you might feel the need to manage your distress by seeking a sense of control, by needing to be perfect, or by staying excessively busy. While it might seem counterintuitive, you can think of this critical or controlling part as a protector who has been working hard to shield you from feeling your pain. When it is left unaddressed, you are more likely to feel stuck in your life or unable to meet your goals.

- Parts work addresses this internal conflict by helping you gain access to the vulnerable exiled parts of yourself that are often hidden underneath your protective defenses. These exiled parts hold the painful emotions, sensations, and memories related to the traumatic events from your past. In time, you can help these exiled parts release their burdens.

- You can release these burdens by connecting to an inner source of wisdom that you carry within you—known as your adult, presented-centered self—which is always available to support your healing journey. You know that you are connected to your center when you feel calm, clearheaded, and courageous. Once you are connected to your wise self, you are able to tap into your intuition and your intellect. This allows your adult self to turn toward all parts of yourself with curiosity and compassion, which is a process that allows you to attend to and heal the wounds from your past.

Understand Emotional Dysregulation as a Part

- Often, when we are afraid to feel certain parts of ourselves, they show up as dysregulated emotions or sensations. Until you bring conscious and compassionate awareness to these feelings, these parts are likely to remain outside of your window of tolerance.

- Take a few moments to notice your feelings of… [*If the client is hyper-aroused, this might involve anxiety, overwhelm, panic, or agitation. If the client is hypo-aroused, this might involve depression, hopelessness, despair, or shame.*]

- See if you can become curious about this feeling. In what ways are these feelings familiar? Can you imagine that this feeling is connected to a part of you that felt this way in the past? Can you recall specific times that you felt this way? How old does this part of you feel? In what ways might this part try to protect you from your vulnerable feelings? Or perhaps this part is carrying your vulnerable feelings. Either way, do you have a sense of what this part of you might need?

Build Awareness of a Part through a Photograph or Imagined Picture

- Would you be willing to bring in a photograph of yourself as a child? [*If the client does not have a photograph, invite them to imagine themselves as a child.*]

- What do you notice as you look at this image of yourself as a child? When you look at the eyes, face, and body language of your young self, what you do imagine you were feeling then? What else do you see in this image?

- As you look at this image, how do you feel toward this part of yourself? What beliefs arise as you look at this image? What emotions are present for you? How do you feel in your body?

- What do you imagine you needed most at that time? Is there anything you wish you could say to your young self?

Explore a Part through the Creative Arts

- Sometimes it is helpful to explore a part through a creative channel, such as creating a drawing or making a collage. I have here a blank piece of art paper, drawing materials, magazines, scissors, and glue. Would you be willing to deepen your awareness of this part of you that… [*e.g., feels hopeless, experiences shame, feels anxious, feels protective, feels like an exile, has a headache*] through a creative process?

- Take some time to reflect upon this part of you. What kinds of thoughts are you having? What emotions are present for you? How do you feel in your body?

- Now explore creating a picture or making a collage that represents your experience of this part. Take some time to create a drawing or to choose images that represent your experience of this part. This creative project does not need to be artistic or perfect. You are creating something that matches the feelings, sensations, images, or thoughts that you carry inside.

- Now take some time to look at the drawing or collage that you have created. Notice the colors or images that you chose. How do you feel as you look at this creative work of art? What emotions or body sensations arise for you now? Is there anything familiar about your experience? Can you recall other times when you felt this way? Do you have a sense of what this part of yourself needs?

- You can create additional drawings or collages of other parts as you would like.

Create a Meeting Place for Your Parts

- Sometimes it is helpful to create a meeting place where you can invite all of your parts to be in one place. For example, you might imagine or draw a conference table, campfire, or any other meeting place that you would like. Would you be interested in creating a meeting place for your parts?

- What kind of meeting place would you like to create? Would you like to draw your meeting place or simply imagine it?

- What parts of yourself would you like to bring to this meeting place? These parts might be different ages, such as a baby, inner child, teenager, or adult. Or you might explore parts that represent different emotions, such as a shameful, fearful, angry, joyful, courageous, or loving part. Parts might also represent different aspects of your personality, such as a creative, hard-working, critical, perfectionistic, or self-sabotaging part.

- Once you have identified your parts, take some time to place each part in your meeting place by either drawing them or simply imagining them. What parts might you place close to one another? Which parts would you separate further apart from one another? How would you describe the relationships between different parts of yourself? Are there any conflicts between parts? Are there any parts who nurture or protect other parts?

Connect to Your Adult Self

This healing strategy can be used to guide clients to connect to their adult self so they can access the 8 C's of the "Self" as described in IFS (Schwartz, 1997): compassion, clarity, confidence, creativity, courage, calmness, connectedness, and curiosity.

- This practice is to help you connect to your adult self. I'd like you to imagine that you are connected to your center. This is a place within you that can serve as a source of clarity, curiosity, and compassion.

- Take a few breaths and notice how you feel in your body. See if you can fine-tune your posture so you feel connected to your core. You might explore how it feels to lengthen your spine as you take a deep breath. Or notice how it feels to stand up tall. Continue to explore your posture until you find a stance that helps you feel strong, courageous, and calm.

- Feel yourself in the body of your adult self. Take a look at your hands and notice that these are the hands of an adult. If you are able, stand up and recognize that you are in an adult body by reaching up to the top of a door frame. Remind yourself that you are an adult now and that you are safe.

- Orient to the time and date by looking at a clock or calendar. Notice the current date and time as a way to reinforce that you are an adult and not a child.

- Think of activities that you can do in your life now that were not possible when you were a child. For example, you can drive a car, go to work, take care of your own children, and vote.

- Explore bringing a warm, gentle smile to your face. Relax your face and slightly lift the corners of your lips. Invite a soft smile to your eyes. As you engage in this smile, allow a relaxed feeling to spread across your face, head, and shoulders. Notice if you can connect to a feeling of peace.

- Bring your attention to your heart by taking several deep breaths into your chest. Perhaps place one or both of your hands over your heart to enhance your connection to this area of your body. As you connect to your physical heart, I also invite you to notice the qualities your heart represents: warmth, generosity, and love. Notice how it feels to know that these qualities are always there inside of you.

- Now take several deep breaths into your belly. Again, you can place one or both hands over this area of your body to enhance your awareness. The area in your lower abdomen, about two inches below your navel, has been called the Dan Tian in the Qigong tradition and is considered a center of inner strength. As you focus your attention here, imagine being connected to a source of stability that can help you from being pulled out of balance by people or situations in your life.

- Now that you are connected to your adult self, take some time to notice your thoughts, emotions, and body sensations. Perhaps you notice that you feel more grounded, are more connected to your center, or have an increased sense of clarity. If so, allow yourself to savor and enjoy this positive experience. You can reconnect here as often as needed by returning to these practices.

Differentiate from a Part

Once the client is connected to their adult self, we can invite them to differentiate from any parts with which they are overidentified. Ideally, this helps the client to have greater clarity about the functions of protective parts and to have compassion for wounds carried by exiled parts. Signs that a client is blended with a protective part include self-criticism, perfectionism, a tendency to be judgmental toward others, or aggressive behavior. Signs that a client is blended with an exiled part include overwhelming emotions of sadness, hopelessness, helplessness, or shame.

This practice asks questions and offers suggestions to help the client unblend from a critical protective part and, when needed, to differentiate from a young exiled part. Ultimately, this will help the client gain access to the vulnerable emotions held by the exiled part so resolution and healing can be achieved. Importantly, it is common to move between the previous healing practices regarding parts work as you explore this practice:

- Now that you are connected to your adult self, I invite you to turn toward the part of you that feels… [*e.g., young, anxious, sad, not enough, worthless, lonely*]. Notice how you feel toward this part of yourself. What is it like to witness this part of you? From the perspective of your adult self, what do you believe about this part of you?

If the client appears blended with a critical or rejecting part of self—limiting the client's ability to explore their younger, more vulnerable part—then explore the following questions and statements.

- I notice that you are feeling critical toward the part of you who is feeling… [*e.g., young, anxious, sad, not enough, worthless, lonely*]. I understand that this criticism once served to protect you. Is the critical part willing to step back and allow you to be present with this vulnerable part of you?

- We are not trying to get rid of this critical part but are asking it to step back for the time being. Rather than casting off this part, I invite you to reflect upon the ways that this part has functioned to protect you.

- Perhaps you might offer appreciation to this part for its job. If you weren't able to be vulnerable when you were a child, this part may have helped you maintain a sense of control. Now ask yourself whether it is still necessary to protect yourself in this way. Might it be safe to soften your defenses?

If the client appears overidentified with the young part of the self, then explore the following questions and statements.

- You seem to be feeling very little or young right now. Can you take a moment to reorient to your adult self? Now that you feel more connected to your center and your strength, is there anything that this young or vulnerable part wants the adult part of you to know? Invite the adult part to give the young part a tour of your life now. Show the young part where you live and where you work. Share the ways that your present-day life is different from the experiences you had in childhood.

Invite a Dialogue with an Inner Critic

This practice offers an additional intervention that is beneficial for clients who struggle with an unrelenting self-critical part. In this case, you invite the client to explore a dialogue between their inner critic and the part of themselves who is being criticized. This is accomplished through an empty chair dialogue between the critic and the young or exiled part of the self. As with all therapeutic interventions, it is important that the client express their willingness to participate with this experiment, so begin by inviting the client's consent. In setting up the dialogue, you will ask the client to identify whether they are more connected to the critical voice or the part that feels criticized. You will then invite them to begin the dialogue by giving voice to the part that they are more identified with. As a result, you will need to tailor the order of the suggested prompts offered here to reflect your understanding of the client's unique presentation and internalized parts.

- I notice that you are… [*e.g., feeling self-critical, calling yourself worthless, feeling like you need to be perfect, dismissing your emotions*]. When you have a strong inner critic, it can be helpful to explore an empty chair dialogue with this part of yourself. This process also invites the part that is being… [*e.g., criticized, put down, controlled, dismissed*] to have a voice. Would you be willing to explore a dialogue between your inner critic and the part of you being criticized?

- It is important to know that this dialogue is not real and does not require that you speak these words to your… [*e.g., mom, dad, abuser*] in real life. We are working with your internalization of their presence and voice as it lives inside of you. This dialogue is to help you find resolution within yourself as you express what you were never able to say in the relationship.

- Let's set up the room so you have an empty chair in front of you. Take a moment and check in with yourself. Do you feel more connected to the part of you that is critical or to the part that feels criticized?

- When giving voice to your inner critic, give yourself permission to really exaggerate this part of you! Notice your tone of voice and posture. Do you notice any familiarity in your body language or in the message communicated by this critical part of you? Does this voice remind you of anyone from your past?

- When giving voice to the part of you who feels criticized, notice how you feel when you are being criticized and judged. What thoughts and emotions arise? From this seat, look at the chair of your inner critic. Give yourself permission to express how it feels to be criticized. You might say, "I feel insignificant when you talk to me like that," "You have unrealistic expectations of me," or "I can never get it right!" Notice your posture and tone of voice as you sit in this chair. Are you aware of times from the past when you felt this way?

- Often, self-criticism and self-aggression are manifestations of anger turned inward. Ask yourself what would have happened had you expressed anger toward… [*e.g., mom, dad, abuser*] when you were a child. Instead of attacking yourself, can you give yourself permission to be angry at… [*e.g., mom, dad, abuser*] now?

- Now cultivate a dialogue by going back and forth between the chair of your inner critic and the part of you that feels criticized. Take your time until both parts have had an opportunity to be heard. Continue to explore any memories or associations that arise related to each part. See if you can understand what motivates the critical part. Is it an attempt to protect you from feeling vulnerable? Is it a remnant of unfinished business of your… [*e.g., mom, dad, abuser*] that had nothing to do with you? Begin to explore the needs of the part of you who feels criticized. Does this part need kindness, nurturance, or protection?

- Since this dialogue is in your imagination, you get to decide how it ends. You are allowed to seek resolution and create a new outcome. What might it be like for the critic to soften and meet the needs of the part who feels criticized? Perhaps, you can imagine that your… [*e.g., mom, dad, abuser*] offers an apology that never happened in real life. This is your internal world, so how do you want to bring this dialogue to completion?

Identify Allies for a Young Part

This healing practice helps clients identify supportive people or imagined allies for a young or exiled part of the self. This practice can be especially helpful if the client feels resentment, hatred, or disgust toward the young part. In this case, the client might not be capable of offering compassion from their adult self toward the young part.

- All children deserve to be nurtured, protected, and wisely guided by caring parents or caregivers. If you did not receive this support in childhood, you might have a hard time feeling compassion for a young part of yourself now. In this case, it can be helpful to identify other people or to imagine allies who can offer nurturance, protection, and wise guidance for this young part. Would you be willing to identify some supportive resources for this part?

- You might have had people at various stages of your life who met these needs, such as a caring relative, neighbor, or teacher. Or you might have people in your life now who support you. Can you identify a supportive person or people who could help you as you work through difficult memories from your past? Is there someone in your life who has supported you, believed in you, stood up for you, or guided you during difficult moments in your life?

- Even if you did not or do not have these people in your life, you can imagine the presence of allies who represent these positive qualities. An ally can be an animal, ancestor, spiritual presence, or fictional character from a movie or book. I'd like you to identify a few imagined allies who could help you as you work through difficult memories from your past. What allies might offer care, warmth, or nurturance? You might also want to imagine allies with a strong presence and fearless capacity to protect you.

- Now bring to mind your young self, and take a few moments to identify the needs of this part of you. Imagine these supportive people and allies providing care, protection, or wise counsel for this young part of yourself. What emotions or sensations arise as you imagine having these supportive people and allies with this part of you?

Facilitate Repair Scenarios

Once the client has unblended from their parts, we can invite them to explore creating a repair scenario to facilitate a resolution of the wounds from the past. The following interventions offer examples of how to identify the needs of a younger, vulnerable part and repair these wounds. As with the previous healing practices, you might notice that the client has difficulty maintaining compassion for this part of the self. If the client begins to blend with a critical part of themselves, it may be necessary to help them connect to their adult self or to invite them to bring in allies by revisiting the previous healing practices in this section.

- I invite you to turn toward the part of you that feels… [*e.g., young, anxious, not enough, worthless, critical*]. Often, these parts of ourselves carry unmet needs, such as the need to be nurtured, supported, accepted, seen, heard, understood, respected, protected, rescued, or removed from an unsafe situation. Once we identify an unmet need, we can explore creating an imagined repair for that part of yourself.

- Take a moment to recall a memory of a time in your life that is connected to this part. Where were you? How old were you? Were you alone or with others? What made this time so difficult? What emotions were you feeling then?

- Now, from the perspective of your adult self, can you imagine what you might have needed in that time?

If the client has difficulty connecting to the need, you can share what you imagine the need might have been. For example, you can say:

- If I were there with you then, here is what I imagine you would have needed. [*Name what you imagine was the missing experience for the client.*] Does that feel accurate to you?

- Imagine your present-day self walking into that scene and nurturing your younger self. Can you imagine gazing at this younger you in a loving and compassionate manner?

- What emotions do you see on the face of your younger self? How does it feel to know that these emotions are now understood and seen? Is there anything that you would like to say to your younger self? Is there anything else you might do to offer a sense of comfort, support, or acceptance for that younger you? Take your time with this process until you feel a sense of completion. What do you notice now as you offer this nurturance to this part of yourself?

- Can you imagine your adult self standing up for this young part? You will not let anyone hurt this part of you! You are allowed to have boundaries. Notice if there is a need to rescue or remove your younger self from an unsafe situation. If so, imagine taking this part of yourself away from danger. Now imagine bringing this young part of yourself to a safe place. Take your time until you have created a sense of safety for this part. Now what do you notice as you offer protection and safety to this part of yourself?

- If you find it difficult to imagine your adult self being a resource for this young part, you can explore bringing in an ally into this scene from your past. In what ways might this person nurture or protect you? Maybe you would like to imagine them helping this part of you stand up against an abuser, or perhaps they help remove this part of you from an unsafe situation. Are there any other allies you would like to bring into this scene? Take your time with this process until you feel a sense of completion. Notice how you feel in your body and any emotions you are feeling.

7

Repatterning the Body
with Somatic Psychology

When we observe the natural world, we see that animals have natural, inborn survival instincts that help them respond to threatening experiences. Animals flee from predators, signal their capacity to fight by baring their teeth and claws, or rely upon a freeze response to survive. For example, a rabbit being chased by a fox might initially run and then hide behind a bush. In order to survive, the rabbit might immobilize by reducing its movements, breathing shallowly, and slowing down its heart rate. This immobilization response reduces the likelihood that it will be perceived by the predator. Once the threat is over, animals typically release the physiological impact of threatening experiences by shaking in order to return to healthy mobilization (Levine, 1997).

Although children often share this natural propensity toward shaking when frightened, many adults tend to suppress this natural tremor response (Berceli, 2015). In part, this is because many of us have grown up within a culture of stillness. We have been taught to sit still in school as a sign of obedience and respect. Many of us have thus learned to disconnect from the body. Moreover, when trauma is ongoing and chronic, that time of safety where we can shake it off doesn't arise. As a result, the body can retain the impact of unresolved stress, sometimes for decades. Many therapists and clients who rely on talk therapy approaches avoid integrating movement into therapy as a continuation of this culture of stillness. **Without interventions that incorporate somatic awareness and movement, many therapeutic approaches are limited in their ability help clients fully release the impact of traumatic events.** In other words, we cannot simply think our way out of traumatic activation.

In contrast, somatic psychology invites both therapists and clients to pay attention to sensations and encourages the integration of mindful movement as part of treatment. *Somatic psychology* is the study of the relationship between our body sensations, thoughts, emotions, and behaviors. Somatic approaches are guided by the viewpoint that what we are thinking becomes a feeling in the body—and similarly, the ways in which we move and breathe impact our thoughts and emotions.

Somatic psychology invites us as therapists to notice our own bodies and to observe our client's nonverbal communications for signals of safety or threat. For example, our bodies respond differently depending on whether we feel safe or threatened. Under conditions of safety, we feel relaxed, but under conditions of threat, we react instinctively out of self-defense. A body-centered approach emphasizes the importance of paying attention to these changes in facial expressions, postures, gestures, and tone of voice as a core part of therapy. It focuses on the use of embodiment practices to build a reservoir of bodily and kinesthetic awareness that enhances our communication, strengthens empathy, and guides the resolution of trauma (Damasio, 1999).

In chapter 5, we focused on increasing mindful body awareness in therapy, and this chapter builds upon that foundation. Focusing on embodiment within trauma treatment allows us to strengthen clients' resources through grounding interventions and boundary development. In addition, somatic psychology helps us move into phase two of trauma treatment, which supports clients in working through traumatic material in a well-paced, regulated manner. With an emphasis on dual awareness and working within the window of tolerance, a body-centered approach to psychotherapy helps clients release the effects of traumatic events on the body.

The field of somatic psychology is made up of a wide range of psychotherapeutic approaches. Two of the most recognized body psychotherapies are somatic experiencing (Levine, 1997, 2010) and sensorimotor psychotherapy (Ogden et al., 2006; Ogden & Fisher, 2015). However, other influential modalities include bioenergetics (Lowen, 1977), integrative body psychotherapy (Rosenberg, Rand, & Asay, 1985), focusing (Gendlin, 1982), the moving cycle (Caldwell, 1996, 1997), body-mind psychotherapy (Aposhyan, 2007), and the Hakomi method (Kurtz, 1990).

In discussing these various models of somatic psychotherapy, this chapter offers a unified approach to somatic psychology that integrates the theoretical and methodological elements shared among different body psychotherapies (Geuter, 2015; Schwartz & Maiberger, 2018). The first of these shared elements is the recognition that our difficult life experiences, especially those from early development, contribute to patterns of tension in the body. A second common factor is the belief that body awareness helps us access an internal source of wisdom that guides the healing process. The third common factor is that we engage clients in body awareness and healing movements at a pace they can tolerate. The healing practices in this chapter will help you increase your awareness of nonverbal communications, build somatic resources, work with your client's postural awareness, and invite clients to explore healing movements.

Embodiment in Psychotherapy

Difficult life experiences, especially those that occur in the course of early development, are carried in the body as patterns of tension referred to as somatic "armoring." It is for this reason that paying attention to your clients' postures, use of gestures, or breathing patterns can provide insight into their life experiences. Attending to these sensations not only increases awareness of tension patterns but also helps clients discover new movements that help them resolve the wounds from the past.

With body-centered approaches, we support clients to increase body awareness at a pace they can tolerate by strengthening their capacity for *dual awareness,* in which they remain aware of their external senses while building their capacity to internally sense and feel the body (Rothschild, 2010). This helps clients build their capacity to stay within their window of tolerance so they can effectively respond to both high arousal and low arousal states. You can think of this as helping clients work through trauma by finding tolerable amounts of traumatic activation that take them to the upper and lower "edges" of their window of tolerance. By working at these edges, we help clients create greater tolerance for sensations and emotions, which is a process known as *titration* (Levine, 1997). Titration is a term used in chemistry that refers to the mixing of chemicals in a slow, modulated manner. For example, if you combine large amounts of vinegar and baking soda together, you will get an explosion. However, if you take a dropper of vinegar and add a small amount to the baking soda, you will find that the mixture bubbles up and settles down. We facilitate titration in psychotherapy when we guide clients to become aware of small amounts of somatic distress and then invite them to breathe or move in a manner that helps discharge their physical and emotional tension.

Tension tends to accumulate in the body when we suppress our natural proclivity toward movement (Fogel, 2009). Most people curl their bodies inward when exposed to traumatic events (Berceli, 2008). This defensive posture is a result of contractions in the psoas and hip flexor muscles, which prepare the body for a fight-or-flight response. Ideally, once we are safe, the muscular contraction releases, which can result in a shaking or trembling through the legs. Discharging tension from the body can also be experienced as a trembling in the upper body or a release of emotions. Through this process, which is referred to as *sequencing*, the tension that we've held in the core of the body begins to move out of the body. Somatic release sometimes happens naturally in response to somatic awareness, though we can also facilitate it in therapy by inviting clients to engage in movements or postures that facilitate shaking or trembling. For example, Tension & Trauma Releasing Exercises (TRE®) is a body-based technique that encourages therapeutic tremoring to release muscle tension and reduce anxiety (Berceli, 2008).

Let's take a closer look at what somatic psychology can look like in therapy through my work with Sharon, a single mother whose only daughter was about to leave for college:

Sharon came into therapy feeling both anxious and depressed. She struggled with irritable bowel syndrome and insomnia. She felt great anxiety about losing her relationship with her daughter even though she knew that this separation was an important and necessary stage of her daughter's development. Nonetheless, she struggled with feelings of rejection and over-dependency on her daughter. Sharon described feeling "stuck" in her life. She presented with a collapsed posture, with her shoulders rolled forward and her arms hanging limply by her sides. Working with Sharon, I discovered that she had a history of feeling rejected by her mother, who was dismissive and withholding. She felt that no matter what she did, she couldn't get her needs met. Her father was often at work, which left her unprotected from her mother. When Sharon was 12, she was sexually abused by a babysitter. Around that same time, her parents got divorced. She moved in with her maternal grandparents along with her mother and brother. Because of the chaos in her family, she never told anyone about the sexual abuse incident.

Sharon cried often in sessions and felt helpless to change her circumstances. She had difficulty asserting herself and was fearful of reaching out to others. I began to integrate somatic awareness into our sessions by inviting Sharon to pay attention to her sensations. By placing her hands over her chest and belly, she increased a sense of connection to these areas. We also began to explore her posture. Initially, I suggested that she nonjudgmentally notice her tendency to lean forward and cast her gaze downward. We explored her posture, and she noticed a desire to curl forward even further. This urge to make herself small was connected to her emotions of helplessness and the grief of her childhood.

Next, we explored how it felt to press her legs into the floor, which provided a sense of support. This helped her find more support in her core and eventually allowed her to lengthen her spine and lift her gaze. As she lifted her gaze, Sharon described feeling unprotected and vulnerable. I invited her to follow her urge to curl downward. This time, she touched into feelings of shame, loneliness, and fear that were connected to the rejection she felt as a little girl and the sexual abuse she experienced as a pre-adolescent.

While these emotions were painful to feel, she also began to discover a new sense of strength within herself. She explored moving back and forth between the inward curling motion and a new sense of length and support in her body. I invited her to explore these two postures on her own between sessions. When she returned, she described feeling more hopeful and less isolated when she lengthened her posture because she was more likely to make eye contact with others as she walked through the world.

As Sharon discovered a new sense of support from her core, she was able to explore reaching for what she wanted through her arms. The first time she explored this movement, she began to cry. She described feeling like a little girl, unable to reach out for her mother. Her arms trembled as she cried. After this emotional and physical release, Sharon described feeling a sense of relief. In the following months, she described a new ability to reach out to people in her life who were kind and caring. With this came a new sense of freedom and hope for her future.

As you can see in Sharon's case, her trauma presented as a lack of support in her core and low muscular tone leading to a collapsed posture. As a result, she continued to feel anxious, depressed, and helpless. In contrast, some clients come in with high levels of tension and muscular holding. For these individuals, somatic interventions can help them learn how to release chronic tension patterns from the body. Let's take a look at Marcus, a Black man, who represents the other end of this continuum:

Marcus came into therapy because his wife was frustrated by his anger outbursts, and his inability to talk about his feelings was interfering with their relationship. Marcus had been in the military and now worked as a first responder. His muscular body led him to carry tension in his chest, shoulders, neck, and jaw. While his strength helped him handle the challenges of life, he also carried underlying fears of being seen as a failure. Marcus felt mistrustful of others and was often concerned that people would take advantage of him. As Marcus and I worked together, I discovered that he was raised by a father who was punitive and emotionally cut off. In his family, "love" was based upon performance. He learned to bury his feelings to avoid disappointing his father. His years in the military further reinforced his stoic approach to the world. Furthermore, as an African American man, he experienced the chronic stress of discrimination and racism for much of his life.

Once Marcus and I got to know each other, I began to guide him to pay attention to his sensations. He became increasingly aware of the tension in his upper body. Instead of trying to make this tension go away, I suggested that he explore amplifying the activation in his muscles to deepen his awareness of the feelings in his body. As he increased the tension in his chest and arms, he shared that he was aware that this gave him a sense of control. He recognized that this helped him keep people from getting too close. We spoke about how being "in control" may have been important for him as a child, but now this pattern backfired when he wanted to be closer to his wife.

Marcus shared that there was a part of him that wanted to let go of this tension and a part of him that was afraid of what might happen. We explored these two parts somatically. We began by amplifying the part that was "holding on" as he made fists while tensing his arms, chest, jaw, and face. Then he focused on the part that wanted to "let go" by releasing the tension in his hands, arms, chest, jaw, and face. When letting go of tension, Marcus initially felt uncomfortable. He described that he suddenly felt agitated and had an urge to walk out of the session. In response, I noticed tension build in my own body and a feeling of fear arose within me. I took a deep breath and focused on grounding through my feet and legs. Then I invited him to check in with his body, and he described feeling an "irritable and tight" feeling in his chest, similar to how he felt when he became angry. I reminded him that he was in charge of the pace of our work, and we discussed the window of tolerance as a tool for helping us recognize when we were moving too quickly. Together, we acknowledged that his tension had protected him for many years. I suggested that he could tell me when he was interested in turning his attention toward the part of him that wanted to "let go," but I also suggested that he could return to the "holding on" part as often as needed.

Over the next several sessions, Marcus and I worked with these two competing needs. This process helped him acknowledge how his physical armoring helped him navigate the world as a Black man. He recognized the anger he felt toward his father and began to acknowledge his own hurt and fear that was hiding underneath his defenses. Most importantly, he shared that he was less angry at home and more willing to open up to his wife.

As evident in both Sharon's and Marcus's stories, building body awareness can be uncomfortable at first. Clients may have difficulty staying present with their sensations. They may feel restless, anxious, and irritable, or they might feel lethargic, tired, and heavy. In some cases, clients may report feeling numb or disconnected from their sensations. In order to help clients reclaim their body at a safe pace, you can use the healing practices in this chapter to assist them in increasing somatic awareness, building greater tolerance for sensations, and developing a capacity to safely work through traumatic material.

Of note, while it is helpful to invite clients to explore their somatic experience with curiosity and an open mind, it is equally important that we, as therapists, approach this process with our own openness to the unknown (Gendlin, 1982; Kurtz, 1990). In this way, we apply somatic psychology in a client-centered manner. **When offering any intervention, we must let go of our expectations about the outcome.** In doing so, we communicate to our clients that we trust their innate wisdom and their instinctual response as it arises from the psyche and soma (body). When inviting a client to explore any movement intervention, it is wise to offer this as a possibility rather than a prescription. In other words, once you invite a client to experiment with a movement or postural change, you must sit back and await their response. If you rush or anticipate certain results, you are likely to inhibit their authentic presence.

Nonverbal Communications in Psychotherapy

Nonverbal communications account for about 60 to 70 percent of all communications. Therefore, paying attention to your own and your clients' use of space, facial expressions, eye contact, gestures, posture, tone of voice, and timing of speech helps increase a sense of connection during therapy. Observing these nonverbal communications helps us better attune to our clients' emotions. Increasing awareness of our own nonverbal communications also asks us to recognize that our embodiment is a reflection of our own histories, including our childhood development and the totality of our social and cultural experiences. **When we build awareness of our own somatic experiences, we have an opportunity to enhance congruence between our words and body language—a trait that increases our trustworthiness.**

Attending to nonverbal communications in therapy is especially important when working with preverbal traumatic events that happened during early childhood or when clients are unable to recall explicit memories for later traumatic events. In these cases, we are only able to work with a client's *felt sense* by asking clients to tap into the emotions and sensations they hold in their body. In some cases, clients have stories that have been told to them about birth trauma, or they may be aware that they experienced a surgery, separation from parents, or a death in the family, even if they have no direct memory for these events. Some clients know that they were adopted from situations where they experienced early neglect. To address these preverbal memories, we can invite clients to cultivate awareness of the body sensations that arise as they reflect on these stories about their past or look at photographs from their childhood. Some clients may never identify an event related to stuck sensations in the body. Nonetheless, working with sensations and emotions can still result in a feeling of resolution in the body.

This is also the case when working with *intergenerational* or *legacy trauma*, in which unresolved trauma of one generation becomes a legacy that is passed down to the next generation. For example, Black people may carry the legacy trauma of their ancestors' experience of slavery and systemic racism. Jewish individuals may carry the trauma of the Holocaust and anti-Semitism. Keep in mind that all genocide traumas, including those that devastated the Native Americans in the United States, Aborigines in Australia, Tutsi in Rwanda, and Darfuris in Sudan, have been found to impact the mental health of family members for at least three generations (Yehuda, 2002). These transgenerational traumatic events are experienced as a generalized anxiety, a predisposition to PTSD after trauma exposure, and patterns of tension, pain, or illness in the body (Wolynn, 2016).

Importantly, embodiment is not a static or unchanging experience. We are in constant flux depending upon our interactions with our environment. We feel differently in our body in response to how well we slept or what we ate. We also feel differently in response to different locations. For example, imagine how you feel when at the beach in contrast to how you feel when in an office building. This concept of *intercorporeality* recognizes that our embodiment is an ever-changing relationship between ourselves and our environment (Merleau-Ponty, 1962; Tanaka, 2015). Moreover, intercorporeality challenges the idea that we are a discrete, interior consciousness. As applied to psychotherapy, we recognize that our embodiment is constantly adapting and changing in response to our clients. For example, you may notice that there are certain clients with whom you feel unexplainably tired even though you had a good night's sleep. Or you may have other clients who evoke a feeling of restlessness within you. As discussed in chapter 4, it is not uncommon for our body sensations to parallel our clients' embodied experiences, a concept referred to as *somatic resonance* (Keleman, 1987).

Furthermore, our clients' embodiment is also a reflection of their experience in relationship to us. Recall that all of our culturally and socially informed experiences are held in our bodies (Bennett & Castiglioni, 2004; Kimmel, 2013; Nickerson, 2017). **Our clients' posture, use of eye contact, use of gestures, and use of space cannot be extracted from the power and privilege dynamics that exist in their external lives and within the therapy room.** We must keep in mind that their inability to speak freely or take up space may be a reflection of their lack of safety inside of the therapy room. It is wise to keep these dynamics in mind as you progress into the next healing practice, which invites you to mindfully study embodied relational experiences that emerge during therapy as related to subtle changes in posture, breathing, use of eye contact, movements, use of space, and tone of voice.

Observe Nonverbal Communications in Therapy

The following practice guides you to become aware of your own somatic experiences during sessions while also guiding you to observe the nonverbal communications of your clients. Explore how it feels to increase somatic awareness during sessions. As with all mindful body awareness practices, explore these questions with curiosity and without judgment. You may notice markedly different body language in yourself in relationship to different clients.

- Notice your posture and whether you are leaning forward or backward in your seat. How comfortable do you feel in your body? Do you feel supported by your spine? Is your core engaged? Do you notice that you feel collapsed or unsupported? Conversely, do you feel constricted or tight?

- Observe the posture of your client. Are they learning forward or backward in their seat? Do they appear slumped or collapsed? Does their posture appear rigid? Or does their posture appear relaxed and natural? Do you notice changes in their posture that suggest a change in emotion or physiological arousal?

- Notice how much space you are taking up in the room. Do you notice a need to make yourself smaller? Do you feel unusually unrestricted in your use of gestures or body language?

- Observe your client's use of space. Do they seem to take up only a small area of the room? Do they take up a lot of space? What do you notice in their expressiveness through their arms or hands as they speak? Do you notice any changes in their use of space that suggest a change in emotion or physiological arousal?

- Notice how much you are moving during the session. Do you notice any urges to fidget? Do you find yourself crossing and uncrossing your legs? Do you reach for your water or tea more frequently than usual? Are you moving less than usual?

- Observe your client's use of movement. Do they move around the space or sit still? Do they fidget with their hands, or are they restless in their legs and feet? Do they appear lethargic or sluggish? Do you notice changes in your client's movements that suggest a change in emotion or physiological arousal?

- Notice the quality of your tone of voice and whether you feel any restriction in your throat as you speak. Notice if you feel an urge to speak quickly. Is your voice louder or softer than usual?

- Observe your client's use of speech. Do you notice any restriction or unusual intensity in their voice? Are they speaking noticeably fast or slow? Does their voice have normal prosody in which their tone rises and falls as they speak, or is their voice relatively flat? Do you notice changes in their tone of voice that suggest a change in emotion or physiological arousal?

- Notice any changes in how you are breathing. Is your breath noticeably shallow or restricted? Or are you breathing freely and easily?

- Observe your client's breathing patterns. Are there any changes in the depth or timing of their breaths that suggest a change in emotion or physiological arousal?

- Notice your use of eye contact. Do you feel an urge to look away from the client? Do you feel that it's necessary to always look directly at your client?

- Observe your client's use of eye contact. Do they avoid making any eye contact? Do their eyes appear fixated on you or on another object in the room? Do you notice changes in eye contact that suggest a change in emotion or physiological arousal?

Enhance Proximity Awareness

One way that somatic therapists attend to safety within the therapeutic relationship is through interventions that attend to the proximity between the therapist and client. *Proximity* refers to our use of space and asks us to consciously reflect on how close or far away we are seated from our clients. In addition, proximity awareness invites us to pay attention to whether we are directly facing our clients or sitting at an angle. Changes in proximity can significantly impact our clients' sense of safety or threat within therapy. Exploring varying seating options with your client empowers them to decide how much space they need to feel safe (Schwartz & Maiberger, 2018). This process is especially important because social and cultural dynamics can impact our use of space. **If a client has had a history of feeling disempowered, marginalized, or disenfranchised, we can empower them by giving them choice about our seating arrangements.**

In addition, there is a common expectation that therapy must be done sitting down. However, within somatic psychology, working with proximity also invites clients to know that they can engage in therapy while standing. The next healing practice guides you to explore proximity awareness with your client. It is noteworthy to mention that it is helpful when both the therapist's and client's chairs are able to move closer or farther away from each other. In addition, you can experiment with letting the client know that any seat in the room is available, including your chair. This practice can reduce power differentials and create a more collaborative dynamic.

Explore Proximity Awareness

- You are welcome to choose any seat in the room that feels comfortable for you. I can adjust where I sit depending upon what you choose.

- Take a moment to check in with the seating arrangement that you have chosen. Does this feel comfortable for you, or is there anything that you would like to change? You are welcome to move your chair closer or farther away, or you can ask me to do the same. Or you might prefer if we were sitting at an angle or side by side.

- How does each position feel in your body? How does your body give you feedback about the position that feels most supportive for you?

- Check in with your body and notice how you feel sitting down right now. If you would like, we can stand up together and explore how that feels for you. Once again, let's explore how it feels to stand face to face, at an angle, or side by side. How does each position feel in your body? How does your body give you feedback about the position that feels most supportive for you?

Build Somatic Resources

In alignment with a phase-based approach to care, somatic psychology offers tools that can increase clients' felt sense of safety. **Somatic psychology proposes that our movement patterns influence our sense of who we are in the world.** When we feel safe, we can relax, move freely to explore our world, reach out for what we want, and push away what we do not want. However, when we do not feel safe, we are not able to access a sense of safety or healthy mobility through the body. This can disrupt our ability to sleep deeply, protect ourselves, feel or express our emotions, and communicate our needs to others. Within somatic psychology, we can reclaim a nourishing relationship to ourselves and others through what is known as the satisfaction cycle (Aposhyan, 2007), which involves five phases: yielding, pushing, reaching, grasping, and pulling actions.

Yielding involves surrendering our weight into gravity. Here, you can imagine the way a child who feels safe and secure can rest in the arms of a loving parent. Yielding is also characterized by a relaxed alertness that allows you to fully and consciously receive support. When clients have experienced childhood abuse and are stuck in a fight pattern, they might carry excessive tension in their muscles, making it hard to relax. Or if they are stuck in a flight pattern, they might be jumpy, agitated, or disconnected from their sensations and emotions. In contrast, if they felt helpless as a child, they might get stuck in a state of collapse. Yielding involves reclaiming a relaxed engagement of the muscles, which can help individuals sense their body in relationship to gravity. You can amplify this feeling by keeping a weighted blanket in your office and inviting clients to place it on their lap. When exploring yielding, it is common for emotions to arise given that this process invites clients to let go of protective somatic patterns that they once needed to help them feel safe.

Once we can successfully yield into gravity, then we can *push* into our connection with the earth, which allows us to feel where we begin and end in space ourselves. Mindfully pushing through the arms and legs helps us support ourselves and assert our independence, which is especially salient for individuals with a history of trauma who often have difficulties with boundaries. In particular, they might have a hard time asserting boundaries, or they might maintain rigid boundaries that keep everyone at a distance. **Developing a healthy relationship with pushing can help clients discover flexible boundaries in which they can engage them as needed for self-protection and soften them as needed for greater intimacy with others.** We can experiment with pushing by pressing into the legs and feet. For example, doing a wall-sit can help clients build tolerance for strong emotions or body sensations. This process helps clients who are prone to dissociation feel grounded and oriented to the here and now. We can also experiment with pushing and releasing through the arms to help clients practice self-assertion or soften their defenses.

A well-developed capacity to yield and push can allow us to *reach* out to others without losing the self. Here, you can imagine how a child who feels loved and supported might reach out toward caring parents. **Reaching allows us to express curiosity for the world around us, move toward what we want, care for others, or ask for what we need from them.** However, when a child has been repeatedly rejected when reaching out to caregivers, they might carry a sense of shame or helplessness into adulthood that can be seen in an unwillingness to reach outward. This can lead to lethargy or low motivation. Importantly, we need to remain connected to our center so our reach doesn't leave us feeling overextended beyond our boundaries or disconnected from the self.

Grasping and *pulling* are two movement patterns that work together to close the gap between the self and the world. When we grasp and pull, we are able to bring what we desire from the world in toward the self. Once again, these actions need to be stabilized through the previous stages of the satisfaction cycle; otherwise, our grasping can become frantic, frustrating, and exhausting. For example, it is quite common to grasp for more than we can successfully digest. It's like arriving at a buffet and stuffing ourselves with too much food. We lose our ability to fully receive, appreciate what we have, or feel nourished by the experience. The antidote to this lack of satisfaction involves consciously returning to the practice of yielding, which allows us to slow down and receive what we have taken in.

The next healing practices provide somatic resources to help clients safely connect to the body. These interventions invite an experiential exploration of each action within the satisfaction cycle. I suggest exploring only one of these movement interventions during a single session. Ideally, integration of any movement pattern in session is relevant to the experience of the client. While each movement is developed to assist the client in discovering a new embodied resource, it is also important to approach these interventions with an openness to the unknown that allows the client's authentic experience to guide the session. For example, if you invite the client to relax into support, they might share an awareness that they feel frightened or unable to relax. If that is the case, you have a choice to explore their fear and to examine their patterns of muscle tension, depending upon the client's window of tolerance for discomfort. Or you might reorient them using cues that they are safe in the therapy room to help them reclaim choice and containment (as discussed in chapter 2).

Build Somatic Resources by Connecting to Support

- Would you be willing to experiment with some movements that focus on relaxing into support? As you explore this process, simply notice what arises for you. There is no right or wrong response. While sitting down, explore resting into your connection with the chair (or couch). Explore how it feels to sense the chair supporting you from below. Can you allow yourself to feel the support of the back of the chair? Notice if you have any unnecessary tension that prevents you from resting into this support. Or notice if you feel an urge to collapse.

- Do you notice any emotions that arise as part of this process? If so, would you like to explore this... [*e.g., tension pattern, feeling of collapse, feeling of fear*]?

Build Somatic Resources through Grounding

- Would you be willing to experiment with some movement that focus on grounding? As you explore this process, simply notice what arises for you. There is no right or wrong response. Let's stand up together and find a space to squat against the wall. Find the depth that is right for you, and place your back against the wall. Take several breaths, pressing your feet firmly to the floor, and allow the muscles in your legs to engage. Notice how you need to breathe in response to this shape. Take several breaths here, and rise up when you feel ready. [*For some clients, it is valuable to stay in this shape for about a minute.*] When you rise up, notice the sensations in your legs. Take a few moments to bend and straighten your legs.

- What are you aware of now? Perhaps you feel a little shaky or a greater sense of aliveness. Make space for any feelings that arise.

Healing Practice

Build Somatic Resources with Boundary Awareness

- Would you be willing to experiment with some movements that focus on connecting you to your boundaries? As you explore this process, simply notice what arises for you. There is no right or wrong response. Let's stand up together and press your hands against the wall. You can experiment with straightening through your arms and finding a bend through your elbows. Explore the placement of your feet. You can also bend through your knees and press into your feet while pressing against the wall.

- Imagine that you are setting a boundary, pushing away anything you do not want. Explore how it feels to say "no" or "go away!" As you soften your arms, imagine that you are making space to let down your guard. Slowly release this pushing action, and notice the sensations throughout your body. Make space for any feelings that arise.

Build Somatic Resources through Reaching and Receiving

- Would you be willing to experiment with some movements focused on reaching out into the world? Choose an object in this room that you would like to experiment reaching for. [*This might be a teacup or a pillow.*] Now begin to stretch out your arms in front of you. As you explore this process, simply notice what arises for you. There is no right or wrong response. Allow yourself to notice how it feels to reach for something that you want. Notice if any emotions arise for you or if you feel an urge to collapse.

- If so, would you like to explore this… [*e.g., sadness, fear of rejection, feeling of collapse*]? If you would like, allow yourself to take hold of this object and to bring it in toward you. Once you have brought the object close, pause and notice what it feels like to fully receive this object. Once again, take your time to notice any emotions that arise for you.

Enhance Postural Awareness

Within somatic psychology, we attend to the ways the body carries the burdens of our historical experiences. This is especially evident in our posture, which is often connected to our emotions and memories. For example, individuals whose gaze is downcast, shoulders are rolled forward, and core is collapsed might be more likely to feel depressed or helpless. They might be more likely to recall previous times that they felt this way. In contrast, individuals whose arms are crossed in front of their chest while maintaining an unyielding stance are more likely to be cut off from their feelings.

You can think of posture as a form of implicit memory. For example, the muscular engagement involved in bracing against a threat is directly connected to the sensory information encoded at the time of a traumatic event. One way to explore this body-mind connection is through slow, mindful changes in our posture while studying related changes in our thoughts or emotions. This is the purpose of the next healing practice, which invites clients to experiment with postural changes. Importantly, this practice is not about simply replacing an old posture with a new one. Rather, we invite the client to explore different postures by repeating and exaggerating this shape in their body. This can allow them to notice how they feel so they can choose how they want to carry themselves through the world.

Enhance Postural Awareness

- Would you be willing to explore a brief experiment around posture? As with all mindfulness practices, I invite you to allow yourself to be curious about your experience and to observe your experience without judgment.

- Take a moment and notice how you are sitting in the chair. Now I would like to invite you to let yourself curl forward. Allow your shoulders to roll forward and bring your gaze downward. Rather than fight against this shape, allow yourself to exaggerate it. You might even just let yourself experience a feeling of collapsing forward until you are slumped over your legs. Feel free to move in and out of this shape. Take your time and notice how you feel. What emotions or thoughts are you aware of now? Is there anything familiar about this shape?

- Now bring your spine back up and straighten through your torso and spine. Once again, exaggerate this shape like you are a soldier preparing for war. Roll your shoulders back, stiffen through your arms, and notice how it feels to brace in your belly and chest. Feel free to move in and out of this shape. Once again, notice any emotions or thoughts. Is there anything familiar about this shape?

- Now allow yourself to find an open but supportive posture. Allow your gaze to softly lift. See if you can feel supported by your spine and core, but notice how it feels to simultaneously open your heart. Once again, notice any emotions or thoughts. Is there anything familiar about this shape?

- Perhaps you feel an impulse to move toward collapse or to tighten across your belly and chest. Continue this exploration until an upright but open stance does not require so much effort.

Reclaim Healing Movement

Paying attention to sensations not only increases awareness of tension patterns but also helps clients discover new movements that allow them to resolve the wounds of their past. Sometimes clients will spontaneously explore reparative movements on their own. For example, clients might bring their hands to their chest or engage in a gesture of reaching out for connection. In these moments, we can invite clients to slow down and repeat these movements. When we move slowly, we are more likely to feel ourselves fully. We repeat these movements to help clients integrate the new movement pattern, but we want to ensure that they are not simply in autopilot, disconnected from their bodies.

Ultimately, the goal is to help clients resolve any movement sequences that they did not get to complete in the past, which can lead to a felt sense of resolution of traumatic experiences. For example, a client might visualize pushing an abuser away while simultaneously engaging a pushing action through the arms. Or, if a client's trauma involved being trapped and unable to escape a dangerous situation, we can help them reclaim a stepping movement while imagining running away. This can help them to find a new sense of healthy mobilization into the body.

Alternatively, if a client was unable to use their voice in the past, we can invite them to explore finding words or to make a sound that releases any blocked or stuck feeling in the throat. If a client expresses feeling shy about making a sound, you can suggest creating a sound together, as this can reduce self-consciousness on the part of the client. For example, Peter Levine suggests making a long, slow "voo" sound on an extended exhale (Levine, 2010). This particular sound engages the vagus nerve and PNS, which can allow clients to come out of an overstimulated SNS state or a shutdown dorsal vagal state.

The next healing practices guide the client to reflect on the relationship between their sensations and their trauma history. It then guides them to explore movements that help resolve any stuck or unfinished movement sequences. You can use these interventions to invite somatic awareness of areas of tension, numbness, or pain as you and your client discuss traumatic events from their history. Not all statements will be relevant to all situations, so adapt these as appropriate to your client.

Repattern the Body through Mindful Movement

- Would you be willing to take a moment to explore and notice your sensations? Are you aware of any areas of tension?

- Sometimes it can be helpful to increase the tension in an area of your body that is already tight. If the feeling is in your face, maybe you scrunch your face up tightly, or perhaps you see what happens if you open your mouth wide and stick out your tongue. If the feeling is in your arms, see what happens if you squeeze your hands into fists and tighten your arms to your chest. If the feeling is in your legs, explore how it feels to tighten the muscles of your legs or bring them close to your chest. Are there any other movements that you would like to explore that help increase the sensations in this part of your body? Make space for any emotions that arise.

- I am aware that you were not able to leave or run away during the traumatic event. Would you be interested in exploring how it feels now to imagine leaving the situation? Begin to mindfully move your legs as if you are walking in place. Feel the movement in your legs now. Know that you are no longer stuck in that situation from your past. What arises for you now?

- Animals in the wild often shake after having a threatening experience. See what happens if you shake your arms. Let's stand up together and shake through your legs and hips. Take a few more breaths as you shake and then return to stillness. See what you notice now.

- Sometimes it can be helpful to find a sound or words that match a feeling in your body. If this feeling in your body had words, what would it say? If there are no words, is there a sound? If you prefer, you can simply imagine making the sound. Or, if you would like, we can explore making a sound together. I suggest creating a long, slow "voo" sound on your exhalation. You can imagine creating a sound of a foghorn. As you do so, notice how this sound creates a vibration in your belly, chest, and throat. This sound can help you come out of a fight, flight, or freeze response. After creating your sound, notice any changes in sensation or emotion.

Repattern the Body by Attending to Areas of Numbness

- Would you be willing to take a moment to explore this area of your body where you feel disconnected or numb? When there is an area of numbness or disconnection, it can be helpful to place your hands over this area and gently bring your attention to this part of your body.

- I suggest that you begin by rubbing your hands together for a few breaths until you feel some warmth in your palms. Now place your palms over the part of your body that is difficult to feel. Send your breath and awareness into this area of your body.

- There is no need to force a change to happen. Simply bring your awareness here with an intention to connect. See if you can notice any subtle changes in sensation or emotion that arise as a result of your intention to connect.

- You might notice thoughts or feelings arise in this process. For example, you might be afraid that you will not be able to feel anything at all or that you will remain numb. Or you might fear that if you open up to your feelings, all of your pain will come to the surface at once. While numbness may have once helped protect you from painful emotions, it can also lead you to feel cut-off and disconnected.

- You can pace yourself as you reclaim your ability to feel. To do so, I invite you to take a few breaths while focusing on the part of your body that feels numb and to then take a break. When you feel ready, return your attention to the area of your body that feels disconnected.

- It can also be helpful to bring your attention to an area of your body that is easier to feel. Scan your body and notice if there is any area where you feel connected. Ideally, see if there is a place in your body that feels positive. Maybe you feel connected to your heart. Perhaps you can find an area of your body that you like. Bring your hands over the part of your body to which you feel connected, and take several breaths focusing your awareness here. Now return your awareness to the part of your body that feels numb. Once again, notice if anything has changed.

Repattern the Body by Pendulating Awareness to Pain

- Would you be willing to take a moment to explore and notice your sensations? Are you aware of any areas of pain? Sometimes pain can be connected to painful memories from the past. This may be the case if your pain tends to come and go or if your pain worsens during times of emotional stress.

- When working with a feeling of pain in your body, it can be helpful to alternate your awareness between the difficult sensation and an area of your body that feels either positive or neutral.

- Take some time to identify an area of your body that is not painful. Ideally, you can find an area that feels positive or neutral. Once you identify this area, see if you can notice if this area has a texture or temperature. If you choose, you can bring your hands over this area of your body. Now focus your attention on this area for several breaths.

- When you are ready, redirect your attention to the part of your body that is feeling pain. Once again, take several breaths as you observe the area of pain. You might notice if this area has a texture or a temperature too. Again, you might choose to bring your hands over this area of your body. Once again, take several breaths as you focus your attention on this area of pain.

- Now take several more rounds of breaths, bringing your attention back and forth between these two places. Take four or five breaths into each area of your body. You can imagine that your awareness is like a pendulum swinging from your sensation of pain to your neutral or positive sensation.

- When you feel ready, pause and notice if there are any changes in the area of your body that felt painful.

8

Reprocessing the Past with Cognitive Behavioral and EMDR Therapies

Throughout history, storytelling has been used as a healing practice. When given a safe space where we know we will be unconditionally accepted, it can be profoundly empowering to share the events of our lives. As we tell and retell our narrative, we are able to work through difficult parts of our past and express emotions that we weren't able to feel at the time of the event. Taking this time to work through a disturbing memory reduces the power that traumatic events have over our lives. We recognize that these events are over and, as a result, have less power over us.

Cognitive behavioral therapies (CBT) have been among the most researched of the therapeutic approaches applied for the treatment of PTSD and complex trauma. Some of the more commonly recognized applications of CBT for trauma include prolonged exposure (Foa, Hembree, & Rothbaum, 2007), cognitive processing therapy (Resick, Monson, & Chard, 2016), and narrative exposure therapy (Schauer, Neuner, & Elbert, 2011). These therapies work by helping clients modify unhelpful thoughts related to trauma and, in some cases, process traumatic memories so that they no longer induce a fear response.

Another treatment method commonly used to address trauma is EMDR therapy, which is a comprehensive approach that combines elements of cognitive behavioral, psychodynamic, and somatic therapies. EMDR helps clients process the images, thoughts, feelings, and body sensations related to traumatic events by adding dual-awareness stimulation (Shapiro, 2018). As previously discussed, dual awareness asks clients to remain aware of the positive aspects of their present-moment experience or bring to mind memories of positive events while simultaneously recalling memories of historical traumatic events. Within EMDR, dual awareness is amplified using short, slow sets of bilateral stimulation, including eye movements, hand-held tactile pulsers, self-tapping, or sounds.

Rather than emphasizing a single CBT method for memory reprocessing, this chapter offers a common factors approach that is based on our understanding of neural networks and the formation of traumatic memories. As discussed in chapter 2, a neural network is a group of interconnected neurons in the brain that fire together, and traumatic memories are thought to be maintained by impaired neural networks that are isolated from memories of positive events (Bergmann, 2012). One common factor underlying CBT and EMDR therapies is that they reactivate the neural networks associated with traumatic memories, which gives clients an opportunity to reprocess disturbing memories as they focus on cognitive reappraisal during exposure. The goal is to help clients desensitize or reduce the amount of emotional or somatic distress they experience when reflecting on the event.

Treatment approaches that focus on the reprocessing of memories ask clients to talk about or write about traumatic events, which gives clients a chance to review associated images, sensory details, thoughts, and feelings. In some cases, clients may only imagine the event if they do not want to describe the details out loud. Importantly, reprocessing traumatic events involves introducing new information that challenges negative beliefs and inaccurate conclusions that the client formed as a result of traumatic experiences. For many individuals, the act of reprocessing a memory through exposure and desensitization can feel empowering as they realize that the past no longer has power over them.

In some cases, prolonged exposure and desensitization interventions can lead clients with C-PTSD to feel flooded or destabilized. Therefore, it is often necessary to focus on extending phase one of treatment so clients can develop the positive resources necessary to cultivate a felt sense of safety and stabilization. Once clients are ready for phase two of trauma treatment, we may still need to slow down the pace of memory reprocessing with modified approaches to exposure and desensitization. The healing practices within this chapter help clients develop positive resources, engage in cognitive reappraisal, and safely reprocess traumatic memories to find emotional resolution.

The Neural Networks of Trauma

As discussed in chapter 2, all of our memories are encoded in neural networks that contain the sensory experiences that were present at the time of the event, including associated sights, sounds, smells, tastes, emotions, and bodily sensations. These neural networks extend across various areas of the brain that are associated with each sensory aspect of our experience. The process of *memory retrieval* can be thought of as the reconstitution of a neural network in which we pull together these separate pieces of information. In other words, we reactivate neurons throughout the brain, allowing us to "recollect" our experience.

In normal, everyday memories, there are gaps in the representation of our experience. These gaps can be considerably wider with developmental trauma and C-PTSD. In some cases, individuals may only recall the memory in fragments or as vague somatic sensations. In these cases, clients fill in the gaps with inferences and knowledge based upon other historical experiences or educated guesses about what most likely occurred. The way we remember an event is also influenced by our current emotional state, our external surroundings, and the people with whom we are interacting. Given the malleability and constructive nature of memory, therapists must be mindful not to influence the construction of false memories by suggesting or inferring events that we or the client do not know to be true.

Each time we retrieve a memory, we reactivate a neural network, and once a neural network has developed, there is a greater probability that we will activate that same neural network in the future. For example, a smell or sound might evoke disturbing reexperiencing symptoms in someone with C-PTSD, causing them to have a flashback and reactivating the neural network associated with distressing emotions, such as fear or rage. When this occurs, the distress associated with the traumatic memory is reinforced, which strengthens the neural network. Therefore, without sufficient support, clients with C-PTSD may have a difficult time experiencing themselves as cognitively constructive or emotionally adaptive. They may have difficulty integrating new, positive information into the current fear-based state (Shapiro, 2018).

A predictive processing model of memory suggests that the primary function of memories is to help us predict or anticipate the next experience, with these predictions being essential for our survival (Chamberlin, 2019). However, when we are confronted with new information that contradicts our expectations, there is a mismatch between our predictions and current information. For individuals with C-PTSD, fostering the development of positive beliefs, emotions, and somatic experiences can facilitate a paradoxical state that contrasts the expectations of their fear-based memories. Our goal is to evoke this state of cognitive dissonance because it requires clients to update their expectations about the future. In other words, cognitive dissonance activates neuroplasticity, allowing clients to create changes in their neural networks (Tryon, 2014). As therapists, we can take advantage of these key transformational moments by encouraging clients to tolerate the "unknown" as an opportunity for change.

When we invite clients to purposefully reflect on a traumatic memory within a safe and supportive environment, we also have an opportunity to introduce new information that reduces the feeling of threat associated with traumatic memories. That is, we capitalize on the reconstructive nature of neural networks by adding in corrective information that facilitates an experience of resolution. As described, memory is a malleable and constructive in that it is influenced by both internal and external factors. When we invite clients to mindfully reflect on traumatic memories, we can imagine that they are opening up a document on a computer, which allows them to modify or revise the information prior to saving the updated version (Ecker et al., 2012).

Build Positive Resources

Individuals with complex trauma may have greater difficulty with exposure and memory-focused treatment. If we move too quickly, they might feel unsafe or re-traumatized, which can lead them to prematurely leave treatment or lose faith in the benefits of therapy. In alignment with a phase-based approach to care, the integrative treatment model in this book emphasizes clients' stability and safety prior to reprocessing traumatic memories, which is why phase one is often the longest and most important phase of C-PTSD treatment. Prior to beginning the reprocessing of traumatic memories, we want to ensure that clients are ready for the demands of revisiting difficult thoughts, emotions, or sensations. This is especially true for clients who are at risk of self-harming behaviors or substance use.

The purpose of *resource development* is to strengthen clients' access to positive states, increase emotion regulation, and help them feel in control about when or how they think about traumatic events. In fact, much of the CBT and EMDR therapy literature supports the integration of coping skills and positive resources into the treatment of C-PTSD (Jackson, Nissenson, & Cloitre, 2009; Shapiro, 2018). Clients build positive resources when they feel safe, connect to their therapist, ground themselves in mindful body awareness, orient to their adult self, imagine nurturing or protective allies, and focus on constructive, affirming beliefs about themselves in the world.

For example, you can invite clients to imagine a time when they felt safe and to notice the related images, thoughts, emotions, and body sensations. If a client cannot recall a time when they felt safe, they can visualize an imagined time or place. You can also help them enhance this positive imagery through guided relaxation and diaphragmatic breathing exercises. As clients experience this positive state, they are creating a new neural network or enhancing an existing one by associating it with this positive state.

Clients with C-PTSD may initially struggle to develop positive resources because the experience of safety and connection can feel threatening. To them, these nourishing experiences can bring up vulnerable emotions of sadness or elicit memories of times when they were rejected or alone. Clients with complex trauma often rely heavily upon defensive coping mechanisms that prevent them from letting in the nourishment of other people or the world. For some, it feels too risky to let in the "good" because it requires that they let down their guard, and they do not believe that they can handle any more pain. In these instances, we need to progress slowly and help clients build tolerance for positive emotions and somatic sensations. Ultimately, we can help them sustain their attention on positive emotions for longer periods of time as they build tolerance for these nourishing feelings.

To help clients achieve safety and stabilization, you can return to the healing practices from the previous chapters that built resources through relational, mindfulness, parts work, and somatic therapies. In addition, you can use the next two healing practices to help clients feel connected to a positive state. The first healing practice invites clients to visualize a real or imagined place where they feel safe, relaxed, peaceful, and calm. In this healing practice, you can introduce clients to a self-tapping practice called the butterfly hug, which draws on EMDR's use of bilateral stimulation to calm the nervous system. If the client's feeling state shifts in a negative direction while engaging in self-tapping, ask them to stop and explore whether any intrusive thoughts or imagery interfered with the peaceful place visualization.

The second healing practice is a tree of life drawing that explores the use of a tree to map out the challenging and positive experiences in a client's life. The purpose of this exercise, which is inspired by narrative exposure therapy, is to help clients contain their distress in a "compost heap" while reorienting their attention to their sources of strength, self-care activities, values, and goals.

Visualize Your Peaceful Place

- I would like to suggest that you take some time to visualize a calm or peaceful place to give your mind and body a chance to feel comfortable and relaxed. This practice is important because we often do not release the impact of traumatic events until we feel safe.

- Is it okay with you if we take a few minutes to identify an image of a place that feels peaceful and calm to you? This place can be real or imaginary. Maybe you can think of a place or time when you felt safe or relaxed in your life. Perhaps you would like to choose a place from a movie or book, or you can create a place from your imagination.

- Use your senses to enhance your imagery. What do you see? What do you hear? Are there any smells that you associate with this place?

- This is *your* imagined place, so you can be creative with your process. You are in charge of this place. You can decide if you want to bring another person or an animal into this place. As you think about your place, are there any changes that you would like to make?

- Let me know if any negative thoughts or intrusive images interfere with your ability to feel safe and relaxed while imagining your peaceful place. If so, continue to take your time to make changes to the imagery until you feel relaxed. For example, you can place a fence or wall around your peaceful place to add a layer of protection.

- If you'd like, we can do a self-tapping practice called the butterfly hug, which can feel calming or relaxing. Cross your arms over your chest so your palms are resting on your sternum, with your fingers extending toward opposite shoulders, and interlock your thumbs to create the image of a butterfly. Go ahead and begin alternately tapping your hands for about 15 to 20 seconds, as if they were the wings of a butterfly. I'll let you know when to pause. As long as this feels positive, we can explore another round of self-tapping while you visualize your calm and peaceful place. If at any point you feel uncomfortable, simply stop the self-tapping.

Draw Your Tree of Life

In this exercise, you will draw a tree to map out the challenging and positive experiences in your life. To begin, you will need a blank piece of paper and some colored pencils or pens. Take a few minutes to draw an outline of a tree. Be sure to include roots, a trunk, and branches. To the side of your tree, draw a box that will hold your compost heap. Feel free to approach this exercise as creatively as you would like. Most importantly, this drawing does not need to be perfect. Take your time to fill in your tree using the following guidelines:

- **Compost heap:** The compost heap, which is the box to the side of your tree, breaks down the "yuck" so you can use it for your growth. Within this box, you can write down traumatic events, experiences of abuse, times when you were neglected or rejected, or any challenging relationships. Be sure to give your compost box a lid. Know that you can contain these events in this space until you have the resources to work through them.

- **Roots:** The roots of your tree represent your sources of strength. Within the roots, take some time to write down any positive influences from your life or sources of pride, such as your hometown or country. Or you might include cultural resources, such as meaningful rites of passage, spiritual teachers, or influential mentors. Add in any other positive family legacies, such as stories of ancestors who were courageous or who overcame challenges.

- **Ground:** The ground represents your current sources of nourishment, such as any self-care activities that you do on a regular basis to help you stay healthy. Examples are healthy nutrition, exercise routines, mindfulness practices, or creative endeavors. Write down your sources of nourishment on the ground beneath your tree.

- **Trunk:** The trunk represents anything that keeps you upright and standing tall. Inside of your trunk is a good place to write down your values and skills. Examples of values include open-mindedness, humility, integrity, honesty, bravery, leadership, lifelong learning, fairness, kindness, forgiving others, social responsibility, and caring for others.

- **Branches:** Your branches represent what you are reaching for. On the branches of your tree, write down your hopes, dreams, and wishes. For example, you might want to create more space in your life for spiritual reflection through journaling or meditation. Or you might want more space in your life for creative projects, such as making music, writing poetry, or painting. Perhaps you would like to focus on developing healthy eating habits or implementing a new exercise routine. What activities would help you find greater enjoyment and fulfillment in your life?

- **Leaves:** Your leaves represent that which helps you gather light to yourself. On your leaves, write down who is a supportive presence in your life, such as such as friends, family, or pets.

- **Flowers and seeds:** The flowers and seeds represent your goals. Draw flowers and seeds at the ends of your branches. Here, you can write down anything that you would like to pass on to others or to the next generation. These are your gifts to the world.

Cognitive Reappraisal

Engaging clients in *cognitive reappraisal* invites them to explore the beliefs that they have constructed about themselves or the world and helps them identify when they have adopted thinking errors. **Negative beliefs from trauma are often related to a sense of being defective or damaged, an inaccurate sense of over-responsibility for the traumatic events, an impaired sense of safety, or a pervasive feeling of helplessness.** These "thinking errors" are often due to overgeneralizations, all-or-nothing thinking, catastrophizing, and emotional reasoning.

Once we have identified clients' negative beliefs, we can invite the client to construct new, accurate beliefs. Often this process involves Socratic inquiry, in which we ask the client a question that they have the ability to answer, even if they do not yet realize it. For example, when working with a client who experienced abuse as a child, we might say, "You were just a child. Do you really believe that you could have been responsible for your father's behavior?" This can empower the client to see new possibilities, question their assumptions, develop new beliefs, and form a new outlook for the future (Heiniger et al., 2018). This facilitates cognitive dissonance, creates a new emotional response, and allows clients to form new meanings about the events of their lives (Tryon, 2014).

For example, the client may realize that they were never to blame for their abuse and that they were always deserving of kindness and respect. Often, this evokes a grief process that involves letting go of limiting beliefs or behaviors with which they have overidentified. Ultimately, grieving can lead to a sense of resolution in which there is a natural reduction in emotional disturbance related to the traumatic event (Cutuli, 2014). In other words, desensitization occurs as a natural result of memory reprocessing.

The next section offers two healing practices. The first focuses on helping clients recognize the importance of cultivating a healthy mind through a garden metaphor. The second practice helps clients identify negative beliefs, explore counterevidence to these beliefs using Socratic inquiry, and form new beliefs they would like to adopt.

Garden of the Mind Metaphor

- Trauma recovery is like creating a garden. You begin by tending to the soil—adding in the right amount of nutrients, sun, and water that create an optimal environment for growth. When planting the garden of your mind, remember that you have a choice about what seeds you are planting. You can think of kindness, compassion, and wisdom as flowers that come from a well-tended garden of the mind.

- You must, at times, also pull up the weeds. These are the thoughts that tell you that you are unworthy of love, not enough, or helpless to change your circumstances. In your garden, you can take the weeds and place them into the compost. There, they can be safely held and, in time, transformed into the rich, fertile earth.

- Now that you have created this space, what new seeds would you like to plant in the garden of your mind? What would you like to believe about yourself now? Perhaps you want to grow a new sense of self rooted in the knowledge that you are worthy of love, kindness, and respect. You get to choose what you want to grow and flourish in yourself and in your life.

- It is important to take care of the new growth in your garden. The seeds you planted may still be fresh, green sprouts that require protection and careful tending. Ultimately, with the sunlight of your awareness, you can guide yourself to bloom into your full potential.

Invite Cognitive Reappraisal

- Let's take a look at the following list of common negative beliefs. Are there any you identify with? If so, do you have a sense of where this belief comes from as related to your history?

    o I am not good enough.

    o I am a bad person.

    o I cannot trust myself.

    o I am not lovable.

    o I am worthless.

    o I am weak.

    o I am damaged.

    o I should have done something.

    o I should have known better.

    o I did something wrong.

    o It is my fault.

    o I am not safe.

    o I can't trust anyone.

    o I can't protect myself.

    o I am not in control.

    o I am powerless.

    o I am helpless.

- Pick one negative belief that you identified on the previous list, and examine this belief by asking yourself a few questions. [*Ask one question at a time until the client exhibits a change in their negative belief. Not all questions will be relevant to all client situations.*]

    o Do you know for sure that what you feel or believe is true?

    o What evidence do you have for this negative thought?

    o Can you find any evidence that suggests this belief is not true?

- o Are you holding yourself to an unrealistically high standard?

- o You were just a child. Do you really believe that a child could be blamed for…?

- o Is the belief that you carry about yourself helpful for you?

- o Will this thought allow you to achieve your goals?

- o If a close friend of yours knew that you were having this thought, what would they say to you?

- o If someone you love was having this thought, what would you tell them?

- o Imagine receiving advice from your future self. What would the future you like to tell you? How does this information change your thoughts or beliefs about yourself?

- Now let's take a look at the following list of positive beliefs. What would you like to believe about yourself now?

    - o I am good enough.
    - o I am a good person.
    - o I can trust myself now.
    - o I am lovable.
    - o I am worthy of love.
    - o I am strong.
    - o I am healthy and whole.
    - o I did the best that I could.
    - o I am doing the best that I can now.
    - o I can learn from difficult experiences.
    - o It was never my fault.
    - o It is over and I am safe now.
    - o I can choose whom to trust now.
    - o I can protect myself and take care of myself now.
    - o I have choices now.
    - o I can stand up for myself now.
    - o I am empowered.

Reprocessing the Past

Clients with a history of complex trauma often develop a wide range of avoidance strategies that temporarily reduce anxiety or distress, but this avoidance does not resolve traumatic activation in the long term. It is for this reason that exposure-based interventions ask clients to purposefully reflect on their traumatic memories while temporarily suspending their avoidance strategies. In time, this allows the client to build confidence in their ability to turn toward the fearful event without becoming flooded by distressing sensations and emotions.

However, exposure can be challenging with clients who have C-PTSD because revisiting traumatic memories can be destabilizing. Given that memories are connected to one another through neural networks, this increases the likelihood that clients will experience flooding or dissociative symptoms during exposure. For example, a client with C-PTSD who was sexually abused in childhood for many years may subsequently enter into an abusive marriage. In this case, the client's fear-based expectancies have been powerfully reinforced across time, and recalling a single traumatic event might pull forth a sequela of related disturbing memories. Furthermore, clients often lead stressful lives that reflect the instability they feel as a result of their traumatic histories. In turn, they often come into our office with repeated crises. In these moments, it is necessary to attend to the current stressor or emotionally disturbing experience with a focus on establishing safety and stabilization.

In cases where the client is prone to destabilization, our work can focus on helping them process current stressors through the experience of co-regulation, in which clients are able to develop a feeling of connection and safety with us as the therapist until they experience a resolution of the distress. Clients with C-PTSD can often tolerate talking about recent traumatic events with us, even if they are not yet ready to work through disturbing memories from the past. When they feel validated and understood, this builds a positive resource state that offers a contrast to the ongoing emotional turmoil that has defined much of their life. Therefore, we help clients process the current event until they achieve a feeling of resolution, which can help them recognize that the current reality is distinct from the historical trauma. Through repetition, clients can internalize this positive state of connection and safety as a resource that is increasingly accessible within and outside of sessions (Courtois, Ford, & Cloitre, 2009). Working in this manner helps clients work through attachment trauma and increase emotion-regulation skills (Karatzias et al., 2018).

At the same time, having too much emphasis on safety and stabilization can unnecessarily delay effective treatment (de Jongh et al., 2016). Therapists who spend too much time focusing on this phase of treatment may be unconsciously colluding with clients' avoidance defenses and, as a result, stop providing opportunities for clients to focus their attention on traumatic material from the past. An overemphasis on resource development might also inadvertently send a message to clients that we view them as "fragile" and incapable of handling the work. In contrast, when we view therapy as a collaborative process, we can have open conversations with clients about the value of resource development, the pacing of therapy, and their readiness for trauma reprocessing.

Even when a client is facing current stressors, we can help them turn toward the pain of their traumatic past in a slow, modulated manner. We create safety during reprocessing of traumatic memories when we invite clients to focus on only one event or a small part of the memory while simultaneously asking them to use a containment strategy (Gonzalez & Mosquera, 2012). This allows clients to focus on small, manageable amounts of discomfort while placing other trauma-related memories into their container (see the choice and containment healing practice from chapter 2).

Given that similar traumatic events tend to share the same neural networks and cognitive distortions, working through one significant traumatic event can help resolve other traumatic events as well. For example, the client who was sexually abused over many years can choose to work through one or two specific incidents as representational of the repeated trauma. It is often relieving for clients to learn that it is not necessary to reprocess every traumatic event from their lives. Once they have achieved a sense of resolution with a specific memory, you and the client can review the relevance of the new information or insights as related to other traumatic events. In addition, you can work together to determine traumatic events that were unaffected and need attention through further reprocessing.

We can also help clients slow down the pace of trauma reprocessing through *pendulation*, a process that invites them to alternate between paying attention to the distressing trauma-related memory and paying attention to cues in the present moment that help them feel safe (Knipe, 2015; Schwartz & Maiberger, 2018). You can liken this process to a pendulum swinging back and forth—in this case, between two emotional states. During this process, we carefully invite clients to focus on the traumatic memory while observing for cues of emotional or physiological dysregulation. We also invite clients to tell us when they feel at risk of dissociation. At that point, we invite them to return their attention to a positive resource. In this manner, we mindfully work at the "edges" of the window of tolerance.

Within EMDR therapy, we enhance memory reprocessing through the addition of *bilateral stimulation* while the client reflects on the traumatic event. Bilateral stimulation appears to work through several related mechanisms in that it: (1) enhances dual awareness, which strengthens clients' awareness of the here and now; (2) facilitates an orienting response in which clients draw their attention to the current environment and realize there is no threat present, which decreases arousal; and (3) mimics rapid eye movement (REM) sleep by alternating between the left and right hemispheres in the brain, which facilitates memory consolidation (Pagani et al., 2017). These mechanisms help the client perceive and accommodate new information to achieve a sense of emotional resolution (Shapiro, 2018). In addition, when clients reflect on a traumatic event, they are bringing the images, thoughts, emotions, and sensations into their working memory. Bilateral stimulation helps to challenge or tax working memory, which has been shown to reduce the vividness of the memory (van Veen, Kang, & van Schie, 2019).

If clients report feeling stuck, overwhelmed, or shutdown during reprocessing, we can also reintroduce cognitive reappraisal through Socratic inquiry to provide greater insight into deeply held beliefs that may be blocking their progress. For example, if a client is blaming themselves for an event that happened when they were a child, we can ask whether these thoughts are helpful or what advice they would give to a friend who was having a similar thought. Ideally, this process invites the client to think about the memory in a new way that challenges their rigid thinking pattern or helps them perceive their situation differently. We can also integrate resources from parts work therapy. For example, the client can imagine a loving or protective ally as they reprocess a traumatic event from childhood. This top-down, cognitive approach can be wisely coupled with bottom-up strategies (such as mindful body awareness and somatic repatterning interventions) to facilitate a holistic, mind-body approach to trauma recovery. Using this integrative approach, we can assist our clients to reprocess memories and develop neural networks that integrate positive states in body and mind.

The following case exemplifies the integration of resources into the reprocessing of memories with a woman diagnosed with C-PTSD from childhood trauma. Helen was a 40-year-old, Caucasian woman.

As you will see, her memory reprocessing involved elements of mindful body awareness, parts work therapy, somatic repatterning, and bilateral dual-awareness stimulation with EMDR:

Helen came into therapy after experiencing a car accident. She suffered from chronic migraines and described feeling "cut off" from herself. She stated that she felt inauthentic and like she was constantly in hiding. She spoke about patterns of taking care of everyone else to the point that she would become ill. She had an ACE score of 5, which reflected her history of being neglected and growing up in a household characterized by mental illness, substance abuse, domestic violence, and divorce.

As we explored Helen's history in greater depth, I learned that she had spent much of her childhood on a military base in another country. Her father was an alcoholic who was often neglectful and dismissive of her needs. Her mother appeared to have strong borderline personality traits and tended to intrude on Helen's boundaries, even now in adulthood. Both of her parents had histories of childhood trauma. There were also many disturbing incidents of domestic violence that Helen had witnessed throughout her childhood.

Despite these difficulties, Helen also had several resilience factors. On the military base, she had neighbors and teachers who were supportive and believed in her when she was a child. She also had fond memories of spending time in nature when she was a young girl. Currently, she is married to a supportive husband and has two children. In addition, she worked as a hospice nurse and found a sense of meaning and purpose in her work.

Helen was eager to work through the difficult events of her childhood but struggled with dissociative symptoms that would arise when we spoke about difficult memories. She would become disconnected from her emotions and described feeling "cut off." She also experienced somatic symptoms, such as dizziness or tension in her body. The initial stages of our work focused on strengthening her social engagement system, building dual awareness, practicing mindful body awareness, anchoring her adult self, and developing allies for her young self. Initially, she struggled with feeling compassion for her young self because she blamed this part of herself for not being able to stop the "bad things" that happened in her childhood home. In time, she was able to recognize that she had internalized this self-blame as a result of the messages she had received from both of her parents over the years.

As Helen and I began to look more closely at the beliefs and emotions she carried, she described feelings of shame, guilt, fear, helplessness, and disgust when she imagined herself as a young girl. She also described feeling undeserving and unworthy of love. Many of these feelings had globalized into a set of beliefs that she carried about herself now. When she was at work or taking care of her family, she felt good about herself. But when she was alone or tried to take care of herself, the feelings of guilt and shame would take over. In those moments, she felt blocked from experiencing any positive or nourishing feelings.

Once she had developed sufficient resources and awareness of her habitual thinking patterns, I asked Helen if she felt ready to explore working with a traumatic memory that stood out from her childhood. She agreed to give it a try, knowing that she could change her mind at any point. While there were many violent incidents, one specific incident happened when Helen was 3 years old. She recalled seeing her father attempt to choke her mother and had an image of her mother collapsed on the floor after her father walked out of the house. She then described going into the kitchen, making her mother a bowl of soup, and attempting to feed her mother as she sat on the bathroom floor.

This one story was representative of the many traumatic events that Helen had chronically and repeatedly experienced. When I asked her what belief arose as she thought about this image, she stated that this memory felt connected to a belief that she was bad if she were to take care of herself. I asked her what she would like to believe about herself instead and she said, "I would like to believe that I can take care of myself and that I deserve good things, but that doesn't feel true to me right now." As she reflected on the memory, she described feeling tightness in her stomach accompanied by a feeling of shame.

At this point in our work together, we progressed slowly using a modified approach to memory reprocessing with pendulation and bilateral eye movements. However, because Helen was experiencing dissociative symptoms, there were several periods in which we removed the bilateral stimulation to help slow down the pace of the session and keep her within her window of tolerance. During these parts of the process, I guided her to focus on resources by connecting to her body and developing self-compassion. The following dialogue reflects our work in processing this specific memory from her childhood:

Me: "Take a moment to bring to mind the image of that time when you witnessed your father hurting your mother."

Helen: "I imagine myself as a little girl feeling ashamed. I carried a burden. I never spoke to anyone about what was happening in my house. I held it together for them."

Me: "Yes, that was difficult. Are you comfortable with adding eye movements as you think about that time?"

Helen: "Okay." [Bilateral eye movements for about 20 seconds]

Me: "What are you noticing now?"

Helen: "I feel stuck, like I'm mute."

Me: "Can you feel yourself as an adult now, witnessing yourself as this little girl?"

Helen: "I see her taking care of her mother. I feel disgusted by that little girl."

Me: "What do you need right now that will allow you to be with this part of yourself?"

Helen: "I need to put my hands over my heart. It's painful to see her pain." [She moves hands over chest and cries. Bilateral eye movements for about 20 seconds]

Me: "What are you noticing now?"

Helen: "I imagine my adult self, hugging the little me."

Me:	*"Let's go with that." [Bilateral eye movements for about 20 seconds]*
Helen:	*"Now I feel disconnected."*
Me:	*"It's hard to feel that much pain."*
Helen:	*"I can see myself as a little girl, I'm in shock. I feel disconnected again. I feel dizzy."*
Me:	*"I'm right here with you."*
Helen:	*"I feel a constriction in my throat. I feel like I'm choking."*
Me:	*"Can you take a look around the room and notice that you are safe here and now?" [Helen looks around and takes several long deep breaths.]*
Helen:	*"I feel a little calmer now, but I'm afraid to look at the little girl again."*
Me:	*"That's okay. Remember, you are in charge of the pace here."*
Helen:	*"Now I feel all zipped up. I don't like this feeling either."*
Me:	*"You're scared to connect to the pain but you don't like feeling all zipped up. Is that correct?"*
Helen:	*"Yes, and when I push away my pain, my little girl feels resigned, like I'm giving up on her."*
Me:	*"What would you like to do now?"*
Helen:	*"Part of me wants to take care of her, and part of me is afraid of her."*
Me:	*"Ah, say more."*
Helen:	*"To feel connected to her feels like death."*
Me:	*"How so?"*
Helen:	*"It wasn't safe for me to exist. I feel a pit in my stomach again."*
Me:	*"Would you like to place your hands on your stomach and take a few deep breaths?" [Helen places her hands on her stomach and cries.]*
Helen:	*"I'm sad. If I take care of myself, then I feel like I'm abandoning my mother!"*
Me:	*"You tried so hard to take care of your mother." [Helen nods and cries silently.]*
Helen:	*"And when I took care of her, I didn't exist."*
Me:	*"You felt lost."*
Helen:	*[nods, cries] "My throat is tight."*
Me:	*"Is there a sound or a word?"*
Helen:	*[crying audibly] "Who am I if I am not taking care of my mother?"*
Me:	*"Ah, that's a big question."*

Helen: "I am scared to have a self."

Me: "Now can be different from then." [Helen nods. We add bilateral eye movements for about 20 seconds.]

Helen: "I hoped that by taking care of her, she would finally take care of me." [Cries]

Me: "But that didn't happen, and you feel sad." [Bilateral eye movements for about 20 seconds]

Helen: "It wasn't my job to take care of her. I was just a little girl. She was the adult."

Me: "And, you're not that little girl anymore." [Bilateral eye movements for about 20 seconds]

Helen: "And now I can take care of myself." [Bilateral eye movements for about 20 seconds]

Me: "Yes, right now, you are taking care of yourself."

Helen: [smiling] "Yes." [Bilateral eye movements for about 20 seconds]

Me: "Let yourself have this good feeling."

Helen: "I'm scared that I can't do this consistently. I don't know how to do this on my own."

Me: "When you're not in therapy?"

Helen: "Yeah. I'm scared I'll go to the zipped-up place again."

Me: "You might, and you feel more connected now."

Helen: "Yes. I don't feel cut off now. I feel lighter, like I have let go of something." [Bilateral eye movements for about 20 seconds]

Me: "Can you let yourself have this good feeling right now?"

Helen: [smiling] "Yes. I can have this now." [Bilateral eye movements for about 20 seconds]

Me: "Take some time with this feeling."

This transcript came from one of several sessions when Helen and I spent reprocessing this specific memory, which served as a representational memory of the many years of exposure to chaotic and violent events in her childhood home. While she did return to the "zipped-up place," she learned how to move out of her disconnected defense with greater choice and was able to sustain greater capacity for self-care over time.

Ultimately, the purpose of reprocessing a traumatic memory is to review an event and to reduce the amount of emotional or somatic distress clients experience when reflecting on that experience. The next healing practice is intended to help clients achieve this level of reprocessing and desensitization. You do so by helping clients stay oriented to their present experience of safety while they recall the traumatic event. We begin this healing practice by working with clients to identify a focus for the session. Often, it is beneficial to start by talking about any current distress they are experiencing, as this will allow the focus of the session to be most relevant to their current needs.

As the client describes their current distress, begin to have them mindfully notice any accompanying beliefs, emotions, and body sensations. If they have difficulty talking about traumatic events from their past, their current experience of distress might be the focus of your session. However, if clients are able to tolerate working with historical traumatic events, invite them to reflect on their current distress and relate it to previous times when they recall experiencing similar thoughts and feelings. If the client describes more than one traumatic event from their past, create a list of these related events, but invite them to choose a single event that stands out as the most significant or that was the earliest they can remember feeling that way. If the client appears flooded or overwhelmed by the memory, help them choose one small part of the traumatic memory and have them place the rest of the events in a container.

Once the client has chosen a focus for the session, deepen their experience by inviting them to describe related images, emotions, body sensations, and negative beliefs about the event. Before moving forward with reprocessing, invite the client to imagine how they would like to feel once this disturbance is resolved and to identify a new, positive belief that they would like to hold about themselves. Reflecting on the imagined positive outcome is like seeing the light at the end of a tunnel and knowing there is a benefit to working through the dark and painful material. Then return your client's attention to the disturbing event and restate any associated negative beliefs they have identified. Have them notice their emotions and sensations, and then ask your client to rate their distress related to the disturbing event using a subjective units of distress (SUDS) scale, with 10 being the "worst distress possible" and 0 being "no distress at all."

Next, move forward with reprocessing by asking the client to mindfully observe their thoughts, emotions, and sensations with regard to the event they have chosen as the focus of the session. Alternate between having the client observe their inner experience related to this event for 30 seconds (about 5 to 10 breaths) and then having them reorient their attention to cues in the here and now that indicate they are safe. If this time period is too long for the client, then work together to determine an appropriate amount of time. After deciding on an agreed-upon period of time, invite the client to describe any thoughts, emotions, or body sensations they are noticing. If you are trained in EMDR therapy, you can also enhance reprocessing by adding bilateral stimulation while they reflect on the traumatic event.

Encourage the client to trust their mind and body even if the images, thoughts, or feelings do not feel logical. Remind the client that they are in charge of the pace and that they can stop or pause this process at any point. Observe your client for somatic cues that suggest that they are leaving their window of tolerance. If a client is prone to dissociation or has difficulty speaking when they feel overwhelmed, then you can establish a nonverbal "stop signal" by asking them to lift a hand when they need a break.

In some cases, it can be too distressing to add bilateral stimulation while the client reflects on the traumatic event. In this case, you can experiment with adding bilateral stimulation only when the client focuses on cues that they are safe in the here and now (Knipe, 2015). If persistent negative beliefs lead the client to feel stuck during reprocessing, you can reintroduce the cognitive reappraisal questions offered in the previous healing practice. Though an interactive exchange, you and your client work as a team to facilitate a sense of resolution.

Reprocess a Traumatic Memory

- Let's take some time to identify a focus for our session. Check in with your body and mind, and begin to notice anything that is bothering you or any current distress that you are experiencing.

- Once you have identified a current stressor, begin to notice any beliefs about yourself that arise. What emotions or body sensations are you experiencing?

- Sometimes our current distress is related to memories from the past. Do you recall other times when you have felt this way? If there are many events that come to mind, I will write these down, and we can choose whether you would like to work with the current disturbing event or one of these memories from your past.

- Now that we have chosen a focus for the session, go ahead and return your awareness to your emotions and body sensations. Begin to notice if there are any images that arise in relationship to this event. Are you aware of any related negative beliefs about yourself? [*If needed, you can review the list of common negative beliefs from the previous healing practice.*]

- I'd like you to take a moment to imagine how you will feel once this disturbing event or experience is resolved. What emotions do you imagine you might feel when you achieve some sort of emotional resolution? What new beliefs would you like to have about yourself? [*As needed, you can review the list of common positive beliefs from the previous healing practice.*]

- Now bring your attention back to the event you have chosen as a focus for this session and the belief that… [*restate the negative belief that the client previously identified*]. On a scale of 0 to 10—with 10 being the "worst distress possible" and 0 being "no distress at all"—how much distress are you aware of right now?

- As you reflect on the event you have chosen as your focus for our session, I would like you to observe your emotions and body sensations. Remember, you are in charge of the pace. You can stop or pause this process at any point either by letting me know verbally or by simply lifting your hand.

- If it feels alright to you, I'll suggest that you keep your focus on this event for about 30 more seconds. I'll let you know when the time is over. If this feels too short or too long, let me know.

- Now go ahead and return your sensory awareness to the room. What are you noticing? Describe any thoughts, images, or sensations that are present for you now.

- When you are ready, once again return your attention to the event for about 30 seconds. [*Continue guiding the client into short periods of mindful reflection on the event with intermittent check-ins about their experience.*]

- If you'd like, let's explore adding bilateral movements while you pay attention to the event you have chosen as a focus for the session. [*You can use the previous butterfly tap exercise, or if you are trained in EMDR, you might also introduce bilateral eye movements, tactile pulsers, or alternating sounds in headphones. Continue short sets of focusing on the traumatic event with added bilateral stimulation.*]

If the client reports associations to other events, trust their process, but periodically return their awareness to the original focus as a way to observe any changes in their level of distress. If a client describes intrusive negative thoughts or beliefs during reprocessing, then reintroduce the cognitive reappraisal questions from the previous healing practice. If a client is working with a memory related to a young part of the self, return to parts work practices from chapter 6. If the client reports thoughts or images, but has little connection to their emotions or sensations, work with them to develop greater embodied self-awareness. If the client reports feeling stuck in their somatic sensations, integrate movement interventions from chapter 7 to facilitate a sense of release or resolution through the body. If you observe cues that the client is dissociating during the exercise, or if the client reports any feelings of being flooded or overwhelmed, then ask them to place the disturbing memory into a container. For example:

- I notice that you are leaving your window of tolerance. Let's go ahead and put the disturbing event into your container and bring your full awareness to the room. Look around the room and observe that you are safe right here and now. The event that we are speaking about is over. If you would like, you can engage in bilateral movements while you focus on the here and now, and see if this helps you feel more connected to a sense of safety. Once again, you can use the butterfly tap exercise. When you feel safe and connected to yourself, we can slowly explore returning your attention to the disturbing event.

Continue reprocessing the memory until the client describes feeling a sense of resolution or a SUDS of 0. At this point, ask them to reflect on any positive changes they have noticed during the session. If the client has difficulty noticing any positive change, you might reflect back to them any positive change or insight that you observed during the course of the session.

- I am aware that we are coming to the end of our session time today. As we prepare to complete our work for today, take a few moments to notice any positive change or insight that you would like to take with you. Notice how you feel in your body as you reflect on this positive change. What beliefs about yourself do you notice now? How do you imagine that you could bring this new awareness into your life? Take some time to explore this new awareness.

If the client continues to exhibit a high level of distress toward the end of a session, invite them to place the event (and any related images, thoughts, emotions, and body sensations) into their container.

- Take a few moments before leaving here to today to place any remaining disturbing images, thoughts, emotions, or body sensations into an imagined container that can hold these experiences until you return to therapy. Remember, you have a choice about when to think about any distressing memories from your past.

9

Restoring Wellness with Complementary and Alternative Medicine

Individuals are increasingly turning to complementary and alternative medicine (CAM), in conjunction with traditional psychotherapy, for the treatment of mental illness, chronic pain, and physical conditions (Berna, 2019; de Jongh et al., 2016). Common forms of CAM include exercise, massage therapy, bodywork, nutrition therapy, acupuncture, meditation, relaxation, yoga, Tai Chi, and Qigong. By definition, *complementary* refers to the use of any of these practices alongside conventional medicine or therapy practices, whereas *alternative* means that the intervention is used to replace conventional medicine or therapy practices. In this chapter, I explore the benefits of CAM and the value of helping clients develop integrative healthcare teams to respond to the impact of trauma on both mental and physical health. The healing practices within this chapter focus on the integration of CAM within therapy. These interventions will allow clients to identify healthcare goals and work through barriers that might otherwise prevent them from integrating exercise, healthy nutrition, mindful eating, meditation, yoga, and relaxation practices into their lives.

Trauma and Health

There is an undeniable correlation between C-PTSD and physical health problems, including chronic pain and illness (Felitti et al., 1998; Harrell et al., 2011; Paradies et al., 2015). For example, individuals with C-PTSD commonly experience obesity, seizures, migraines, gastrointestinal problems, autoimmune disorders, fibromyalgia, chronic fatigue, and an array of medically unexplained symptoms. In part, trauma disrupts physical health because of its impact on the ANS. Under ordinary conditions, the SNS and PNS are meant to work in a rhythmic fashion that supports healthy digestion, sleep, and immune system functioning. Unresolved trauma disrupts this balance, resulting in prolonged dysregulation of the ANS, which changes the functioning of the HPA axis and alters how the body processes cortisol. More specifically, clients who are stuck in a state of hyper-arousal have chronic SNS activation and increased cortisol levels. Due to the inverse relationship between bloodstream cortisol levels and immune system functioning (Scaer, 2005), the prolonged fight-or-flight activation that accompanies this state suppresses the immune system, making these individuals more susceptible to frequent colds, high blood pressure, blood sugar imbalances, cravings for salty or sugary snacks, obesity, sluggish digestion, and cancer.

In contrast, individuals who are stuck in a hypo-aroused state have an imbalanced expression of the PNS associated with the dorsal vagal complex, which is related to lower baseline levels of cortisol (Yehuda, 2002). These reductions in cortisol serve to increase immune system functioning, which can lead to inflammation and pain throughout the body. An unrestrained immune system may also target tissues and organ systems within the body, leading to greater likelihood of autoimmune disorders (Bergmann, 2012). Digestive disturbances are common as well—including constipation, diarrhea, gastroesophageal reflux disease, irritable bowel syndrome, and ulcerative colitis—as are sleep disturbances and hormonal imbalances. Individuals in this hypo-aroused state may also be subjected to invasive medical procedures, medical mismanagement, or misdiagnoses as they attempt to navigate their chronic pain, leading to further traumatization.

The *microbiota–gut–brain (MGB) axis* also plays an important role in the functioning of the HPA axis as related to traumatic stress reactions (Malan-Muller et al., 2018). The MGB axis refers to a bidirectional set of interactions between the gut and the brain. Our microbiota reflects all of the microorganisms that live within the human body, including bacteria and viruses. Trillions of these microorganisms and their genetic material live within the intestinal tract and are often referred to as the "gut microbiome." The gut has also been called our second or "enteric" brain, in part because the intestines are capable of producing the same neurotransmitters found in the brain. These neurochemicals facilitate communications between our digestive system and our nervous system.

When individuals experience mental and emotional stress, this is associated with imbalances in the gut microbiome, referred to as "dysbiosis," which contribute to immune system dysfunction and inflammation. This can lead to a vicious cycle in which imbalances in the body can worsen anxiety, depression, and traumatic stress reactions (Foster, Rinaman, & Cryan, 2017). While most psychotherapy focuses on mental and emotional changes, many CAM treatments focus on creating balance in the body in order to improve the mind. For instance, nutrition therapy focuses on identifying and treating nutritional deficiencies, managing blood sugar imbalances, and eliminating food allergies or sensitivities in order to improve immune system functioning, reduce inflammation, and treat mental health conditions. As an example, magnesium deficiency can contribute to anxiety, and gluten sensitivity can exacerbate depression (Korn, 2016).

Many CAM treatments, such as massage therapy, meditation, and yoga, are effective because they bring about physiological changes in the ANS as measured by changes in vagal tone and heart rate variability (Trakroo & Bhavanani, 2016). Healthy vagal tone involves a rhythmic increase in heart rate on each inhale and a decrease in heart rate during each exhale. This creates a healthy balance between SNS and PNS actions. Each inhale subtly engages the SNS as the heartbeat speeds up, and each exhale engages the PNS as the heart rate slows back down. This balance is referred to as heart rate variability (HRV), which is a marker for resiliency. In fact, HRV is one of the ways that researchers measure the changes that happen in mind-body therapies. HRV is measured by the rhythmic oscillations of your heart rate that occur with the breath. Your heart rate is a measure of the number of beats per minute, whereas HRV is a measure of the intervals between your heartbeats. High HRV means there is greater variability between the number of heartbeats, which is typically associated with a greater ability to tolerate or recover from stress. In contrast, low HRV is associated with stress, anxiety, and depression. Practices that increase HRV help build flexibility and resilience within the ANS. As a result, it becomes easier to move between feelings of excitement and ease.

The yogic tradition of *pranayama* or conscious breathing has been found to enhance HRV and is associated with improved immune system health, as well as reduced anxiety, depression, and PTSD symptoms (Brown & Gerbarg, 2005a, 2005b; Rhodes et al., 2016; Seppälä et al., 2014). Similarly, CAM treatments that involve meditation, such as the loving-kindness meditation, are associated with greater autonomic flexibility, increased vagal tone, more positive emotions, and an increased sense of social connectedness (Kok & Fredrickson, 2010; Kok et al., 2013). The loving-kindness meditation has also been associated with improvements in chronic pain (Carson et al., 2005). In addition, meditation practices that focus on gratitude, such as keeping a daily gratitude journal, are associated with positive mood, increased optimism, a sense of connection to others, decreased pain, and better sleep (Emmons, 2007; Emmons & McCullough, 2003).

Integrating gentle forms of acupressure and self-massage into psychotherapy also has benefits for trauma recovery. For example, the emotional freedom technique is a therapeutic modality based on Chinese medicine that involves self-tapping on traditional acupressure points on the face and upper body. Applied to psychotherapy, therapists teach clients the tapping technique while they incorporate the cognitive process of stating a psychological concern aloud with an intention of unconditional self-acceptance. Research has shown that this practice is associated with significant reductions in PTSD symptoms and improvements in the regulation of stress hormones (Church & Feinstein, 2017). In addition, research from the Touch Research Institute has shown the benefits of massage therapy in alleviating depression, reducing pain, and improving immune system functioning (Field, 2014).

Although there is some support for touch as a therapeutic intervention, it also carries significant potential risks, including the potential for clients to feel violated by therapist-touch behaviors. As a result, the use of touch is often contraindicated in psychotherapy because of the complexity of transference dynamics and risks around the blurring of boundaries between therapists and clients. Instead, we can introduce clients to the Havening Technique (Ruden, 2011), which involves having clients engage in self-touch of the face, arms, and hands while reflecting on a stressful or traumatic event. In this way, we bring the benefits of touch into psychotherapy.

Integrating Complementary and Alternative Medicine into Therapy

It is often necessary to focus on basic healthcare needs to facilitate stabilization when working with clients with C-PSTD. Here, we explore with clients whether they are getting enough sleep, eating at regular intervals, staying hydrated, and sufficiently digesting their food. As needed, we can then prioritize interventions to address these basic needs by ensuring that clients have access to food, set reminders to drink water, or learn sleep hygiene strategies to assist with debilitating insomnia. For example, we can encourage clients to reduce caffeine use during the day or manage computer or phone screen exposure after dark by wearing blue light blocking glasses. Given that insomnia can lead to irritability, anxiety, poor concentration, confusion, and depression, we can also partner with other medical professionals to help clients access pharmaceutical medications, natural supplements, herbal medicines, bodywork, or acupuncture to assist with sleep.

The integration of CAM into therapy falls into two categories: referring clients to outside practitioners and offering interventions within sessions. When referring to other treatment providers, we can help clients develop an integrative healthcare team. For example, this team might include conventional medical professionals, a nutritionist, an exercise coach, a massage therapist, an acupuncturist, and a meditation or therapeutic yoga teacher. With a signed release from clients, we can discuss their mental and physical healthcare goals with members of this team. These sorts of CAM treatments are becoming increasingly accessible. For example, many community mental health centers offer group auricular acupuncture, which has demonstrated benefits in the treatment of anxiety, depression, insomnia, digestive issues, substance use, migraines, and chronic pain (Murakami, Fox, & Dijkers, 2017). Likewise, meditation and therapeutic yoga for trauma recovery have become increasingly available, with ample research demonstrating their effectiveness in reducing sympathetic activation, blood pressure, inflammation, opiate use, and PTSD symptoms, while also improving neuroendocrine activity, endocrine system health, and heart rate variability (Bolton et al., 2020; Emerson, 2015; Price et al., 2017; Rhodes et al., 2016; Tyagi & Cohen, 2016; van der Kolk et al., 2014).

However, it can be challenging to integrate CAM into mental health treatment due to issues with insurance coverage, lack of affordable options, lack of trauma-informed referral sources, and time constraints (Schwartz, 2014). As a solution, we can offer these interventions in more easily accessible way. For example, as appropriate, we can provide guided mindfulness and relaxation practices through a variety of technologies, such *Insight Timer*, which is a free downloadable app that has a wide variety of guided meditations. As therapists, we can also provide some CAM interventions in therapy sessions to increase accessibility to these treatments without having to rely upon outside practitioners. Let's take a closer look at the value of increasing availability to CAM through my experience of working with Ruby, a middle-aged, African American woman struggling with C-PTSD and myalgic encephalomyelitis/chronic fatigue syndrome (ME/CFS):

Ruby was in her early forties when she was referred to therapy by her doctor after an episode of depression and fatigue that kept her in bed for approximately three months. At that time, she was diagnosed with ME/CFS. When she entered therapy, I learned that she was suffering from symptoms of depression, anxiety, brain fog, dizziness, fatigue, joint pain, and digestive difficulties. In her worst moments, Ruby felt hopeless and carried a sense of despair about her future. This often corresponded to times when her pain and fatigue were debilitating, which interfered with her ability to parent her children or enjoy her life.

When exploring Ruby's history, I learned that her mother was emotionally unavailable and disengaged, while her father was an alcoholic. As a child, Ruby would often "hang out" with her father while he was drunk, and during these times, she became his confidant as he talked about his own childhood abuse. When Ruby was 12 years old, she began to drink and use drugs with friends at school. She engaged in increasingly risky and dangerous behaviors that led to multiple sexual traumas, including a gang rape that occurred when she was 17. Ruby eventually became sober in her late twenties, after which she married and had two children.

In session, Ruby and I explored her window of tolerance and discussed her symptoms of depression, dizziness, brain fog, and fatigue as related to hypo-arousal. She learned to mindfully pay attention to her body in session and explored changes in her breathing and posture that helped her feel grounded and connected to her body. Ruby and I also explored her healthcare goals as related to therapy. In doing so, she shared that she was beginning to understand the connection between her trauma and her physical health. She wanted to heal from her past, and we developed a plan to help her integrate healthy nutrition, meditation, and gentle exercise into her life. I also suggested that she begin working with a craniosacral therapist to help support her nervous system.

Between sessions, she began to practice relaxing and mindful resting using a free guided Yoga Nidra practice available through Insight Timer. She also began craniosacral therapy. After a month, Ruby already began to notice a reduction in her symptoms of brain fog and dizziness. This stabilization allowed us to begin addressing the traumatic events from her past using somatic psychology and EMDR therapy. We progressed in a titrated manner with careful attention to nervous system regulation. During this process, Ruby and I both noticed that she would often feel foggy just prior to having an emotional release, and her fog would lift once she expressed her feelings.

Despite this progress, Ruby had difficulty meeting her lifestyle goals of creating dietary changes and incorporating exercise into her routine. She knew she would feel better if she ate less sugar, walked, and began a gentle yoga practice, but she struggled with the legitimate concern that too much exercise would exacerbate her ME/CFS symptoms. She also expressed the fear that nothing she did would make a difference, so she felt that maybe it wasn't worth trying.

As we compassionately explored these barriers, she identified an underlying blocking belief that she didn't deserve good things. Through parts work therapy, she grew curious about the part of her that carried this feeling of unworthiness and discovered a connection to the shame she felt as a 12-year-old when she began drinking and using drugs. She was able to achieve resolution with this part of herself, which allowed her to commit to making dietary changes and engaging in a gentle exercise program that didn't worsen her ME/CFS symptoms. While Ruby's fatigue and pain didn't completely resolve, her hopelessness and despair were significantly reduced, which allowed her to respond more compassionately and effectively to her physical needs for rest and relaxation. As a result, her episodes of fatigue and pain were more transient than they had been in the past, which helped her feel more in control and engaged in her life.

You can use the next healing practice to identify your clients' physical health concerns and healthcare goals. Within this practice, explore with clients their history of illness and injury, making sure to gain an understanding of their current symptoms and chronic pain. As you explore lifestyle changes that the client would like to make to facilitate their recovery, it is important that you identify current strengths and work with the client to create shared healthcare goals.

Explore Physical Health and Identify Healthcare Goals

- I would like to know a little about your physical health. Let's start with some basics. Do you have difficulty sleeping at night and, if so, how does this impact your life? Do you eat regular meals and have access to food that is nutritious? Do you drink enough water throughout the day? How is your digestion? [*If the client shares that they are struggling with any of these areas, begin to explore ways to support these basic needs prior to exploring other aspects of their health history.*]

- It can also be helpful to know more about your physical health history. Have you had or do you currently have any physical health challenges, such as digestive challenges, heart disease, headaches, skin conditions, allergies, thyroid imbalances, or autoimmune conditions? Do you experience any areas of chronic pain? Do you have any current health concerns for which you have not received any diagnosis?

- Let's take a look at the care that you have already received for your physical health concerns. What treatments have you had or are you currently using for your condition? Were or are these treatments helpful or successful? As a result of any illness or pain, have you had any invasive or traumatic medical procedures? Do you find yourself fearful of or avoiding medical care? Do you feel understood and respected by healthcare providers?

- In addition to traditional or conventional medical care, have you explored any complementary or alternative healthcare modalities, such as acupuncture, massage therapy, or bodywork? Have these helped reduce your symptoms?

- Have you ever worked with a nutritionist? Are you aware of any food sensitivities, intolerances, or allergies?

- Do you currently have an exercise routine? Does this help reduce your symptoms, or do you notice any symptoms that worsen after exercise?

- Do you currently engage in any mindfulness or relaxation practices, such as meditation, yoga, Tai Chi, or Qigong? If so, do you find these practices helpful in reducing your symptoms? Do you notice any exacerbation of symptoms during relaxation practices?

- Are there any lifestyle changes that you would like to create or goals that you would like to set for your physical health? These goals might include integrating an exercise routine into your life, creating more time for meditation or yoga, committing to writing in your journal, or focusing on dietary changes. Let's write down a list of these goals together.

Overcoming Barriers to Healthcare Goals

Some clients might desire to integrate lifestyle changes, such as exercise, nutritional changes, or meditation, but have difficulty sustaining these health-promoting behaviors. It is common for a vicious cycle of shame to ensue in which clients feel powerless to meet their healthcare goals. For example, clients might know that they need to change their diet, exercise more, or set up a visit with a doctor to address a medical problem. However, they might also believe that nothing they do will make a difference, that they don't deserve to be healthy, or that change is impossible. Or they might not feel safe with or trusting of medical professionals, or they might fear that they will lose access to financial or emotional resources if they get better. As a result, they avoid doing the very activities that would promote their health. If left unaddressed, these factors can lead to the worsening of physical health problems.

Use the next healing practice to help clients identify beliefs that interfere with their healing, such as the notion that nothing they do will make a difference or that they don't deserve to be healthy. This practice can also help clients identify and compassionately work with any feelings of shame, helplessness, fear, or distrust that impact their recovery. If you and the client identify a pattern of self-sabotage, you can return to the parts work practices from chapter 6. Or you and the client might identify a blocking belief or emotion that is connected to a traumatic event from the client's past. In this case, you can use the somatic repatterning or cognitive reprocessing healing practices from chapters 7 and 8. It is also important to consider that some physical health problems will not go away. In this case, it may be necessary to help clients work toward grieving and accepting their chronic illness or autoimmune conditions as unresolvable. This process can allow clients to more successfully focus on the aspects of their healthcare that are under their control. As with the other healing practices in this book, tailor the intervention to meet the needs of your client.

Overcome Barriers to Healthcare Goals

- **Identify blocking beliefs:** Sometimes we carry beliefs about ourselves or the world that interfere with our ability to get better or meet our healthcare goals. Would you be willing to take a look at the following list of blocking beliefs and explore if there are any you identify with?

    o I can never get better.

    o I do not have the strength to heal or recover.

    o I do not deserve to get better.

    o I deserve to be sick.

    o Nothing I do will make a difference in my health.

    o If I get better, I will lose a part of who I really am.

    o I am afraid of what this change will bring.

    o I am permanently damaged.

    o I am powerless or helpless to change my situation.

    o People will only care for me if I am sick.

- **Identify blocking emotions:** Sometimes difficult emotions arise that sabotage your efforts toward healing. You might notice feelings of shame come up because you have put on weight or have had difficulty exercising. Or you might feel helpless to change your situation. Perhaps you feel distrusting of medical providers, which leads you to avoid getting necessary care. If left unattended, these emotions can interfere with your ability to meet your healthcare goals. Take a few moments to notice if there are any emotions that arise when you think about your healthcare goal to… [*e.g., stop eating sugar, see the doctor, begin exercising, stop smoking*]. Are you aware of any emotions that prevent you from following through with this goal?

- Sometimes these emotions might be difficult to identify, but you might notice uncomfortable feelings in your body that lead you to avoid creating positive change. Can your turn toward these emotions and sensations with acceptance and compassion? You might try saying to yourself, "all of my feelings are welcome here" or "I fully accept myself even though I am having difficult feelings about creating change in my life."

- **Explore sabotaging parts:** You might notice a conflict between a part of you who wants to… [*e.g., stop eating sugar, see the doctor, begin exercising, stop smoking*] and a part of you who… [*e.g., is afraid of change, feels helpless, doesn't believe healing is possible*]. I invite you to turn toward the belief that… [*e.g., you can never get better, you do not deserve to get better, you are powerless to change your situation*] or the feeling of [*e.g., shame, anger, sadness, helplessness, confusion, fear*]. Do you recall other times in your life when you felt this way? Do you have any memories connected to this belief or these feelings? How old does this part feel? Notice how you feel toward this part of yourself. Is there anything that this part needs from you?

- **Build acceptance and compassion:** I invite you to turn toward the belief that… [*e.g., you can never get better, you do not deserve to get better, you are powerless to change your situation*] or the feeling of… [*e.g., shame, anger, sadness, helplessness, confusion, fear*]. What would it feel like to fully accept yourself, just as you are, with these thoughts and feelings? You might say to yourself, "I am okay just as I am" or "I am willing to accept myself even if I cannot completely recover." Notice how it feels to be with your experience without needing to change, control, or fix yourself.

- **Engage with change:** Take a moment to review your healthcare goals. Now that you have identified some of the barriers that interfere with your ability to reach these goals, you are ready to focus your attention on new beliefs and behaviors that will enhance your health. I'd like for you to choose one action that you would like to take during the week to support your health. This might involve making a dietary change, choosing an exercise goal, committing to a mindfulness practice, or engaging in a reflective activity, such as journaling or a creative project. Explore the kinds of support that you need to help you to be most successful with this new behavior. Take a moment to identify the best time in your day or week to engage in this activity. Where is the best location that will help you to be successful? Allow yourself to imagine completing the new behavior successfully. If you notice any blocking beliefs or feelings, explore if there is anything else that you need to navigate around or remove this barrier.

Natural Vagus Nerve Stimulation

Irregularities in the vagus nerve can cause tremendous disruptions to physical and emotional health. Physical consequences can include gastroesophageal reflux disease, irritable bowel syndrome, nausea or vomiting, fainting, migraines, tinnitus, autoimmune disorders, or seizures. Mental health consequences can include fatigue, depression, panic attacks, or a classic alternation between feeling overwhelmed and shutdown. Traditional vagus nerve stimulation treatment, also referred to as *neuromodulation*, involves surgically implanting a bioelectronic device that provides stimulation for the vagus nerve. However, it is also possible to indirectly stimulate the vagus nerve naturally. Recall that the vagus nerve passes through the belly, diaphragm, lungs, throat, inner ear, and facial muscles. Therefore, practices that change or control the actions of these areas of the body can influence the functioning of the vagus nerve through the mind-body feedback loop, especially since 80 percent of the nerve fibers are sensory or afferent, meaning that they communicate messages from the body to the central nervous system.

Vagus nerve stimulation helps regulate both sympathetic hyper-arousal and parasympathetic hypo-arousal. When the vagus nerve is activated, it keeps the immune system in check and releases an assortment of hormones and neurotransmitters into the body, such as acetylcholine and oxytocin, which result in reductions in inflammation, improvements in allergies, relief from tension headaches, improvements in memory, and feelings of relaxation (Groves & Brown, 2005).

Since all vagus nerve stimulation initiates a relaxation response, it is important to help clients develop tolerance for being in a parasympathetic state without moving into a state of dysfunctional hypo-arousal in which they feel collapsed or shutdown. Initially, clients might routinely fall asleep when exploring relaxation or vagus nerve interventions. So long as this pattern of sleeping does not worsen symptoms, we can simply encourage clients to allow themselves to be nourished by the experience and trust that sleeping can be medicinal for their nervous system. However, we also want to help clients differentiate between a dorsal vagal response and a healthy yielding into gravity as discussed in chapter 7. If the client describes that physical health symptoms worsen in response to any vagal stimulation exercises, help them discover a relaxed yet alert state by asking them to experiment with sitting up instead of laying down or keeping their eyes open during the practice.

You can explore natural vagus stimulation through gentle yoga breath and movement interventions that aim to stimulate and balance the vagus nerve. Slowing down the exhale is considered the most direct way to balance the vagus nerve, as an emphasis on a slow, lengthened out-breath stimulates nerve fibers in the lungs to initiate a relaxation response. This is particularly the case when there is an emphasis on fully emptying the lungs through engagement of the diaphragm and abdominal muscles, which also provides a gentle massage to the digestive organs. You can teach clients to lengthen the exhale with gentle yoga breath practices, such as adding a slight constriction in the throat and an audible quality to the breath by making a "ha" sound. Humming also stimulates the vagus nerve as it passes through the throat and inner ear.

Another way to engage the vagus nerve is by relaxing the eyes and releasing the muscles in the neck. The eyes are regulated by twelve extraocular muscles that extend down into the suboccipital muscles surrounding the upper cervical vertebrae. The extraocular nerve endings have a direct connection to the vagus nerve, which explains why we can often see in our clients' eyes whether they feel stressed or relaxed. When we relax the muscles in the eyes, this engages an innate reflex called the oculocardiac reflex (OCR), which initiates a parasympathetic response to slow down the heart rate and lower blood pressure. Individuals can faint if this response happens too quickly. However, we can also stimulate the OCR by providing gentle pressure on the eyes, which can have a calming effect on the nervous system. This can be accomplished by placing an eye pillow over the eyes during relaxation or by placing the palms of the hand over the eyes and applying very light pressure.

We can also stimulate the vagus nerve through eye movements, which increase blood flow to the vertebral artery and stimulate the vagus nerve as it passes through the upper neck. For example, oculocardiac convergence visual therapy, which involves having clients repeatedly converge their eyes on a nearby focal point (about four inches away from the face) and then shift to a distant focal point, has been found to reduce anxiety and panic (Merrill & Bowan, 2008). In addition, the vagus nerve passes right behind the sternocleidomastoid muscles (SCM) and in front of the scalenes, which tend to be the tightest muscles in the neck. Therefore, exercises that involve moving the eyes to the right and left with accompanying stretching of the SCM and scalenes in the neck also tend to produce a relaxation response by engaging the vagus nerve (Rosenberg, 2017).

The final healing practices in this chapter offer yoga, self-tapping, Havening, and meditation-based interventions that you can introduce to clients. **When offering any therapeutic practice for individuals who have experienced trauma, it is important to ensure that clients feel safe.** We accomplish this by helping clients know that they have a choice about whether or not they want to engage in any practice. They have a choice about how to move their bodies and how to breathe. Depending upon their trauma and health history, any breath-focused intervention, especially those that involve holding the breath, might trigger them into a state of sympathetic hyper-arousal or shut them down into a state of collapse. **Make sure clients know that they can say no and opt out of any practice.**

While several of these breath practices have specific instructions, it is equally important to let clients know that they can adapt or change any practice. For example, they can choose to practice with their eyes open or closed, or they can choose to stand up, be seated, or lay down on a couch. This emphasis on choice is especially important when offering the guided yogic relaxation intervention since relaxing the body into stillness can feel very vulnerable for clients with an extended trauma history or who have a tendency toward dissociation and immobilization.

With an emphasis on choice, we reduce the likelihood that these interventions will come across as forceful, and we decrease the likelihood that the client will approach the practice in a perfectionistic or self-aggressive manner. I suggest introducing only one healing practice at time, and then invite the client to mindfully observe and share their experience. Remember, not all practices will work for all clients.

Discover Yogic Breath Practices (Pranayama)

- In yoga, pranayama is the practice of breathing consciously to change how we think and feel. Slowing down and deepening the breath can have a calming effect on the mind and body. As with all practices, I invite you to allow yourself to be curious about your experience and to observe your experience without judgment. Please let me know if you feel any distress or disturbance; we can stop the practice at any time.

- If you would like, begin to explore how it feels to take a four-count breath in and a four-count breath out. In yoga, this breath practice is called *Sama Vritti*, which can be translated as equal or balanced breathing. As you breathe, allow your breath to move your belly by expanding your diaphragm on each inhale and allowing your belly to soften on each exhale. If the four-count breath feels too short, explore how it feels to extend to a six- or eight-count breath. Repeat for another five breaths or about a minute. Once you are complete, notice any changes in how you feel mentally, emotionally, and physically.

- Stressful and traumatic situations can cause shallow breathing, holding of the breath, or tightness in the chest. Each inhale engages the SNS, while each exhale stimulates the PNS. Slowing down and giving resistance to your exhale trains your body to use the diaphragm when breathing, which can help you to feel calmer and more relaxed.

- This next breath involves imagining having a straw between your lips. You can practice this breath with a physical straw as well. To begin, take a gentle inhale. Then purse your lips and exhale very slowly through your imagined straw until your lungs are 80 percent empty. Then close your mouth and slowly exhale the last 20 percent through your nose as you engage the muscles in your abdomen and diaphragm to expel all of the air from your lungs. Allow your next inhale to come naturally, and take three regular breaths. If you would like, repeat this exercise two or three more times. Once you are complete, notice any changes in how you feel mentally, physically, and emotionally.

- Another way to explore your breath is to add a sound that creates a slight constriction in the throat. Let's begin with a breath called *Haakara pranayama* in Sanskrit, which is translated as the "ha" sounding breath. To begin, relax your shoulders and jaw as you allow a deep belly inhale.

Exhale slowly while you create a soft and whispered "ha" sound until you have emptied your lungs. You can imagine that you are trying to fog up a mirror as you make the "ha" sound. Continue to breathe in this manner, or if you would like, you can keep the same slight constriction in your throat and audible quality to the breath as you breathe in and out of your nose. In yoga, this breath practice is referred to as *Ujayii pranayama*, which translates to the victorious breath. The victory is over the mind. Continue for five to ten more breaths, and once you are complete, notice how you feel mentally, physically, and emotionally.

- If you would like, I'd like to share with you the yogic practice of *Bhamari Pranayama*, which is translated as the honeybee breath. For this breath, you can explore humming on the exhale to create a vibration in the eardrums. Since the vagus nerve passes by the vocal chords and inner ear, this breath can be calming for your body and mind. You can also explore how it feels to take place your palms over your ears to amplify the feeling and sound in your ears. Continue for five rounds of this breath—taking a deep breath in and then humming on the exhale—and notice the sensations in your chest, throat, and head. Once you are complete, take a moment to notice how you feel mentally, physically, and emotionally.

Stretch and Relax Your Eyes and Neck

- The vagus nerve is deeply connected to the muscles in and around your eyes. Since the vagus nerve also passes through the neck, stretching the muscles in the neck can also increase blood flow to the vagus nerve.

- If you would like, begin to explore stretching and engaging the eye muscles, which can ultimately help these muscles relax. You can start by holding a pencil or small object about four to six inches in front of your face. Allow your eyes to focus on this object for about 20 seconds, and then shift your focus to look off in the distance for about 20 seconds. Continue back and forth for about four cycles, and then softly relax your eyes.

- You can also engage and stretch your eyes by moving them to the right and left. If you'd like, you can explore how it feels to bring your eyes to the right, as if trying to look over your right shoulder without turning your head. Then allow your head to turn toward the right, and continue to take several breaths with your eyes in this position. Stretch only to the point that you feel your neck stops naturally, and then breathe into the sensations. If you would like, keep your head in this position as you send your eyes to the left for a few breaths. Then bring your eyes back to the right and notice if the muscles in your neck soften, allowing your head to turn farther in this direction. As you feel complete, allow your head and eyes to come back to center. Take a few breaths and repeat this exercise on the other side.

- If you would like, you can explore bringing your right ear toward your right shoulder without turning your head. Then bring your eyes toward the right. Take several breaths into the left side of your neck, and then bring your head back to center as your eyes come forward again. Repeat this on the left side and notice how you feel. You can also explore how it feels to bring your right ear to the right shoulder as you send your eyes and gaze to the left. Once again, hold this shape for about 30 seconds and then switch sides.

- You might also want to explore how it feels to lift both of your eyes upward as if looking at the center of your forehead. After a few breaths, allow your head to follow your eyes by lifting your chin. Notice how it feels to breathe into the sensations in your upper chest, neck, and throat. After several breaths, bring your head and eyes to center. Finally, turn your eyes downward as if looking at the tip of your nose. After a few breaths, allow your head to follow by tucking your chin toward your chest. Notice how it feels to breathe into the sensations of your upper back, neck, and the base of your skull. To complete, allow your head and eyes to soften toward your center, and notice any subtle shifts in your body and mind. Notice any changes in how you feel mentally, emotionally, and physically.

- We can also balance the vagus nerve by covering our eyes, which can have a calming effect on the body. If you'd like, explore how it feels to lift your hands and place your palms over your eyes. Allow your hands to create a gentle pressure over the eyes and take several breaths, softening your eyes in this position. Notice how you feel mentally, physically, and emotionally.

Find Emotional Freedom with Self-Tapping

- Would you be open to exploring a self-tapping practice to help reduce emotional distress? This practice invites you to tap on traditional acupuncture meridian points.

- To begin, I would like you to choose one area of concern or distress that you are experiencing right now. Notice your emotions and sensations, and identify a level of distress from 0 to 10, with 10 being the "worst distress possible" and 0 being "no distress at all."

- Once you have chosen a focus for the practice, I invite you to repeat the following "setup" phrase three times with me while tapping with one hand on the side of your opposite hand: "Even though I have… [*name the client's area of concern*], I deeply and completely accept myself."

- Now name just the area of concern while you tap each of the following points five times. Usually, you choose just one side of your body.

    o The inside edge of your eyebrow

    o The outside of your eye

    o Under your eye

    o Under your nose

    o Under your lips in the crease of your chin

    o Under your collarbones (you can use both hands to tap both sides)

    o Under your arm near your ribcage

- Now observe how you are feeling. Take a moment to reflect on your area of concern, and rate your level of distress on a scale of 0 to 10, with 10 being the "worst distress possible" and 0 being "no distress at all."

- Notice if the sensation has changed or if a new area of concern has come to the surface. If so, repeat the steps with this new area of concern. Continue until the level of distress is reduced to a tolerable level or gone.

Self-Soothe with Self-Havening

- Would you be open to exploring a self-soothing practice that uses touch to help reduce emotional distress? This practice invites you to touch your face and arms while thinking about a stressful or traumatic event.

- To begin, I would like you to choose one area of concern or distress, either something you are experiencing right now or a memory of a historical trauma. Notice your emotions and sensations, and identify a level of distress, with 10 being the "worst distress possible" and 0 being "no distress at all."

- Now I'd like to invite you to put the disturbing thought to the side and to bring to mind a peaceful place where you can imagine going for a barefoot walk. This might be a beach or a grassy field.

- Now cross your arms, and place your right hand on the top of your left shoulder and your left hand on top of your right shoulder. Begin to move your hands from your shoulders down past your elbows to opposite hands. Repeat this action 5 to 10 times as feels good to you. Move slowly enough to sense the feeling of your hands on your arms. See if you can allow yourself to fully receive the experience of your own touch. Let yourself be nourished.

- As you continue to move both of your hands from your shoulders down to the elbows, imagine yourself taking a walk through this peaceful place as I count each step up to 20.

- Continue moving your hands on your arms as you slowly and rhythmically add eye movements to the left and right.

- Now bring your hands to your forehead, and smooth your hands across the top of your face, from the center out to your temples. Bring your hands up to your hairline and stroke outward, and then repeat this same movement from the crown of your head down toward your ears.

- Now bring your hands to your cheeks and move them gently from the center out as if comforting your face.

- Observe how you are feeling. Take a moment to reflect on your area of concern, and rate your level of distress on a scale of 0 to 10, with 10 being the "worst distress possible" and 0 being "no distress at all."

- Notice if the sensation has changed or if a new area of concern has come to the surface. If so, repeat the steps with this new area of concern. Continue until the level of distress is reduced to a tolerable level or gone.

Explore Therapeutic Chair Yoga

- Would you be open to exploring a little bit of yoga movement right now? These seated stretches can help balance the vagus nerve as you move the spine, belly, chest, and throat. If you would like to continue, it is helpful to come to the front of your chair or couch.

- First bring your hands to your shoulders. Inhale as you expand across the front of your chest by extending your spine forward as you open your elbows wide and lift your chin. Exhale as you curl your spine inward while contracting your elbows in front of your heart and tucking your chin. Take several deep breaths, inhaling to open and exhaling to close in this moving meditation. After several breaths, come back to stillness and notice how you feel mentally, physically, and emotionally.

- If you would like to continue, you can come into a twist by placing your left hand on the outside of your right leg while placing your right hand behind you toward the center of your chair. On the inhale, lengthen your spine, and on your exhale, deepen the twist of your spine toward the right. You can also bring your chin to the right and gaze over your shoulder. Take several breaths here to massage your digestive organs and then return to center. When you are ready, switch sides by placing your right hand on the outside of your left leg while placing your left hand behind you toward the center of your chair. On the inhale, lengthen your spine, and on your exhale, deepen the twist of your spine toward the left. You can also bring your chin to the left and gaze over your shoulder. Take several breaths here then return to center. Once again, notice how you feel mentally, physically, and emotionally.

Release Tension through Guided Relaxation

- Would you be open to exploring a guided relaxation practice? This can be useful to help you reclaim the health of your parasympathetic nervous system. If you would like, I will guide you to relax each area of your body. It is up to you if you want to remain seated, or you are welcome to lie down if you feel comfortable doing so. Over the next several minutes, I invite you to relax each area of your body. Most importantly, you are in charge of this practice, and you can stop the practice at any point.

- Begin this practice by relaxing your eyes, ears, mouth, and entire head. Now allow yourself to relax through your neck and throat. As you continue, begin to relax your shoulders. Bring your attention to your left arm, and relax this arm from your shoulder all the way to your hand. Now bring your attention to your right arm, and relax this arm from your shoulder all the way to your hand. Feel both arms relaxed at the same time. You might find it difficult to relax the muscles in your face, shoulders, and arms. If so, explore tensing these areas of your body briefly and then releasing the muscles. Repeat two more times and notice if you can feel a relaxation response.

- Remember, you can choose to end this practice, move, or change positions at any time. If you would like to continue, bring your awareness to your torso. Take a breath into your chest and upper back. Notice these areas of your body and relax. Now bring your awareness to your belly and lower back. Notice these areas of your body and relax. Now bring your awareness to your pelvis and hips and relax. Again, you might explore tightening and relaxing these areas of your body. Notice if this allows you to let go of any unnecessary tension.

- It is okay if thoughts, emotions, or sensations arise during this practice. Allow these to rise and fall like waves on the ocean. Remember, you can move in any way that helps you relax and be comfortable.

- If you would like to continue, bring your awareness to your legs. Feel your left leg from your hip to your toes and relax this leg. Now feel your right leg from your hip to your toes and relax this leg. Notice both legs relaxed at the same time. As needed, explore tensing and releasing the muscles of your legs until you feel a relaxation response.

- Now feel the entire right side of your body relaxed. Notice the entire left side of your body relaxed. Feel your entire body fully relaxed. Continue to breathe here for the next minute, and when you feel ready, begin to bring your awareness to your external surroundings. Take as long as you would like to make this transition, and notice how you feel in your mind, body, and emotions.

Connect to Your Heart with a Gratitude Meditation

- Would you be open to exploring a brief meditation practice focused on gratitude? This practice invites you to focus on three things that you are grateful for in this moment. I will guide you through this practice in this moment, and then I invite you to explore including this practice as part of a daily routine throughout your week.

- To begin, I invite you to place your hands over your heart and take a few deep breaths. Bring to mind one thing for which you are grateful about yourself. You might appreciate yourself for your commitment to healing, your smile, or being a good friend. [*You can tailor these statements to share what you observe as positive traits in your client.*]

- Next, take a moment to reflect on one thing for which you are grateful in terms of your connection to another person. Perhaps you can bring to mind one person who has been kind or supportive to you. [*Again, you can tailor this statement by mentioning a specific person in the client's life who serves as a positive resource.*]

- The third focus for our gratitude practice invites you to focus on one thing for which you are thankful related to the world around you. For example, you might be grateful for your home, your pet, your garden, the water you drink, or a tree that brings you shade.

- Now take a final moment and repeat to yourself the three things you are grateful for about yourself, another person, and the world around you. Once again, I invite you to place your hands over your heart and to take a few deep breaths. Notice how you feel in body and mind.

10

Nurturing Resilience and Post-Traumatic Growth

··

The tender places and wounds left behind from chronic and repeated traumatic events often do not completely go away. However, when clients make a commitment to trauma recovery, they have an opportunity to recognize that the traumatic events of their past do not need to define their future. They can learn to accept themselves as they are and hold themselves with compassion. This journey toward acceptance often evokes grief as clients confront the painful truth that they cannot change the past. It can be difficult to let go of the fantasy that they will finally receive the love, attention, or protection that they needed when they were a child. It can also be difficult to let go of any hopes for redemption or retaliation against an abuser. All of these feelings are valid. While some individuals may choose to work toward forgiveness of their abusers, forgiveness is not the same as forgetting, and it does not mean that what happened was acceptable.

This concluding chapter focuses on the third phase of trauma recovery by helping clients work through lingering feelings of anger, resentment, and sadness in order to cultivate a feeling of hope for the future. Over time, the hard work of trauma reprocessing helps clients discover their resilience and illuminates areas of post-traumatic growth. As a result, they may discover a greater willingness to stay engaged in life even with the knowledge that they risk facing additional difficult events. They can discover the unique skills and strengths that they have gained as a result of the difficult events from their past. **Ultimately, clients can learn to weave together their strengths and struggles to create a sense of self that feels increasingly integrated and whole.**

Within this phase of treatment, we support clients to apply the wisdom gained from therapy into their lives. However, it is wise to remember that trauma recovery is not linear. For example, clients might work through some of their traumatic memories and move into a meaning-making process prior to reengaging with trauma reprocessing. Regardless of the course that your clients' healing path takes, you can use the final healing practices in this book to focus on forgiveness and invite clients to reflect on their strengths as related to post-traumatic growth.

Living a Meaningful Life

One of the tasks of healing from complex trauma involves working through impaired meaning making as related to self-perception. It is common for individuals with C-PTSD to experience intense shame and confusion as a result of abuse, especially when this originates in childhood.

This shame is driven by distorted beliefs about being at fault, bad, or damaged. Most often, shame and self-blame reflect anger that has been turned inward toward the self. Here, we may need to guide clients to return the responsibility to the abuser. For example, they might blame themselves because they didn't say no to their abuser or didn't tell anyone about the abuse. In this case, we can remind clients that a child is never responsible for the abusive actions of an adult and that many children do not speak up because they believe they must obey their abuser and are afraid of being further harmed.

When we return responsibility to the abuser, it is common for anger to arise. Although healthy anger is necessary for self-protection, anger can also linger in a way that is deep, long-lasting, and disruptive. This kind of anger can lead clients to lose sleep, ruminate about past events, or become obsessed with retaliation fantasies. Often, our work involves encouraging them to express these feelings of betrayal and resentment. This process may evoke the painful recognition that they cannot change the past, which can open up underlying feelings of sadness, loss, and hurt. However, grieving the past can also bring about a sense of resolution, acceptance, and forgiveness.

Importantly, forgiveness should never be a forced process. **When clients feel stuck around the concept of forgiveness, it may be important to remind them that forgiveness is a choice and that it does not require that they reconcile with someone who has harmed them.** Moreover, the benefit of forgiveness is that it supports the client in feeling a greater sense of freedom. In some cases, forgiveness arises as clients recognize that the actions of another person were never personal to them at all. Perhaps they realize that the perpetrator of abuse had faced their own hardship or suffered from their own trauma. Such realizations can facilitate a sense of compassion for these individuals despite their harmful actions.

In addition, trauma often forces us to come to terms with the lack of reason or overpowering senselessness that surrounds acts of violence or abuse. It is common to wonder how or why such atrocities or evil can exist in this world. For many trauma survivors, therapy serves as an introspective journey and search for meaning (Frankl, 1946/2006). There is no universal meaning that can be generalized to all people or situations. Rather, meaning making is a personal process that arises as individuals work through feelings of despair until they find resolution with the past and hope for the future.

We support the process of meaning making when we invite clients to reflect on the ways that they have grown or changed as a result of the work of trauma recovery. Turning toward pain helps clients build a sense of character and allows them to realize that they are stronger than they previously believed (Tedeschi et al., 2018). Often, they feel more capable of handling life's challenges. This "post-traumatic growth" has been associated with enhanced interpersonal relationships, increased willingness to ask for or accept help, increased willingness to be vulnerable, increased recognition of social supports that had previously been ignored, increased appreciation of life, increased ability to "take it easy," newly found interests or passions, and spiritual discoveries (Schwartz, 2020).

According to the principles of ACT (Hayes, 2005), a meaningful life occurs when we live in alignment with our strengths and values. Examples of strengths and values include being open-minded, treating others with kindness, having a sense of social responsibility, being creative, connecting with nature, spending time with others, or learning new things. If there is a gap between our values and our behaviors, we are more likely to feel stuck, depressed, or unsatisfied in our lives. As clients identify their earned strengths and values, we can invite them to explore how they would like to bring these capacities into the world. For example, a woman who suffered from childhood abuse became an advocate for other survivors, and a man who experienced discrimination as a result of racism focused his work on social justice. It can be deeply satisfying to know that suffering can serve a cause that is greater than ourselves.

Let's take a closer look at meaning making through my experience of working with Lilah, a Jewish woman in her mid-forties who was diagnosed with C-PTSD due to childhood trauma and who carried intergenerational, legacy trauma related to the Holocaust. Lilah struggled with severe anxiety and mild dissociative symptoms:

Lilah came into therapy with "unmanageable anxiety" that interfered with her ability to sleep, drive, or work. She described feeling intense separation anxiety each time her husband left the house. She worried that something bad would happen to him and she carried a belief that she "couldn't handle it" if he died. This led her to worry about her future when he left for business trips. In sessions, Lilah shared that she had a difficult relationship with both of her parents and that she grew up as the middle child of three daughters. She often described having to "survive on scraps" and that she had to fight for love and attention in her family. This pattern of scarcity in her family system went back for several generations. Lilah shared that her grandmother was a survivor of the Holocaust who had experienced the trauma of losing both of her parents and her brother. She described her grandmother as rigid, cold, and unexpressive, and while her grandfather was warmer, he could lose his temper. The person to whom she felt most connected in her family was her father, but he died of cancer several years before I met Lilah.

In one particularly moving session, Lilah described the fears that would arise when her husband left the house. She intuitively felt that this anxiety was connected to her grandmother's losses related to the Holocaust. She said, "I can't let go. The world is not safe" and described feeling as if a wall was holding back a tidal wave of grief. I observed that she was holding her breath and appeared frozen in her body. As we acknowledged the grief, she described an ache in her heart and a tightness in her throat. She said, "There is so much grief. It is mine, but it isn't mine."

When I asked her to explore what she needed to find resolution with these feelings, she identified that she wished her grandmother could have had support for her grief. Lilah described remembering her grandmother's closed-off body language and stoic facial expressions when she visited as a little girl. As Lilah connected these memories, she began to cry. Lilah grieved as she recognized that her grandmother carried this pain until she died. This pain had prevented her grandmother from bonding to Lilah's mother and impaired her mother's ability to love her. As she realized that her grandmother couldn't handle any more loss, Lilah said, "I'm afraid of loss too. I don't have a relationship with my mother, and I have lost my father. I can't face another loss."

I acknowledged Lilah's fear that she couldn't handle another loss and also reflected her strength in persevering despite these challenges. I also identified how she had chosen to be in relationship with her husband even though she feared losing him. She took in this positive feedback and paused. She then said, "I feel like I am carrying this fear for my grandmother." At this point, Lilah realized that she was doing what her grandmother and mother were never able to do. She was feeling her sadness and talking about her fears. She sat up just a little bit taller and looked me squarely in the eyes as she stated, "I am learning to let go." This began her courageous journey of trusting in her own strengths as a survivor and gaining greater trust that she could relax when her husband was away.

As evidenced by Lilah's story, clients can develop the capacity to reflect on challenging life events while cultivating awareness of their strengths. This process can help them realize that all of their life experiences collectively make them who they are. This facilitates what Dr. Daniel Siegel (2010) calls *coherence*, a characteristic that helps us feel integrated, whole, and capable of reflecting on our complex and diverse life experiences. Coherence helps us relate to dichotomies and contradictions within ourselves, our interpersonal relationships, and our world with equanimity. We understand that all relationships will inevitably have challenges and times of disconnection. We recognize that opening our hearts to the world entails the risk of rejection or loss. We build our capacity to handle conflicts. Moreover, we recognize that although other people may have different beliefs or feelings than us, we can still treat them (and ourselves) with respect and kindness. These final two healing practices focus on forgiveness and invite clients to reflect on their earned strengths and post-traumatic growth so they can create a life that fulfills a deeper sense of meaning and purpose.

Find Freedom Through Forgiveness

While forgiveness should never be a forced process, you can guide clients through a process that can help them resolve lingering feelings of anger and resentment specific to a relationship in their life. As you move through this practice, give them time to process any related emotions and allow for any grief that arises.

- Would you be willing to make space for your feelings of anger, resentment, and hurt in relationship to... [*name the person from the client's life*]? What feels incomplete about this relationship? Is there anything that you wish you could say to this person? What do you want them to know? Ask yourself if you feel a desire to punish or retaliate against this person. If so, give yourself space for your anger. How do you feel as you speak these words out loud? Can you create more space for you and your feelings? What do you notice in your body?

- Take a moment to imagine this other person. What do you think caused them to behave the way they did? What do you imagine motivated their actions toward you? Are you aware of any trauma or losses that they suffered? Once again, notice how you feel in your body and make space for your emotions.

- This is completely optional, but if you would like, explore how it feels to imagine forgiving this person. Perhaps, explore saying the words "I forgive you." Or, if this doesn't feel right, perhaps explore how it feels to say the words, "I release you." Once again, take some time to notice how you feel emotionally and in your body.

Explore Earned Strengths and Post-Traumatic Growth

- Take some time to reflect on the traumatic events that you have faced in your life. How have you grown as a result of working through difficult experiences? Are you aware of any strengths that you have discovered as a result of your commitment to your healing process? What do you believe about yourself as a result of your recovery? [*You might take this time to share with your clients the strengths or positive changes that you have observed as a result of their commitment to therapy.*]

- Who were the people who helped you the most through your journey of trauma recovery? How have your relationships changed as a result of your commitment to healing your trauma? Do you notice that it is easier to be vulnerable with others? Or are you more willing to ask for or accept help?

- Have you discovered any new interests, passions, or spiritual discoveries as a result of working through traumatic events? What brings you a sense of meaning or purpose? In what ways do you currently spend time doing the things that help you connect to this sense of meaning? What changes would you like to make to live a life that is more in alignment with this sense of meaning? What are the barriers to living your life in this way? What would support you to make changes that help you live in alignment with your sense of meaning and purpose?

- What hopes do you have for your future? In what ways do you hope to continue to grow?

- What wisdom or gifts have you gained as a result of your healing journey? In what ways might you share these gifts with the world?

Conclusion

I invite you to take a moment to reflect upon your own process of reading this book. In what ways do you imagine this content will assist you in your work with your clients? What barriers might arise that inhibit your ability to integrate these practices into your work? And what would best support you to continue to thrive in your work with clients who have experienced trauma? Perhaps you would like to seek out additional supervision aligned with this mind-body treatment model. Or maybe you will decide to further your education through additional trainings. I also suggest that you to return to this book regularly. You might find yourself revisiting particular passages or healing practices that illuminate another perspective or that help you feel refreshed when you feel fatigued.

Most importantly, I encourage you to stay the course when the path to healing seems to take unexpected twists and turns. Recovery from trauma, especially C-PTSD, is rarely linear. However, there is growth and healing on the other side. Each insight or new positive development makes a difference. In time, these seemingly insignificant moments of growth accumulate and help your clients develop trust in the process and in themselves. Moreover, my hope is that you feel supported to grow through your work with your clients. In closing, I would like to personally thank you for your willingness to turn toward the suffering of others—your commitment to bringing care and compassion to the world makes a difference.

References

....

For your convenience, the practices in this book
are available for download at www.pesi.com/cptsd

Amen, D. G. (2015). *Change your brain, change your life: The breakthrough program for conquering anxiety, depression, obsessiveness, lack of focus, anger, and memory problems.* Easton, PA: Harmony.

American Psychiatric Association. (2013). *Diagnostic and statistical manual of mental disorders* (5th ed.). Arlington, VA: Author.

Anderson, F. G., Sweezy, M., & Schwartz, R. D. (2017). *Internal family systems skills training manual: Trauma-informed treatment for anxiety, depression, PTSD & substance abuse.* Eau Claire, WI: PESI Publishing & Media.

Aposhyan, S. (2007). *Natural intelligence: Body-mind integration and human development.* Boulder, CO: NOW Press.

Banks, A. (2006). Relational therapy for trauma. *Journal of Trauma Practice, 5*(1), 25–47.

Bardeen, J. R., & Orcutt, H. K. (2011). Attentional control as a moderator of the relationship between posttraumatic stress symptoms and attentional threat bias. *Journal of Anxiety Disorders, 25*(8), 1008–1018.

Bennett, M. J., & Castiglioni, I. (2004). Embodied ethnocentrism and the feeling of culture: A key to training for intercultural competence. In D. Landis, J. Bennett, & M. Bennett (Eds.), *Handbook of Intercultural Training* (3rd ed., pp. 249–265). Thousand Oaks, CA: Sage.

Berceli, D. (2008). *The revolutionary trauma release process: Transcend your toughest times.* Vancouver, Canada: Namaste.

Berceli, D. (2015). *Shake it off naturally: Reduce stress, anxiety, and tension with (TRE).* Charleston, SC: CreateSpace.

Bergmann, U. (2012). *Neurobiological foundations for EMDR practice.* New York: Springer.

Berna, F., Göritz, A. S., Mengin, A., Evrard, R., Kopferschmitt, J., & Moritz, S. (2019). Alternative or complementary attitudes toward alternative and complementary medicines. *BMC Complementary and Alternative Medicine, 19*(1), Article 83.

Boffa, J. W., Short, N. A., Gibby, B. A., Stentz, L. A., & Schmidt, N. B. (2018). Distress tolerance as a mechanism of PTSD symptom change: Evidence for mediation in a treatment-seeking sample. *Psychiatry Research, 267,* 400–408.

Bolton, R. E., Fix, G. M., VanDeusen Lukas, C., Elwy, A. R., & Bokhour, B. G. (2020). Biopsychosocial benefits of movement-based complementary and integrative health therapies for patients with chronic conditions. *Chronic Illness, 16*(1), 41–54.

Bornstein, M. H., & Suess, P. E. (2000). Child and mother cardiac vagal tone: Continuity, stability, and concordance across the first 5 years. *Developmental Psychology, 36*(1), 54–65.

Böttche, M., Ehring, T., Krüger-Gottschalk, A., Rau, H., Schäfer, I., Schellong, J., ... Knaevelsrud, C. (2018). Testing the ICD-11 proposal for complex PTSD in trauma-exposed adults: Factor structure and symptom profiles. *European Journal of Psychotraumatology, 9*(1), Article 1512264.

Bowan, M. D. (2008). Treatment of panic attack with vergence therapy: An unexpected visual-vagus connection. *Journal of Behavioral Optometry*, *19*(6), 155–158.

Bromberg, P. M. (2011). *The shadow of the tsunami and the growth of the relational mind*. New York: Routledge.

Brown, R. P., & Gerbarg, P. L. (2005a). Sudarshan Kriya yogic breathing in the treatment of stress, anxiety, and depression: Part I—neurophysiologic model. *Journal of Alternative & Complementary Medicine*, *11*(1), 189–201.

Brown, R. P., & Gerbarg, P. L. (2005b). Sudarshan Kriya Yogic breathing in the treatment of stress, anxiety, and depression: Part II—clinical applications and guidelines. *Journal of Alternative & Complementary Medicine*, *11*(4), 711–717.

Caldwell, C. (1996). *Getting our bodies back: Recovery, healing, and transformation through body-centered psychotherapy*. Boston: Shambhala Publications.

Caldwell, C. (1997). *Getting in touch: The guide to new body-centered therapies*. Wheaton, IL: Theosophical.

Caldwell, C. (2018). *Bodyfulness: Somatic practices for presence, empowerment, and waking up in this life*. Boulder, CO: Shambhala Publications.

Carson, J. W., Keefe, F. J., Lynch, T. R., Carson, K. M., Goli, V., Fras, A. M., & Thorp, S. R. (2005). Loving-kindness meditation for chronic low back pain: results from a pilot trial. *Holistic Nursing*, *23*(3), 287–304.

Chamberlin, D. E. (2019). The predictive processing model of EMDR. *Frontiers in Psychology*, *10*, Article 2267.

Church, D., & Feinstein, D. (2017). The manual stimulation of acupuncture points in the treatment of post-traumatic stress disorder: A review of clinical emotional freedom techniques. *Medical Acupuncture*, *29*(4), 194–205.

Cloitre, M., Courtois, C. A., Ford, J. D., Green, B. L., Alexander, P., Briere, J., … van der Hart, O. (2012). The ISTSS expert consensus treatment guidelines for complex PTSD in adults. Retrieved from https://www.istss.org/ISTSS_Main/media/Documents/ISTSS-Expert-Concesnsus-Guidelines-for-Complex-PTSD-Updated-060315.pdf

Cloitre, M., Garvert, D. W., Weiss, B., Carlson, E. B., & Bryant, R. A. (2014). Distinguishing PTSD, complex PTSD, and borderline personality disorder: A latent class analysis. *European Journal of Psychotraumatology*, *5*(1), Article 25097.

Corrigan, F. M. (2002). Mindfulness, dissociation, EMDR and the anterior cingulate cortex: A hypothesis. *Contemporary Hypnosis*, *19*(1), 8–17.

Corrigan, F. M., & Hull, A. M. (2015). Neglect of the complex: Why psychotherapy for post-traumatic clinical presentations is often ineffective. *British Journal of Psychology Bulletin*, *39*(2), 86–89.

Courtois, C. A., & Ford, J. D. (Eds.). (2009). *Treating complex traumatic stress disorders: An evidence-based guide*. New York: Guilford Press.

Courtois, C. A., Ford, J. D., & Cloitre, M. (2009). Best practices in psychotherapy for adults. In C. A. Courtois & J. D. Ford (Eds.), *Treating complex traumatic stress disorders: An evidence-based guide* (pp. 82–103). New York: Guilford Press.

Cutuli, D. (2014). Cognitive reappraisal and expressive suppression strategies role in the emotion regulation: An overview on their modulatory effects and neural correlates. *Frontiers in Systems Neuroscience*, *8*, Article 175.

Damasio, A. (1999). *The feeling of what happens: Body and emotion in the making of consciousness*. New York: Harcourt Brace.

Dana, D. A. (2018). *The polyvagal theory in therapy: Engaging the rhythm of regulation*. New York: W. W. Norton.

Daniels, J. K., Frewen, P., McKinnon, M. C., & Lanius, R. A. (2011). Default mode alterations in posttraumatic stress disorder related to early-life trauma: A developmental perspective. *Journal of Psychiatry & Neuroscience, 36*(1), 56–59.

da Silva, H. C., Furtado da Rosa, M. M., Berger, W., Luz, M. P., Mendlowicz, M., Coutinho, E. S., ... Ventura, P. (2019). PTSD in mental health outpatient settings: Highly prevalent and under-recognized. *Brazilian Journal of Psychiatry, 41*(3), 213–217.

de Jongh, A., Resick, P. A., Zoellner, L. A., van Minnen, A., Lee, C. W., Monson, C. M., ... Bicanic, I. A. (2016). Critical analysis of the current treatment guidelines for complex PTSD in adults. *Depression and Anxiety, 33*, 359–369.

Doidge, N. (2007). *The brain that changes itself: Stories of personal triumph from the frontiers of brain science.* London: Penguin Books.

Ecker, B., Ticic, R., & Hulley, L. (2012). *Unlocking the emotional brain: Eliminating symptoms at their roots using memory reconsolidation.* Abingdon, UK: Routledge.

Edelkott, N., Engstrom, D. W., Hernandez-Wolfe, P., & Gangsei, D. (2016). Vicarious resilience: Complexities and variations. *American Journal of Orthopsychiatry, 86*(6), 713–724.

Ehlers, A., Maercker, A., & Boos, A. (2000). Posttraumatic stress disorder following political imprisonment: The role of mental defeat, alienation, and perceived permanent change. *Journal of Abnormal Psychology, 109*(1), 45–55.

Emerson, D. (2015). *Trauma-sensitive yoga in therapy: Bringing the body into treatment.* New York: W. W. Norton.

Emmons, R. A. (2007). Gratitude, subjective well-being, and the brain. In M. Eid & R. J. Larsen (Eds.), *The science of subjective well-being* (pp. 469–492). New York: Guilford Press.

Emmons, R. A., & McCullough, M. E. (2003). Counting blessings versus burdens: An experimental investigation of gratitude and subjective well-being in daily life. *Journal of Personality and Social Psychology, 84*(2), 377–389.

Felitti, V. J., Anda, R. F., Nordenberg, D., Williamson, D. F., Spitz, A. M., Edwards, V., ... Marks, J. S. (1998). Relationship of child abuse and household dysfunction to many of the leading causes of death in adults. *American Journal of Preventive Medicine, 14*(4), 245–258.

Felmingham, K., Kemp, A. H., Williams, L., Falconer, E., Olivieri, G., Peduto, A., & Bryant, R. (2008). Dissociative responses to conscious and non-conscious fear impact underlying brain function in post-traumatic stress disorder. *Psychological Medicine, 38*, 1771–1780.

Field, T. (2014). *Touch.* Cambridge, MA: MIT Press.

Fisher, J. (2017). *Healing the fragmented selves of trauma survivors: Overcoming internal self-alienation.* New York: Routledge.

Foa, E., Hembree, E., & Rothbaum, B. O. (2007). *Prolonged exposure therapy for PTSD: Emotional processing of traumatic experiences therapist guide.* New York: Oxford University Press.

Fogel, A. (2009). *Body sense: The science and practice of embodied self-awareness.* New York: W. W. Norton.

Ford, J. D. (2018). Trauma memory processing in posttraumatic stress disorder psychotherapy: A unifying framework. *Journal of Traumatic Stress, 31*(6), 933–942.

Ford, J. D., Grasso, D. J., Elhai, J. D., & Courtois, C. A. (2015). *Posttraumatic stress disorder: Scientific and professional dimensions* (2nd ed.). Oxford, UK: Elsevier.

Forgash, C., & Copeley, M. (Eds.). (2008). *Healing the heart of trauma and dissociation with EMDR and ego state therapy.* New York: Springer.

Foster, J. A., Rinaman, L., & Cryan, J. F. (2017). Stress & the gut-brain axis: Regulation by the microbiome. *Neurobiology of Stress, 7*, 124–136.

Frankl, V. E. (1946/2006). *Man's search for meaning.* Boston: Beacon Press.

Franklin, C. L., Raines, A. M., Chambliss, J. L., Walton, J. L., & Maieritsch, K. P. (2018). Examining various subthreshold definitions of PTSD using the clinician administered PTSD Scale for DSM-5. *Journal of Affective Disorders, 234*, 256–260.

Frey, L. L. (2013). Relational-cultural therapy: Theory, research, and application to counseling competencies. *Professional Psychology: Research and Practice, 44*(3), 177–185.

Fuller-Thompson, E., & Hooper, S. R. (2014). The association between childhood physical abuse and dyslexia: Findings from a population-based study. *Journal of Interpersonal Violence, 30*(9), 1583–1592.

Gatchel, R. J. (2004). Comorbidity of chronic pain and mental health disorders: The biopsychosocial perspective. *American Psychologist, 59*(8), 795–805.

Gendlin, E. (1982). *Focusing*. New York: Bantam.

Germer, C., & Neff, K. (2019). *Teaching the mindful self-compassion program: A guide for professionals*. New York: Guilford Press.

Geuter, U. (2015). The history and scope of body psychotherapy. In G. Marlock, H. Weiss, C. Young, & M. Soth (Eds.), *The handbook of body psychotherapy and somatic psychology* (pp. 22–39). Berkeley: North Atlantic Books.

Goleman, D. (1995/2006). *Emotional intelligence: Why it can matter more than IQ*. New York: Bantam Books.

Gonzalez, A., & Mosquera, D. (2012). *EMDR and dissociation: The progressive approach*. Charleston, SC: Amazon Imprint.

Grant, M. (2016). *Change your brain, change your pain: Based on EMDR*. Australia: Trauma and Pain Management Services.

Groves, D. A., & Brown, V. J. (2005). Vagal nerve stimulation: A review of its applications and potential mechanisms that mediate its clinical effects. *Neuroscience & Biobehavioral Reviews, 29*(3), 493–500.

Haggerty, R. J., Sherrod, L. R., Garmezy, N., & Rutter, M. (1996). *Stress, risk, and resilience in children and adolescents: Processes, mechanisms, and interventions*. New York: Cambridge University Press.

Harrell, C. J. P., Burford, T. I., Cage, B. N., Nelson, T. M., Shearon, S., Thompson, A., & Green, S. (2011). Multiple pathways linking racism to health outcomes. *Du Bois Review: Social Science Research on Race, 8*(1), 143–157.

Hayes, S. C. (2005). *Get out of your mind and into your life: The new acceptance and commitment therapy*. Oakland, CA: New Harbinger.

Heim, C. M., Mayberg, H. S., Mletzko, T., Nemeroff, C. B., & Pruessner, J. C. (2013). Decreased cortical representation of genital somatosensory field after childhood sexual abuse. *American Journal of Psychiatry, 170*(6), 616–623.

Heiniger, L. E., Clark, G. I., & Egan, S. J. (2018). Perceptions of Socratic and non-Socratic presentation of information in cognitive behaviour therapy. *Journal of Behavior Therapy and Experimental Psychiatry, 58*, 106–113.

Herman, J. (1997). *Trauma and recovery: The aftermath of violence—from domestic abuse to political terror*. New York: Basic Books.

Hopwood, T. L., & Schutte, N. S. (2017). A meta-analytic investigation of the impact of mindfulness-based interventions on post traumatic stress. *Clinical Psychology Review, 57*, 12–20.

Insel, T. R. (2000). Toward a neurobiology of attachment. *Review of General Psychology, 4*(2), 176–185.

Jackson, C., Nissenson, K., & Cloitre, M. (2009). Cognitive-behavioral therapy. In C. A. Courtois & J. D. Ford (Eds.), *Treating complex traumatic stress disorders: An evidence-based guide* (pp. 243–263). New York: Guilford Press.

Kabat-Zinn, J. (1990). *Full catastrophe living: Using the wisdom of your body and mind to face stress, pain, and illness.* New York: Delacorte Press.

Kain, K. L., & Terrell, S. J. (2018). *Nurturing resilience: Helping clients move forward from developmental trauma.* Berkeley: North Atlantic Books.

Karatzias, T., Shevlin, M., Hyland, P., Brewin, C. R., Cloitre, M., Bradley, A., ... Roberts, N. P. (2018). The role of negative cognitions, emotion regulation strategies, and attachment style in complex post-traumatic stress disorder: Implications for new and existing therapies. *British Journal of Clinical Psychology, 57*(2), 177–185.

Keleman, S. (1987). *Bonding: A somatic-emotional approach to transference.* Berkeley, CA: Center Press.

Killian, K., Hernandez-Wolfe, P., Engstrom, D., & Gangsei, D. (2017). Development of the Vicarious Resilience Scale (VRS): A measure of positive effects of working with trauma survivors. *Psychological Trauma: Theory, Research, Practice, and Policy, 9*(1), 23–31.

Kilpatrick, D. G., Resnick, H. S., Milanak, M. E., Miller, M. W., Keyes, K. M., & Friedman, M. J. (2013). National estimates of exposure to traumatic events and PTSD prevalence using DSM-IV and DSM-5 criteria. *Journal of Traumatic Stress, 26*(5), 537–547.

Kimmel, M. (2013). The arc from the body to culture: How affect, proprioception, kinesthesia, and perceptual imagery shape cultural knowledge (and vice versa). *Integral Review, 9*(2), 300–348.

Knipe, J. (2015). *EMDR toolbox: Theory and treatment of complex PTSD and dissociation.* New York: Springer.

Kok, B. E., Coffey, K. A., Cohn, M. A., Catalino, L. I., Vacharkulksemsuk, T., Algoe, ... Fredrickson, B. L. (2013). How positive emotions build physical health: Perceived positive social connections account for the upward spiral between positive emotions and vagal tone. *Psychological Science, 24*(7), 1123–1132.

Kok, B. E., & Fredrickson, B. L. (2010). Upward spirals of the heart: Autonomic flexibility, as indexed by vagal tone, reciprocally and prospectively predicts positive emotions and social connectedness. *Biological Psychology, 85*(3), 432–436.

Korn, L. (2016). *Nutrition essentials for mental health: A complete guide to the food-mood connection.* New York: W. W. Norton.

Kurtz, R. (1990). *Body-centered psychotherapy: The Hakomi method.* Mendocino, CA: Life Rhythm.

Lanius, R. A., Brand, B., Vermetten, E., Frewen, P. A., & Spiegel, D. (2012). The dissociative subtype of posttraumatic stress disorder: Rationale, clinical and neurobiological evidence, and implications. *Depression and Anxiety, 29,* 701–708.

Larrivee, D., & Echarte, L. (2018). Contemplative meditation and neuroscience: Prospects for mental health. *Journal of Religion and Health, 57*(3), 960–978.

LeDoux, J. (1996). *The emotional brain: The mysterious underpinnings of emotional life.* New York: Touchstone.

Levine, P. (1997). *Waking the tiger: Healing trauma.* Berkeley: North Atlantic Books.

Levine, P. (2010). *In an unspoken voice: How the body releases trauma and restores goodness.* Berkley: North Atlantic Books.

Lewis, C., Raisanen, L., Bisson, J. I., Jones, I., & Zammit, S. (2018). Trauma exposure and undetected posttraumatic stress disorder among adults with a mental disorder. *Depression and Anxiety, 35*(2), 178–184.

Linehan, M. (1993). *Cognitive-behavioral treatment of borderline personality disorder.* New York: Guilford Press.

Lowen, A. (1977). *Bioenergetics: The revolutionary therapy that uses the language of the body to heal the problems of the mind.* New York: Penguin.

Malan-Muller, S., Valles-Colomer, M., Raes, J., Lowry, C. A., Seedat, S., & Hemmings, S. M. (2018). The gut microbiome and mental health: Implications for anxiety- and trauma-related disorders. *Omics: A Journal of Integrative Biology, 22*(2), 90–107.

Maté, G. (2010). *In the realm of hungry ghosts: Close encounters with addictions*. Berkeley: North Atlantic Books.

Matheson, C. (2016). A new diagnosis of complex post-traumatic stress disorder, PTSD—a window of opportunity for the treatment of patients in the NHS? *Psychoanalytic Psychotherapy, 30*(4), 329–344.

Matthews, S. G., & McGowan, P. O. (2019). Developmental programming of the HPA axis and related behaviours: Epigenetic mechanisms. *Journal of Endocrinology, 242*(1), T69–T79.

McElroy, E., Shevlin, M., Murphy, S., Roberts, B., Makhashvili, N., Javakhishvili, J., ... Hyland, P. (2019). ICD-11 PTSD and complex PTSD: Structural validation using network analysis. *World Psychiatry, 18*(2), 236–237.

Merleau-Ponty, M. (1962). *Phenomenology of perception*. London: Routledge and Kegan Paul.

Murakami, M., Fox, L., & Dijkers, M. P. (2017). Ear acupuncture for immediate pain relief—a systematic review and meta-analysis of randomized controlled trials. *Pain Medicine, 18*(3), 551–564.

Nicholson, A. A., Friston, K. J., Zeidman, P., Harricharan, S., McKinnon, M. C., Densmore, M., ... Lanius, R. A. (2017). Dynamic causal modeling in PTSD and its dissociative subtype: Bottom-up versus top-down processing within fear and emotion regulation circuitry. *Human Brain Mapping, 38*(11), 5551–5561.

Nickerson, M. (Ed.) (2017). *Cultural competence and healing culturally based trauma with EMDR therapy*. New York: Springer.

Ogden, P., & Fisher, J. (2014). Integrating body and mind: Sensorimotor psychotherapy and treatment of dissociation, defense, and dysregulation. In U. F. Lanius, S. L. Paulsen, & F. M. Corrigan (Eds.), *Neurobiology and treatment of traumatic dissociation: Toward an embodied self* (pp. 399–422). New York: Springer.

Ogden, P., & Fisher, J. (2015). *Sensorimotor psychotherapy: Interventions for trauma and attachment*. New York: W. W. Norton.

Ogden, P., Minton, K., & Pain, C. (2006). *Trauma and the body: A sensorimotor approach to psychotherapy*. New York: W. W. Norton.

Pagani, M., Amann, B. L., Landin-Romero, R., & Carletto, S. (2017). Eye movement desensitization and reprocessing and slow wave sleep: A putative mechanism of action. *Frontiers in Psychology, 8*, Article 1935.

Paradies, Y., Ben, J., Denson, N., Elias, A., Priest, N., Pieterse, A., ... Gee, G. (2015). Racism as a determinant of health: A systematic review and meta-analysis. *PloS One, 10*(9), 1–48.

Pearlman, L., & Courtois, C. A. (2005). Clinical applications of the attachment framework: Relational treatment of complex trauma. *Journal of Trauma Stress, 18*(5), 449–459.

Perls, F. (1992). *Gestalt therapy verbatim*. Gouldsboro, ME: The Gestalt Journal Press.

Porges, S. (2011). *The polyvagal theory: Neurophysiological foundations of emotions, attachment, communication, and self-regulation*. New York: W. W. Norton.

Price, M., Spinazzola, J., Musicaro, R., Turner, J., Suvak, M., Emerson, D., & van der Kolk, B. (2017). Effectiveness of an extended yoga treatment for women with chronic posttraumatic stress disorder. *Journal of Alternative and Complementary Medicine, 23*(4), 300–309.

Raffone, A., Tagini, A., & Srinivasan, N. (2010). Mindfulness and the cognitive neuroscience of attention and awareness. *Zygon, 45*(3), 627–646.

Resick, P. A., Monson, C. M., & Chard, K. M. (2016). *Cognitive processing therapy for PTSD: A comprehensive manual*. New York: Guilford Press.

Rhodes, A., Spinazzola, J., & van der Kolk, B. (2016). Yoga for adult women with chronic PTSD: A long-term follow-up study. *The Journal of Alternative and Complementary Medicine, 22*(3), 189–196.

Rosenberg, S. (2017). *Accessing the healing power of the vagus nerve: Self-help exercises for anxiety, depression, trauma, and autism.* Berkeley: North Atlantic Books.

Rosenberg, J., Rand, M., & Asay, D. (1985). *Body, self, and soul: Sustaining integration.* Atlanta, GA: Humanics Trade Group.

Rothschild, B. (2010). *8 keys to safe trauma recovery: Take-charge strategies to empower your healing.* New York: W. W. Norton.

Rousseau, P. F., El Khoury-Malhame, M., Reynaud, E., Boukezzi, S., Cancel, A., Zendjidjian, X., ... Khalfa, S. (2019). Fear extinction learning improvement in PTSD after EMDR therapy: An fMRI study. *European Journal of Psychotraumatology, 10*(1), Article 1568132.

Ruden, R. A. (2011). *When the past is always present: Emotional traumatization, causes, and cures.* New York: Routledge.

Sachser, C., Keller, F., & Goldbeck, L. (2017). Complex PTSD as proposed for ICD-11: Validation of a new disorder in children and adolescents and their response to trauma-focused cognitive behavioral therapy. *Journal of Child Psychology and Psychiatry, 58*(2), 160–168.

Scaer, R. (2005). *The trauma spectrum: Hidden wounds and human resiliency.* New York: W. W. Norton.

Scaer, R. (2014). *The body bears the burden: Trauma, dissociation, and disease* (3rd ed.). New York: Routledge.

Schauer, M., & Elbert, T. (2010). Dissociation following traumatic stress: Etiology and treatment. *Zeitschrift für Psychologie/Journal of Psychology, 218*(2), 109–127.

Schauer, M., Neuner, F., & Elbert, T. (2011). *Narrative exposure therapy: A short-term treatment for traumatic stress disorders after war, terror, or torture* (2nd ed.). Ashland, OH: Hogrefe.

Schore, A. N. (2001). Effects of a secure attachment relationship on right brain development, affect regulation, and infant mental health. *Infant Mental Health Journal, 22*(1–2), 7–66.

Schore, A. N. (2010). Relational trauma and the developing right brain: The neurobiology of broken attachment bonds. In T. Baradon (Ed.), *Relational trauma in infancy: Psychoanalytic, attachment and neuropsychological contributions to parent-infant psychotherapy* (pp. 19–47). New York: Routledge.

Schore, A. N. (2019). *Right brain psychotherapy.* New York: W. W. Norton.

Schwartz, A. (2014). *Mind-body therapies: Beliefs and practices of APA member professional psychologists* (Fielding Monograph Series, Vol. 2). Santa Barbara, CA: Fielding University Press.

Schwartz, A. (2016). *The complex PTSD workbook: A mind-body approach to regaining emotional control and becoming whole.* Berkeley: Althea Press.

Schwartz, A. (2020). *The post-traumatic growth guidebook: Practical mind-body tools to heal trauma, foster resilience, and awaken your potential.* Eau Claire, WI: PESI Publishing & Media.

Schwartz, A., & Maiberger, B. (2018). *EMDR therapy and somatic psychology: Interventions to enhance embodiment in trauma treatment.* New York: W. W. Norton.

Schwartz, R. (1997). *Internal family systems therapy.* New York: Guilford Press.

Seligman, M. E. (1975/1992). *Helplessness: On depression, development, and death.* San Francisco: W. H. Freeman.

Seppälä, E. M., Nitschke, J. B., Tudorascu, D. L., Hayes, A., Goldstein, M. R., Nguyen, D. T., ... Davidson, R. J. (2014). Breathing-based meditation decreases posttraumatic stress disorder symptoms in US military veterans: A randomized controlled longitudinal study. *Journal of Traumatic Stress, 27*(4), 397–405.

Shapiro, F. (2018). *Eye movement desensitization and reprocessing (EMDR) therapy: Basic principles, protocols, and procedures* (3rd ed.). New York: Guilford Press.

Shapiro, R. (2016). *Easy ego state interventions: Strategies for working with parts.* New York: W. W. Norton.

Siegel, D. J. (1999). *The developing mind: How relationships and the brain interact to shape who we are.* New York: Guilford Press.

Siegel, D. J. (2001). Memory: An overview, with emphasis on developmental, interpersonal, and neurobiological aspects. *Journal of the American Academy of Child and Adolescent Psychiatry, 40*(9), 997–1011.

Siegel, D. J. (2010). *Mindsight: The new science of personal transformation.* New York: Bantam Books.

Silberman, E. K., & Weingartner, H. (1986). Hemispheric lateralization of functions related to emotion. *Brain and Cognition, 5*(3), 322–353.

Steuwe, C., Daniels, J. K., Frewen, P. A., Densmore, M., Pannasch, S., Beblo, T., ... Lanius, R. A. (2014). Effect of direct eye contact in PTSD related to interpersonal trauma: An fMRI study of activation of an innate alarm system. *Social Cognitive and Affective Neuroscience, 9*(1), 88–97.

Szczygiel, P. (2018). On the value and meaning of trauma-informed practice: Honoring safety, complexity, and relationship. *Smith College Studies in Social Work, 88*(2), 115–134.

Tanaka, S. (2015). Intercorporeality as a theory of social cognition. *Theory and Psychology, 25*(4), 455–472.

Tedeschi, R. G., Shakespeare-Finch, J., Taku, K., & Calhoun, L. G. (2018). *Posttraumatic growth: Theory, research, and applications.* New York: Routledge.

Teicher, M. H., & Samson, J. A. (2016). Annual research review: Enduring neurobiological effects of childhood abuse and neglect. *Journal of Child Psychology and Psychiatry, 57*(3), 241–266.

Trakroo, M., & Bhavanani, A. B. (2016). Physiological benefits of yogic practices: A brief review. *International Journal of Traditional and Complementary Medicine, 1*(1), 0031-0043.

Tryon, W. (2014). *Cognitive neuroscience and psychotherapy: Network principles for a unified theory.* New York: Academic Press.

Tyagi, A., & Cohen, M. (2016). Yoga and heart rate variability: A comprehensive review of the literature. *International Journal of Yoga, 9*(2), 97–113.

Vaish, A., Grossmann, T., & Woodward, A. (2008). Not all emotions are created equal: The negativity bias in social-emotional development. *Psychological Bulletin, 134*(3), 383–403.

van der Hart, O., Nijenhuis, E., & Steele, K. (2006). *The haunted self: Structural dissociation and the treatment of chronic traumatization.* New York: W. W. Norton.

van der Kolk, B. (2006). Clinical implications of neuroscience research in PTSD. *Annals of the New York Academy of Science, 1071,* 277–293.

van der Kolk, B. (2014). *The body keeps the score: Brain, mind, and body in the healing of trauma.* New York: Viking Press.

van der Kolk, B. A., Stone, L., West, J., Rhodes, A., Emerson, D., Suvak, M., & Spinazzola, J. (2014). Yoga as an adjunctive treatment for posttraumatic stress disorder: A randomized controlled trial. *Journal of Clinical Psychiatry, 75*(6), e559–e565.

van Veen, S. C., Kang, S., & van Schie, K. (2019). On EMDR: Measuring the working memory taxation of various types of eye (non-)movement conditions. *Journal of Behavior Therapy and Experimental Psychiatry, 65,* Article 101494.

van Vliet, N. I., Huntjens, R. J., van Dijk, M. K., & de Jongh, A. (2018). Phase-based treatment versus immediate trauma-focused treatment in patients with childhood trauma-related posttraumatic stress disorder: Study protocol for a randomized controlled trial. *Trials, 19*(1), Article 138.

Walker, P. (2013). *Complex PTSD: From surviving to thriving: A guide and map for recovering from childhood trauma.* Lafayette, CA: Azure Coyote.

Wampold, B. E. (2010). The research evidence for the common factors models: A historically situated perspective. In B. L. Duncan, S. D. Miller, B. E. Wampold, & M. A. Hubble (Eds.), *The heart and soul of change: Delivering what works in therapy* (2nd ed.) (pp. 49–81). Washington, DC: American Psychological Association.

Wampold, B. E. (2015). How important are the common factors in psychotherapy? An update. *World Psychiatry, 14*(3), 270–277.

Wampold, B. E., & Imel, Z. E. (2015). *The great psychotherapy debate: The evidence for what makes psychotherapy work* (2nd ed.). New York: Routledge.

Watkins, J., & Watkins, H. (1997). *Ego states: Theory and therapy.* New York: W. W. Norton.

Wolynn, M. (2016). *It didn't start with you: How inherited family trauma shapes who we are and how to end the cycle.* New York: Viking Press.

World Health Organization. (2018). *International statistical classification of diseases and related health problems* (11th revision). Geneva, Switzerland: WHO.

Yehuda, R. (2002). *Treating trauma survivors with PTSD.* Washington, DC: American Psychiatric Press.

Yehuda, R. (2009). Status of glucocorticoid alterations in post-traumatic stress disorder. *Annals of the New York Academy of Sciences, 1179*(1), 56–69.

Yehuda, R., Cai, G., Golier, J. A., Sarapas, C., Galea, S., Ising, M., ... Buxbaum, J. D. (2009). Gene expression patterns associated with posttraumatic stress disorder following exposure to the World Trade Center attacks. *Biological Psychiatry, 66*(7), 708–711.

Yehuda, R., Daskalakis, N. P., Bierer, L. M., Bader, H. N., Klengel, T., Holsboer, F., & Binder, E. B. (2016). Holocaust exposure induced intergenerational effects on FKBP5 methylation. *Biological Psychiatry, 80*(5), 372–380.

Yehuda, R., Mulherin Engel, S., Brand, S. R., Seckl, J., Marcus, S. M., & Berkowitz, G. S. (2005). Transgenerational effects of posttraumatic stress disorder in babies of mothers exposed to the World Trade Center attacks during pregnancy. *Journal of Clinical Endocrinology and Metabolism, 90*(7), 4115–4118.

Zaba, M., Kirmeier, T., Ionescu, I. A., Wollweber, B., Buell, D. R., Gall-Kleebach, D. J., ... Schmidt, U. (2015). Identification and characterization of HPA-axis reactivity endophenotypes in a cohort of female PTSD patients. *Psychoneuroendocrinology, 55*, 102–115.

Zammit, S., Lewis, C., Dawson, S., Colley, H., McCann, H., Piekarski, A., ... Bisson, J. (2018). Undetected post-traumatic stress disorder in secondary-care mental health services: Systematic review. *The British Journal of Psychiatry, 212*(1), 11–18.

Zarbo, C., Tasca, G. A., Cattafi, F., & Compare, A. (2016). Integrative psychotherapy works. *Frontiers in Psychology, 6*, Article 2021.